全国职业技能英语系列教材

English for Agriculture and Forestry
农林英语

主　编：张永萍　吴江梅
副主编：吕丽塔　马碧英
编　者：吴江梅　张永萍　吕丽塔　孙　莹
　　　　徐淑兰　马碧英　刘　真　赵劲鹰
　　　　陈　曦　张兰英

图书在版编目(CIP)数据

农林英语/张永萍,吴江梅主编.—北京：北京大学出版社,2009.12
（全国职业技能英语系列教材）
ISBN 978-7-301-16166-1

Ⅰ.农… Ⅱ.①张…②吴… Ⅲ.①农业-英语-高等学校：技术学校-教材 ②林业-英语-高等学校：技术学校-教材 Ⅳ.H31

中国版本图书馆CIP数据核字(2009)第208434号

书　　　名：农林英语

著作责任者：张永萍　吴江梅 主编
责 任 编 辑：李　颖
标 准 书 号：ISBN 978-7-301-16166-1/H·2376
出 版 发 行：北京大学出版社
地　　　　址：北京市海淀区成府路205号　100871
网　　　　址：http://www.pup.cn
电　　　　话：邮购部 62752015　发行部 62750672　编辑部 62755217　出版部 62754962
电 子 邮 箱：zbing@pup.pku.edu.cn
印　刷　者：北京虎彩文化传播有限公司
经　销　者：新华书店
　　　　　　787毫米×1092毫米　16开本　14印张　326千字
　　　　　　2009年12月第1版　2022年8月第4次印刷
定　　　　价：28.00元(配有光盘)

未经许可，不得以任何方式复制或抄袭本书之部分或全部内容。
版权所有，侵权必究　举报电话：010-62752024
电子邮箱：fd@pup.pku.edu.cn

总 序

我国高职高专教育的春天到来了。随着国家对高职高专教育重视程度的加深,职业技能教材体系的建设成为了当务之急。高职高专过去沿用和压缩大学本科教材的时代一去不复返了。

语言学家 Harmer 指出:"如果我们希望学生学到的语言是在真实生活中能够使用的语言,那么在教材编写中接受技能和产出技能的培养也应该像在生活中那样有机地结合在一起。"

教改的关键在教师,教师的关键在教材,教材的关键在理念。我们依据《高职高专教育英语课程教学基本要求》的精神和编者做了大量调查,秉承"实用为主,够用为度,学以致用,触类旁通"的原则,历经两年艰辛,为高职高专学生编写了这套专业技能课和实训课的英语教材。

本套教材的内容贴近工作岗位,突出岗位情景英语,是一套职场英语教材,具有很强的实用性、仿真性、职业性,其特色体现在以下几个方面:

1. 开放性

本套教材在坚持编写理念、原则及体例的前提下,不断增加新的行业或岗位技能英语分册作为教材的延续。

2. 国际性

本套教材以国内自编为主,以国外引进为辅,取长补短,浑然一体。目前已从德国引进了某些行业的技能英语教材,还将从德国或他国引进优秀教材经过本土化后奉献给广大师生。

3. 职业性

本套教材是由高校教师与行业专家针对具体工作岗位、情景过程共同设计编写,同时注重与行业资格证书相结合。

4. 任务性

基于完成某岗位工作任务而需要的英语知识和技能是本套教材的由来与初衷。因此,各分册均以任务型练习为主。

5. 实用性

本教材注重基础词汇的复习和专业词汇的补充。适合于在校最后一学期的英语教学，着重培养和训练学生初步具有与其日后职业生涯所必需的英语交际能力。

本教材在编写过程中，参考和引用了国内外作者的相关资料，得到了北京大学出版社外语编辑部的倾力奉献，在此，一并向他们表示敬意和感谢。由于本套教材是一种创新和尝试，书中瑕疵必定不少，敬请指正。

丁国声

教育部高职高专英语类专业教学指导委员会委员

河北省高校外语教学研究会副会长

河北外国语职业学院院长

2008 年 6 月

前 言

本书为大农科院校高等职业学生学习英语编写,农、林、生物、环境等专业的学生均可使用。鉴于本书特点,本科生也可选用。

编写本书的依据有二。一、语言学习需求调查。本书主编近年对英语学习者、英语教师以及用人单位进行了广泛的调查,结果表明:各方面一致认为除英语阅读能力之外,口语表达能力也很重要,并对于听和写也提出了高于以往的要求。二、教学与语言教学理论。建构主义的教学理论是源于心理学家皮亚杰的认知学习理论,其中一个重要的概念是图式。其形成和变化受到三个过程的影响:同化,学习者个体对输入的刺激进行过滤和改变的过程,也就是把感受到的刺激纳入头脑中原有的图式之内,成为其中一部分;顺应,学习者个体调节内部结构、适应特定的刺激情境的过程;平衡,学习者个体通过自我调节机制使认知发展从一个平衡状态向另一个平衡状态过渡的过程。强调以学生为中心,主动探索、发现、建构知识及其意义。这样就涉及四大要素:情境,教学设计要同时考虑教学目标和创设利于学习者建构意义的情景;协作,指师生、生生间在学习资料搜集与分析、假说的提出与验证、意义的建构中的合作;对话,是协作的重要方式,从制订计划完成任务到分享思维成果,都很重要;意义建构,学习者深入认识学习内容的性质、规律及相关联系。这种长期存储于大脑的形式就是图式。语言教学理论主要依据语言交际能力理论,基于乔姆斯基的 competence 和 performance、海姆斯修正的 communicative competence 和威多森区分得交际行为和语言形式。在卡内尔、斯旺理论的基础上,巴其曼和科恩完善了交际能力的模式,我国学者文秋芳在跨文化交际理论框架下,对其做了进一步修订,称为跨文化交际理论:由语言能力、语用能力、学习策略组成的交际能力,还有敏感性、宽容度、灵活性合成的跨文化交际能力。具体地说,就是应该具备目标语语法、语篇的能力;语言功能——语言形式、社交语言的能力;进行语言补偿和商讨完成交际目的的能力;由于文化背景差异,在调整交际行为、应对交际冲突时对目标语文化的敏感性、宽容度和灵活性。

此外,考虑到大农科所涉及的专业其实很多,基础英语课本事实上不可能面面俱到,它的功能并不等同于专业英语书。因此本书在内容上的定位是:拓展学习者的农业观,介绍世界范围内大农业领域较新的信息,引发学习者对专业内新事物的关注,激发他们基于已有知识观察新事物、阐述观感,并试图启发他们的创新精神。

鉴于上述理论,编写本书的指导思想是:在教师引导下进行以学生为中心的教学活动,在大量阅读的基础上构建一个事物的意义,通过听说写活动进一步深化意义的构建。这个指导思想体现在四方面:(1)学习者要构件的事物应该是新鲜有趣的,即:在大农科专业中应具备学科前沿性,才可引起学习者的兴趣,因而在信息、语言、技能方面才具备意义构建的前提。(2)在练习设计中尽可能做到内容互补、循序渐进,各项活动为同一个主题服务,揭示一个事物的不同层面,使意义的建构不断深化。(3)尽可能做到一项活动兼有多重训练目的。例如,阅读课文中的提问兼有帮助学习者选用学习策略、分析篇章结构、提取重要信息的功能;再例如口语练习帮助学习者深入理解建构的意义、内化输入刺激的语言形式,还通过辅助手段帮助他们组织篇章、使用篇章标记语、习得语言功能、训练口语表达中的逻辑思维并提高学习兴趣和自信心。同时设计了同伴间对话的练习,为意义建构的过程和交际能力的提高提供机会。(4)充分注意语言形式的学习,词汇、词法的练习也有一定量的比例。生词给予较详尽的注释。

但愿这本书能够为学习者带来一定的收益,这将是编者最大的心愿。

由于时间和水平有限,书中难免有缺陷和不足之处,欢迎广大读者不吝指正。

吴江梅　张永萍

2009 年 10 月

课本使用说明

　　课本由两大部分组成。第一部分是主体,第二部分为补充教材。第一部分对主题进行宏观、概念的介绍;第二部分注重深入、细化的概念、局部典型和具体方案的实施,是对主体课文的深化和推进。第二部分可为水平较高或课时较多的班级使用,也可任意选取练习作为辅助教材,或者作为课外阅读。

　　每个部分的结构大体一致,全面、循序渐进地由输入过渡到输出,引导学生学习语言知识、习得语言技能并发展语言交际能力。可根据学生的程度、兴趣和学习需求张驰有度地利用教材,或修订、改变,或扩展、压缩、取消,以期生动活泼地达到既定教学目标。

　　尤其要提出的是:根据新的教学基本要求,练习中提供了大量的常用专业词汇,并随之附有汉语注释,包括重复出现的术语。其目的是帮助学生认识、熟悉并培养接受难度大读物的良好心理,因此不必强求熟练掌握。首先应引导、训练学习心理,一不惧怕,二能习得敏感、有效的学习策略,以便在二次见面时认识,在今后使用时借助词典正确提取。

　　开始的导入(Warming Up)应是短平快的节奏,千万不能拖沓。其目的是引发兴趣、促进后面内容顺利有效地进行;同时顺便训练一定的语言技能,或复习一些相关的词汇。如果学生有困难,可进行以教师为中心的活动,例如以问答形式做简单讲解,或在教师控制下集体完成。切忌使学生生厌,前功尽弃,适得其反。

　　阅读课文(Reading)为该单元讨论话题输入了主要信息,全部来源于真实语料,竭力保持原汁原味。在一定篇章内设计一个问题或活动,帮助理解课文并训练阅读技巧。不同于在全文之前或之后一并给题,缩小了寻找答案的范围,从而减小了难度。在启发学生的同时,应及时适度地鼓励学生,潜移默化地提高他们的自信心和成就感。活动形式多样,可在激发兴趣的前提下完成。课文后生词表,以字母顺序排列,便于多次出现生词一次和数次查阅,但可根据阅读技巧训练目的确定查阅时间(阅读前、中、后)。

词汇练习(Vocabulary Exercises)紧贴新教学基本要求,以便学生熟悉常用词、词组、构词法以及农林常用功能用语的使用。但所提供的语境,则是该单元的相关内容,取材于真实语料,从另一些侧面补充完善了主题,其中的生词、专业词汇随时给予注释。教学要点是词汇,但个别情况下可简单涉及语境内容。涉及到近年新出现的词汇,有些词典还没有来得及收录,课文中没有改动,目的是让学生了解语言的发展规律,并具备认识这类新词的敏感性和心理接受能力。

听力练习(Listening)本来就容易使学生产生畏惧感。本教材以该单元相关主题为内容,更会遇到困难。但采用得当的方法坚持进行练习非常必要,要让学生感受到成效。因此,听力练习的设计不惜时间和篇幅做了大量的铺垫练习,深入浅出地导入;同时,听力练习的形式化难为易,例如填空、填表等。语言呈示形式丰富,试图以趣味性干扰对难度的感知。在实际操作中,第一听可作为泛听,让学生根据前期练习和熟悉的词汇猜测并总结主题,第二听再完成题目要求。还可以提取语料中相关内容为教学目标服务,例如对话中的社交功能用语等。

口语练习(Speaking)看似有难度,但实际上给出很多相关资料、数据,同时提供了表述的简单句型和组织篇章的词语(农林专业英语中最常用的功能用语,例如表示程序、方法等)。教师可先作示范,然后让学生在小组成员的互助下完成,或在全班引导学生共同完成。应经常组织不同的方式、调换不同的小组成员、搭配男女生和强弱生。虽然组织教学损失了一两分钟,但给学生带来的新鲜感和兴奋度往往事半功倍。因此,教师在教室中的权威性和对学生的洞察力非常重要。教师的巡查要高效,不仅帮助个别组解决特定困难,还要发现普遍的问题在全班及时处理。保证教学活动不流于形式,否则后面的口语活动将无法进行,效果甚微。

口语活动的成功为下一步的书面输出(Writing)奠定基础。学生依据口头表达的内容延伸、转化便可完成写作。口语练习的重点是语言的流利性,而写作练习则重于语言的准确性和思维的逻辑性。教师应认真给学生反馈。

练习答案(Answer to Exercises)给出所有练习的答案或参考。教师还可参考它为听说练习做导入,给示范,或设计其他后续活动。背景知识介绍(Background Knowledge)可供教师备课,也可给学生做课外阅读。

教学是一项创造性的多方位的活动,它的全过程不仅帮助学习者学习语言知识、习得语言交际能力,使听说读写的技能在不断转换使用中得到内化,语言、专业知识、新观点获得主观能动的构建,还能激发学习者的认知冲动、培养对新生事物的兴趣、促进逻辑思维、判断能力、批评精神和创造动力,并在师生、生生互动中,学习沟通交流并互相启发。同时,可使学习者树立崭新的职业观。教师面对的不仅是语言的方方面面,还是学生的方方面面,相同的班不同的课不能永远使用相同的方法,不同的班相同的课也永远不能使用相同的方法。这就是优秀的教师之所以优秀的原因。

Contents

Unit 1 Organic Farming 有机农业 **1**
    Part I   The Principles of Organic Agriculture 1
    Part II   Green Manuring 12

Unit 2 Soilless Cultivation 无土栽培 **20**
    Part I   Soilless Agriculture Helps Save Planet 20
    Part II   Hydroponically Grown Tomato 32

Unit 3 Gene Technology in Agriculture 农业中的转基因技术 **43**
    Part I   The Application of Transgenic Technology in Agriculture 43
    Part II   Genetic Engineering of Rice: *Bt* Rice 55

Unit 4 Ecological Footprint 生态脚印 **62**
    Part I   Ecological Footprint 62
    Part II   How Can We Reduce Our Ecological Footprint? 75

Unit 5 Food Safety 食品安全 **84**
    Part I   Food Safety—A Global Problem 84
    Part II   Pesticides and Food: How We Test for Safety 97

Unit 6 Ecotourism 生态旅游 **107**
    Part I   Ecotourism 107
    Part II   Can China Embrace Ecotourism? 119

Unit 7　Vertical Farming 垂直农场 ··· **127**
　　Part I　　Vertical Farming ··· 127
　　Part II　　Top Issues of the Vertical Farm Tower ······························· 137

Unit 8　Bioenergy 生物能源 ·· **146**
　　Part I　　An Overview of Biomass Energy ··· 146
　　Part II　　Biofuels ··· 155

Unit 9　Remote Sensing 遥感 ··· **163**
　　Part I　　Remote Sensing in Agriculture ··· 163
　　Part II　　Applications of Remote Sensing to Conservation
　　　　　　　of Forest Ecosystems ·· 173

Unit 10　Carbon Sequestration 碳汇 ·· **181**
　　Part I　　Carbon Sequestration in Agriculture and Forestry ············ 181
　　Part II　　Farmers Cashing in on Carbon Credits Contracts with Firms
　　　　　　　Aiming to Reduce CO_2 Emissions ··································· 190

Vocabulary ·· **198**

Unit 1

Organic Farming

有机农业

Part I The Principles of Organic Agriculture

Warming up

I. Faced with pressing food problems, almost all countries are trying to increase food productivity. Could you give some methods that have helped increase productivity? The following pictures may serve as hints.

> *Discussion assistant*
>
> Farmers use ... to (do) ...
>
> The technology of ... is used (for) ...
>
> ... can help incresase / improve / boost / enhance (提高) ... by (doing) ...
>
> For example, ertilizers can help increase food productity by providing more nutrients.

> animal manure (粪肥); chemical fertilizer (化肥); organic fertilizer (有机肥); insecticide (杀虫剂); fungicide (杀真菌剂); rodenticide (杀鼠剂); herbicide (除草剂); high-yielding crop breeding (高产作物培育); crop rotation (轮作); tansgenic (转基因的) technology;
>
> effective weather-warning sysytem; improve soil quality; nutrient (营养成分, 养分); resistant to harmful weather disasters such as floods, droughts and hailstorms

II. Do you think the above methods damage people's health while increasing productivity?

> *Discussion assistant*
>
> Yes, …does. It harms / damages / endangers (威胁) people's health.
> No, … doesn't.
>
> *conventional manure* (传统肥料): infectious (传染性的) diseases; properly used; animal wastes; viruses or bacteria
>
> *synthetic or chemical fertilizers* (化肥): effective; raising yields (产量); easily transported; pollute; soil, water and air; harm; consumers; for example; damage; immune system (免疫系统); the functions of some organs (器官); infants (婴幼儿)
>
> *green manure* (绿色肥料): better; compared with; contribute to; energy recycle; sustainable (可持续的) development
>
> *genetically-modifying method* (转基因方法): a mixed blessing (喜忧参半的事物); genetically modified produces (转基因农产品); fruits, vegetables and poultry (家禽); a threat to humans; genetically modified varieties (转基因变体); moral problems (道德问题)
>
> For example, Yes, conventional manure does. It can cause infectious diseases if not properly used because it carries bacteria (细菌) and viruses (病毒).

Reading

The Principles of Organic Agriculture

Question 1: How would you define "organic farming"? (Paras. 1—2)

1   One researcher recently found that vegetables in the 1950s contained more than eight times as many trace elements as modern crops. The change could be attributed to the excessive use of nitrate fertilizers. As a consumer reaction against the chemical-based food production, organic farming has come about.

2   Organic farming is the production of food using all natural methods—avoiding all synthetic chemicals and genetically modified organisms, with "zero impact" on environment and leaving the earth in its natural state after the harvest.

3   In order for organic farmers and practitioners to have a clear path to follow, several principles have been formulated. These principles apply to agriculture in the broadest sense, including the way people tend soils, waters, plants and animals in order to produce, prepare and distribute food and other goods.

4   Organic agriculture is based on the principle of health, the principle of ecology, the principle of fairness and the principle of care. These principles are to be used as a whole.

5   *Principle of health:* Organic agriculture should sustain and improve the health of soil, plants, animals, human beings and the planet as one and indivisible.

Question 2: What is a healthy ecosystem? (Para. 6)

6   This principle points out that the health of individuals and communities cannot be separated from the health of ecosystems—healthy soils produce healthy crops that foster the health of animals and people. Health is not simply the absence of illness, but the maintenance of physical, mental, social and ecological well-being. Immunity, resilience and regeneration are key characteristics of health.

Question 3: How is the food produced by organic agriculture different from that we usually see on the market? (Para. 7)

7   The role of organic agriculture, whether in farming, processing, distribution, or consumption, is to sustain and improve the health of ecosystems and organisms from the smallest in the soil to human beings. In particular, organic agriculture aims to produce high-quality, nutritious food that contributes to preventive health care and well-being. In view of this, it should avoid the use of fertilizers, pesticides, animal drugs and food additives that may have harmful health effects.

8   *Principle of ecology*: Organic agriculture should be based on living ecological systems and cycles, work with them, emulate them and help sustain them.

Question 4: Can you fill out other elements of "specific production environment" and "common environment" in the following diagrams? (Paras. 9—10)

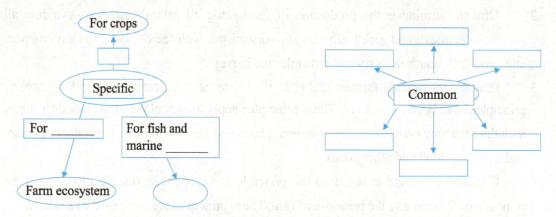

9   This principle roots organic agriculture within living ecological systems. It states that production is to be based on ecological processes and recycling. Nourishment and well-being are achieved through the ecology of the specific production environment. For example, in the case of crops, this is the living soil; for animals, it is the farm ecosystem; for fish and marine organisms, the aquatic environment.

10   Organic management must be adapted to local conditions, ecology, culture and scale. Inputs should be reduced by reuse, recycling and efficient management of materials and energy in order to maintain and improve environmental quality and conserve resources. Those who produce, process, trade, or consume organic products should protect and benefit the common environment including landscapes, climate, habitats, biodiversity, air and water.

11   *Principle of fairness:* Organic agriculture should build on relationships that ensure fairness with regard to the common environment and life opportunities.

12   Fairness is characterized by equity, respect, justice and active control of the shared world, both among people and in their relations to other living beings.

Question 5: What are the aims of organic agriculture? (Para. 13)

13   This principle emphasizes that organic agriculture should ensure fairness at all levels and to all parties—farmers, workers, processors, distributors, traders and consumers. The aims of organic agriculture should include a good quality of life, food and reduction of poverty.

14   *Principle of care:* Organic agriculture should be managed in a precautionary and responsible manner to protect the health and well-being of current and future generations and the environment.

Question 6: Why is organic agriculture a living and dynamic system? (Para. 15)

15   Organic agriculture is a living and dynamic system that coordinates internal and external demands and conditions. Practitioners of organic agriculture can improve efficiency and increase productivity, but this should not be at the risk of damaging health and well-being.

16   These principles state that precaution and responsibility are the key concerns in all stages and process of organic agriculture. Science, practical experience, accumulated wisdom, traditional and indigenous knowledge offer valid solutions.

Vocabulary

accumulate	/ə'kju:mjuleit/	vt.&vi.	积累,堆积
additive	/'æditiv/	n.	添加剂
aquatic	/ə'kwætik/	a.	水栖的,水中的
biodiversity	/ˌbaiəuˌdai'və:siti/	n.	生物多样性
characteristic	/ˌkæriktə'ristik/	n.&a.	特点,特征;特有的,典型的
conserve	/kən'sə:v/	vt.	保护,保存
coordinate	/kəu'ɔ:dinit/	vt.	使协调
distribute	/dis'tribju:t/	vt.	分配,散播
distributor	/dis'tribjutə/	n.	发行人,产品配送人
dynamic	/dai'næmik/	a.	有活力的,动态的
ecology	/i'kɔlədʒi/	n.	生态(学)
ecosystem	/i:kəuˌsistəm/	n.	生态系统
efficiency	/i'fiʃənsi/	n.	效率,效能
emulate	/'emjuleit/	vt.	与……竞争
ensure	/in'ʃuə/	vt.	确保,担保
equity	/'ekwiti/	n.	公平,公正
excessive	/ik'sesiv/	a.	过度的,过分的
external	/ik'stə:nl/	a.	外部的,外观的
fertilizer	/'fə:tiˌlaizə/	n.	肥料,化肥
formulate	/'fɔ:mjuleit/	vt.	构想,规划,阐述
habitat	/'hæbitæt/	n.	栖息地,住处
impact	/'impækt/	n.	影响,作用,冲击
internal	/in'tə:nl/	a.	内部的,内政的,体内的
indigenous	/in'didʒənəs/	a.	本土的,固有的
indivisible	/ˌindi'vizəbəl/	a.	不可分的
landscape	/'lændskeip/	n.	风景,景观,地形
maintenance	/'meintənəns/	n.	维修,维护

marine	/mə'riːn/	a.	海的，海运的，海事的
modify	/'mɔdifai/	vt.	修改，更改
nitrate	/'naitreit/	n.	硝酸盐
nutritious	/njuː'triʃəs/	a.	(有)营养的
organic	/ɔː'gænik/	a.	有机的
organism	/'ɔːgənizəm/	n.	有机体，生物(体)
pesticide	/'pestisaid/	n.	杀虫剂
practitioner	/præk'tiʃənə/	n.	从业者，实习者
precautionary	/pri'kɔːʃənri/	a.	预防的
preventive	/pri'ventiv/	a.&n.	预防的；预防措施
processor	/'prəusesə/	n.	食品加工人，办理事务的人，处理器
productivity	/ˌprɔdʌk'tiviti/	n.	生产率，生产力
regeneration	/riˌdʒenəreit/	n.	再生，重建
resilience	/ri'ziliəns/	n.	恢复力，弹力
sustain	/sə'stein/	vt.	支撑，使继续
synthetic	/sin'θetik/	a.	合成的，人造的
tend	/tend/	vt.&vi.	照顾；倾向，易于(to)
valid	/'vælid/	a.	有效的，有根据的
well-being	/'wel'biːŋ/	n.	健康，幸福
free-living organism			非寄生生物
trace element			微量元素
with regard to			关于

Vocabulary exercises

I. Match each phrase with its Chinese meaning.

1. ____ be attributed to   a. 转基因的
2. ____ harmful effects   b. 以……为特色
3. ____ contribute to   c. 食品添加剂
4. ____ genetically modified   d. 关于
5. ____ food additives   e. 为……作贡献；导致
6. ____ trace elements   f. 归因于……
7. ____ with regard to   g. 冒着……的危险
8. ____ in a ... manner   h. 微量元素

9. _____ at the risk of ...   i. 有害影响
10. _____ be characterized by ...   j. 以……的方式/方法

II. Fill in each blank with the right word from the following box.

| excessive | modified | impact | distribute | sustainable |
| fertilizers | conserve | habitat | accumulated | coordinate |

1. The essence (实质，根本) of modern economy is to _____ energy without hampering (妨碍) the growing economy.
2. A healthy diet is not to take in _____ amount of any kind of food.
3. Genetically _____ species can ensure higher productivity. Meanwhile arguments on their negative effects on human body and morality have arisen.
4. The ways in which people carry out agricultural and industrial productin have long-lasting _____ on the existence of human beings.
5. Organic agriculture aims to _____ the relationships between human demands and the environment we are living in.
6. Modern ecological means should be taken to protect the original (本土的) Metasequoia (水杉) population and its _____.
7. Some species varieties only _____ in areas where living conditions are favorable (有利的) to them.
8. Organic farmers try to avoid the use of _____, pesticides, animal drugs and food additives that may have harmful health effects.
9. With people's awareness of environment growing, the strategy (战略) of _____ development has become the core (核心，重心) of most countries.
10. Plants and animals will adapt better to the environment when some favorable traits (特性) have been _____ in them.

III. It's important to correctly express multiples of numbers in English. Complete the following sentences based on the given Chinese.

1. This piece of land is _____ the size of that one.
   这片田地的面积是那片田地的六倍。
2. This new breeding method is expected to improve the productivity to a level _____ that of last year.
   这一新的培育方法有望将产量提高到去年的两倍。
3. The probabilities of being attacked by pests or diseases are about _____ higher in traditionally grown crops than in crops grown by crop rotation.
   传统耕作的农作物遭受病虫害侵袭的几率比轮作作物大概高出两倍。

4. The price of organically grown vegetables is _____ higher than that of vegetables grown in traditional methods.

   有机农业方法种植的蔬菜的价格比传统方法种植的蔬菜价格高出一倍。

5. A research shows that crops in the 1950s contain _____ as many trace elements as crops of today.

   一项研究结果表明20世纪50年代的作物中微量元素含量是现代作物的八倍。

Listening

Learn the following words and phrases, and then listen to a science report to fill in the blanks with missing information.

Words and phrases			
agrochemical	/ˌægrəʊˈkemɪkl/	n.	农药
bonus	/ˈbəʊnəs/	n.	红利,额外收获
earthworm	/ˈɜːθwɜːm/	n.	蚯蚓
yield	/jiːld/	n.	产量
mycorrhizal fungi			菌根真菌

A latest study shows how organic agriculture can protect biodiversity, save energy, and keep soil healthy.

The researchers (1)_____ data from 76 studies of farms in the United States, Canada, Europe, and New Zealand. They also compared biodiversity levels on (2)_____ and organic farms. More than (3)_____ of the comparisons showed that organic farming benefited (4)_____ more than farms using chemicals and pesticides.

Another study found that while organic crops can have lower (5)_____, which are about 20 percent lower, and the ecology and (6)_____ gains more than just make up for it. The biggest bonus may be soil health: (7)_____ soils have three times as many earthworms, twice as many (8)_____, and 40 percent more mycorrhizal

8

fungi on plant roots than soils polluted with (9) _____ and other chemicals. And in places where farmers cannot afford expensive agrochemicals, organic agriculture can actually (10) _____ yields.

Speaking

I. Please discuss the following points. You may refer to the following passage.

1. Your definition of "organic farming".
2. Advantages of organic produce (农产品).
3. Problems and difficulties that organic farming is now faced with.

Organic farming is the process of producing food naturally. This method avoids the use of synthetic chemical fertilizers and genetically modified organisms. The main idea behind organic farming is "zero impact" on the environment. The definition (定义) of organic varies (变化,不同) from place to place, but it always includes a minimum (最小,最少) time period during which a field is free of chemical use before the field is used for organic farming.

The organic movement began in the 1930s and 1940s as a reaction to agriculture's growing reliance (依赖) on synthetic fertilizers. Artificial fertilizers had been created during the 18th century. These early fertilizers were cheap, powerful, and easy to transport in bulk (大批,大量). Similar advances (进步) occurred in chemical pesticides in the 1940s, leading to the decade being referred to as the "pesticide era".

Farmers and gardeners plan to grow their crops without the aid of artificial (人工的) fertilizers and harmful chemical pesticides. Organic ranchers (农场主) and dairymen (乳牛场主) raise their livestock (牲畜) free of drugs and animal hormones (激素). Supporters of the organic lifestyle believe that food produced in this manner is of higher quality and possesses higher nutritional (营养的) value. Organic farming practice also contributes to soil conservation (水土保持) and biodiversity.

Organic farming on a large scale is both difficult, and time-and-labor-consuming (费时费力的) as well as costly (昂贵的). Researches also show that organic farms have lower yields than conventional ones. Sales and marketing is another problem for organic farmers due to higher prices and people's lack of knowledge about organic produce.

II. Read this passage and discuss what crop rotation (轮作) is.

Growing the same crop over the same piece of land exhausts

(耗竭) soil nutrients (养分) and may lead to more pest disasters and lower yields. Crop rotation, as one technique in organic farming, is a good solution to those problems. Rotating a crop is to change to a different type of crop after the harvest on a particular piece of land. Also, in crop rotation, both crops (previous and following) can yield more, especially if the previous crop is a legume (豆类). As legume crops have the ability of N fixation (固氮) from the air to the soil, the following crop will benefit from it and yield more.

The following pictures illustrate a plan for a four-field crop rotation. Please briefly describe the plan: what is planted in each field in the second year.

(1) First year of rotation   A. lupine (羽扇豆) B. rye (黑麦)   C. potatoes   D. oat (燕麦)

(2) Second year of rotation   A. rye   B. potatoes   C. oat   D. lupine)

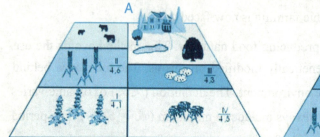
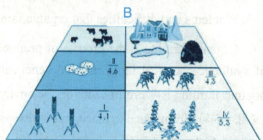

> *Discussion assistant*
>
> first; then; after...; so...; in order to...; as well as; as illustrated in...
>
> divide the piece of land into; equal sections (同等大小的部分); decide; crops to grow; group (把……分类); make a reasonable decision; be familiar with; characteristics and soil requirements; plant family; resistance to pests and diseases; soil benefits; form a crop rotation; rotate the beds (换床,换地); move to the field originally occupied by...; move back; one space (一个格, 一块地)

III. Like vitamins, minerals can be divided into two groups—those needed in larger quantities (major minerals) and those only required in tiny amounts (trace elements). Trace elements are vital for good health. The shortage of trace elements in the body may result in slowed growth (生长迟缓) or even death, but their presence in higher amounts is also harmful. Discuss with a partner and link each element with its functions and food sources.

- Essential for healthy bones
- Contributes to healthy cells, bones and teeth
- Helps to use energy and your muscles to function effectively

1. Phosphorous 磷
2. Calcium 钙
3. Sodium 钠

- Milk and dairy products, dark green leafy vegetables
- Milk, cheese, fish, meat and eggs
- Dark green leafy vegetables, such as cabbage and broccoli

- Helps your body to regulate its water content and your nerves to function effectively
- Helps your cells and body fluids to function properly
- Essential for the body to reach sexual maturity and aids the repair of damaged tissue
- Helps the body to use iron properly
- Ensures healthy cells
- Helps to make thyroid hormones, which control metabolic activity

4. Magnesium 镁

5. Zinc 锌

6. Potassium 钾

7. Iodine (trace element) 碘

8. Copper (trace element) 铜

9. Selenium (trace element) 硒

- Almost all foods as sodium chloride (table salt)
- In most foods, apart from fats, oil and sugar. Particularly found in fruit and vegetables
- Meat, fish, milk, cheese and eggs
- Green vegetables and fish
- Meat, fish, cereals, eggs and cheese
- Seafood and dairy products

> *Expressions for reference*
> muscle (肌肉); function (功能运行); effectively (有效地); regulate (调节); nerve (神经); body fluid (体液); sexual maturity (性成熟); thyroid hormone (甲状腺激素); metabolic activity (新陈代谢活动); dairy (奶制品); cabbage (卷心菜); broccoli (花椰菜); sodium chloride (氯化钠); table salt (食盐)

With people's increasing awareness of food quality and safety, most of them are trying to get the best-quality food they can get. Can you describe some ways people can get healthier food?

How to Obtain Healthier Food

> *Writing assistant*
> first; then; also; additionally; what's more; moreover...
> bear in mind...; not always more expensive;
> location (地点); in season (当季); food items; be lower priced; fresh; grow your own food; local market; more visits; know the shop owner; pick the vegetables on the farm by your own

Part II Green Manuring

Warming up

Different from green manure, organic manures not only provide organic matter (matter from once living organism such as leaves, grass, worms...) but also a mix of nutrients including trace elements essential for good crop growth, and most bagged chemical fertilizers do not offer this added value.

Some sources of organic manure on farms are animal waste, weed, rotten leaves, and urine (尿).

1. Do you know what green manure is? Try to list some of its sources.
2. Can you tell the difference between "organic manure" and "green manure"?

> *Discussion assistant*
> *organic manure:* not only... but also...; organic matter; a mix of nutrients; including trace elements; essential for; crop growth
> *green manure*; a balanced mixture; silage (储藏的饲料); grains (颗粒); when sprinkled (喷洒); soil; spring; late summer; quickly grow into; lush (茂密的) green mass (大块, 大片); young plants; when dug (掘) in; rot (腐烂) down; add valuable nutrients and vegetable matter; feeding (增加营养); improve its structure

Reading

Green Manuring

Question 1: How could green manure increase productivity of the soil? (Para. 1)

1 Green manuring is the practice of turning undecomposed green plant tissue into the soil. The function of a green manure crop is to add organic matter to the soil. As a result of the addition, the nitrogen supply of the soil may be increased and certain nutrients made more readily available, thereby increasing the productivity of the soil.

Question 2: Complete the following table based on the information in paragraph 2.

Country or region	Practice of green manuring	Time

2   The practice of green manuring is very ancient. The Greeks turned broad beans into the soil around 300 B.C., and the planting of beans and lupines for soil improvement was a common practice in the early years of the Roman Empire. The Chinese wrote about the fertilizing value of grass and weeds hundreds of years ago and the early colonists in North America commonly used buckwheat, oats, and rye to add organic matter to the soil. Early in the 18th century, farmers in the southeastern United States recognized the value of green manure crops, especially the legumes, but the usage of green manure in North America peaked in the 1940s, with a notable go-down in planted acreage since that time. With the current trend toward the use of "organic" fertilizers, many people are again looking at green manuring as an economical, practical, and even aesthetically pleasing method of restoring productivity to idle or overworked land.

3   Some of the positive aspects of green manuring as well as some soil science basics will be presented here, which are necessary to the use of this method of fertilization.

4   The major benefits of using green manure in a crop rotation system include organic matter and nitrogen addition, nutrient conservation, and protection of the soil surface during erosion-prone periods of the year.

Question 3: What is "free-living organism"? Please give two examples. (Para. 5)

5   *Organic Matter and Nitrogen Addition*—The organic matter added by the decomposition of green manures encourages the activities of the "free-living" organisms. The organic residues from green manures also help to stabilize the soil structure, increase the water holding capacity of the soil, and increase the infiltration of moisture into the soil and percolation through the soil.

Question 4: What's the function of green manure's decomposing process? (Para. 6)

6   Additional Nutrients Added —Some green manure crops may use less available nutrients than the main crop; hence, when they are ploughed under, they may increase the availability of some nutrients for the main crop. In addition, by decomposing rapidly, the plant residues liberate large quantities of carbon dioxide and weak acids, which act on insoluble soil minerals to release nutrients for plant growth.

Question 5: What causes soil erosion? (Para. 7)

7   Nutrient and Soil Conservation —These two benefits of green manuring are closely related. Since green manure crops are often planted in the late summer or fall after a primary crop, the green manure covers use excess fertilizer not taken up by the main crop. When they are incorporated into the soil the following spring, they not only protect the soil from erosion due to fall and early spring rains and winter runoff, but also conserve nutrients which might have leached away or caused the pollution of streams and lakes.

8   Green manures might be the hardest-working plants you'll ever grow. They are easy to plant and require only basic care to thrive. But remember, despite the above-mentioned contribution to main crops and soil, green manures supplement rather than replace manures and fertilizers.

Vocabulary

acid	/ˈæsid/	n.&a.	酸；酸性的
acreage	/ˈeikəridʒ/	n.	英亩数
aesthetically	/iːsˈθetikəli/	ad.	审美地，美学地
available	/əˈveiləbl/	a.	可用的，可得到的
bean	/biːn/	n.	豆类
buckwheat	/ˈbʌkwiːt/	n.	荞麦属植物
colonist	/ˈkɔlənist/	n.	殖民主义者
decompose	/ˌdiːkəmˈpəuz/	vt.	变坏，分解
erosion	/iˈrəuʒən/	n.	腐蚀
excess	/ikˈses, ˈekses/	a.&n.	过多的，额外的；过量
fertilize	/ˈfəːtilaiz/	vt.	给……施肥
incorporate	/inˈkɔːpəreit/	vt.	包含，合并
infiltration	/ˌinfilˈtreiʃən/	n.	渗透
insoluble	/inˈsɔljubl/	a.	不溶解的

leach	/liːtʃ/	vt.	沥滤
legume	/ˈleɡjuːm/	n.	豆类,豆英
liberate	/ˈlibəreit/	vt.	解放,释放
lupine	/ˈljuːpin/	n.	羽扇豆
moisture	/ˈmɔistʃə/	n.	水分,湿气
nitrogen	/ˈnaitrədʒən/	n.	氮
notable	/ˈnəutəbəl/	a.	显著的
oat	/əut/	n.	燕麦
peak	/piːk/	vi.	达到高峰
percolation	/ˈpəːkəleiən/	n.	过滤,渗透
plough	/plau/	vt.	耕,犁
positive	/ˈpɔzətiv/	a.	正面的,积极的,肯定的
practical	/ˈpræktikəl/	a.	实用的,实践的
release	/riˈliːs/	vt.	释放,发行
replace	/riˈpleis/	vt.	取代
residue	/ˈrezidjuː/	n.	剩余,余渣
restore	/riˈstɔː/	vt.	修复,重建
rotation	/rəuˈteiʃən/	n.	旋转,轮换
runoff	/ˈrʌnɔf/	n.	流走之物
rye	/rai/	n.	黑麦
stabilize	/ˈsteibilaiz/	vt.&vi.	(使)稳定,(使)稳固
supplement	/ˈsʌplimənt/	vt.	增补,补充
thrive	/θraiv/	vt.	兴盛,兴隆
tissue	/ˈtiʃuː/	n.	组织,薄纸
trend	/trend/	n.	趋势,倾向
water holding capacity			水容量

Vocabulary exercises

I. Match each word with its explanation.

1. ____ supplement   a. the ability or power to contain, absorb, or hold
2. ____ residue   b. any substance that nourishes (滋养) an organism
3. ____ release   c. worthy of being noted or remembered; remarkable
4. ____ capacity   d. using the minimum required; not wasteful

5. ____ nutrient   e. matter remaining after something has been removed
6. ____ notable   f. the output of an industrial concern in relation to the materials, labor, and so on that it employs
7. ____ productivity   g. to provide something extra in order to remedy (修正) a deficiency (不足)
8. ____ economical   h. to free (something) from; let go or fall

II. Fill in each blank with the right word from the following box. Change the form when necessary.

| replace | pollution | related | productivity | organic matter |
| decomposition | release | positive | crop rotation | addition |

1. Despite its _____ effects on both soil and human body, organic farming presents some difficulties for farmers.
2. The function of green manure is to add _____ to the soil.
3. By decomposing, the plant residue of green manure crops will _____ certain nutrients for a crop.
4. Crop rotation, green manure, compost (堆肥), biological pest control, and mechanical cultivation (机械耕作), the main practices in organic farming are actually closely _____.
5. The organic matter added by the _____ of green manures encourages the activities of the "free-living" organisms.
6. The core in properly employing green manuring is that it supplements rather than _____ manures and fertilizers.
7. By monitoring the air and water conditions while taking effective measures we can actually reduce biological _____ of our environment.
8. As a result of the _____, the nitrogen supply of the soil may be increased and certain nutrients made more readily available.
9. _____ is one of the oldest and most effective agricultural control strategies. It means that the planned order of specific crops are planted on the same field. It also means that the followed crop belongs to a different family than the previous (先前的) one.
10. Mechanical cultivation will help do away with heavy manual labor (体力劳动) and raise _____.

Listening

Listen to a dialogue and fill in the following blanks with missing information.

Reporter: Mr. Byron, we know that organic farming is quite (1) _____ in recent years. Do you think there exist some risks or trouble in the practical (2)_____ of the new method?

Byron: Yes. There are two (3)_____ types of risks in organic farming: one is pest outbreaks and the other one is (4)_____ and financial risks.

Reporter: What will be the consequence of these risks?

Byron: Pest outbreaks will (5)_____ in lower yield and inferior products, and marketing and financial risks can lead to the stop of an organic farm.

Reporter: Can farmers do something to (6)_____ or avoid the risks?

Byron: Fortunately yes. Pest outbreaks can be (7)_____ through managing ecological system while the solution to marketing and financial problems is rather (8)_____.
For example, many organic food producers are much smaller than the buyers in the (9)_____ market, so they are always at a disadvantage when in a dispute with the buyers. Many can tell stories of selling some of their grain to a company and never receiving (10)_____ for it. Also, organic producers need to develop good marketing skills.

Reporter: Thanks for your informative talk, Mr. Byron.

Speaking

I. Cattle dung (牛粪) has been used as organic manure for many years. This practice not only reduces pollution of the soil, drinking water and rivers, but also contributes to energy conservation. In recent decades cattle dung also works its way into our daily life and industry. Look at the following picture carefully and describe the cycle of a different use of cattle dung—biomass energy, a kind of driving-power source.

STEAM CYCLE

> **Discussion assistant**
>
> *Describe a sequence:* first; then; next; after that; finally; eventually
>
> For example, First the cattle on a feedlot produce a lot of cattle dung. Then the dung will be loaded on a truck and transported to a specified site of an ethanol factory.
>
> pass by; transport (运输); load (装货); unload (卸货); dump (抛弃,倾倒); gasify (使……汽化); get fermented and gasified; generate; serve as...; produce; recycle; ferment (发酵); time; driving-power source; feed (饲料); ranch (农场); steam (蒸汽); WDGS (酒糟); feedlot (饲养场); ethanol facility (制酒设备); in bulk (成批,大量); selectively (有选择地); eventually

II. Read the following passage on agricultural pest management and describe how each pest management tool works based on the reference words and phrases in the table.

A pest is any organism harmful to humans; agricultural pests include insects, mites (螨类), nematodes (线虫类), plant pathogens (病菌,病原体), weeds, and vertebrates (脊椎动物). If pests are not managed, crop yield and quality will drop. Pest management is a key issue in farming and its philosophy is that "pests should be managed, not eradicated (清除)" because pests are inevitable (不可避免的) components (组成部分) of an agricultural system.

There are four broad categories (类别) of pest management tools. In the table below some key words and phrases are given on each category.

Chemical management	*Goal:* repel (驱走); kill pests *Technique:* large number; chemical pesticide; mixtures (混合物); active ingredients (成分); each has a different spectrum (范围) of pest control
Cultural management	*Goal:* all designed to make the environment less favorable (有利的) for pests *Technique:* include; mechanical cultivation (机械耕作); adjusting (调整) planting / harvesting dates; crop rotations
Biological management	*Goal:* force pests out; repel pests *Technique:* accommodate (留宿,容纳); predators (捕食者); parasites (寄生物); pathogens (病原体); competitors (竞争者); and antagonistic (对抗的) microorganisms (微生物); all believed to have little health or environmental threat; another; biological technique; the use of biopesticides (生物杀虫剂)

Bioengineered crops	*Goal:* cultivate; varieties; genetically engineered with traits (特性) for pest management
	Technique: genetic engineering; a more precise (精确的) change of a plant's traits; without the undesirable (不合需要的) characteristics that may occur with traditional breeding (培育) methods.

Background Reading

What is organic farming?
What is green manure?
Soil Conservation.

Please refer to the attached disk.

Unit 2

Soilless Cultivation

无土栽培

Part I Soilless Agriculture Helps Save Planet

Warming up

I. Some natural disasters (自然灾害) like hurricane (飓风), tsunami (海啸), drought (干旱), sandstorm, ice storm, wildfire, snowstorm, earthquake, flood, and volcano (火山) may cause food production problems. What's the specific disaster shown in each of the following pictures?

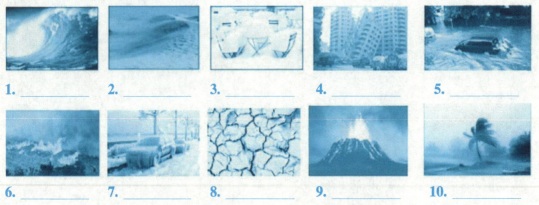

1. _____ 2. _____ 3. _____ 4. _____ 5. _____

6. _____ 7. _____ 8. _____ 9. _____ 10. _____

II. The following statements show some advantages and disadvantages of traditional soil agriculture. Please tick (√) the ones you think of as its disadvantages.

____ 1. Plants cannot be grown anywhere since it needs soil.

____ 2. It does not need high technology and high management skills.

____ 3. It is difficult to keep plant nutrition and water in control and a big part of them is wasted as a result.

____ 4. The animal waste improves the quality of soil and costs very little.

_____ 5. It needs a lot of energy.

_____ 6. It can lead to an increase in the pollution of land and streams with high levels of runoff fertilizers (肥料).

_____ 7. The crops produced in this system are probably tasty, nutritious and natural.

_____ 8. The use of heavy machines results in damage to the soil structure, which may lead to serious soil erosion (流失,侵蚀) problems.

_____ 9. The rotation of crops (庄稼轮作) might prevent soil erosion.

_____ 10. High residues of pesticides pose a health hazard to consumers.

_____ 11. Good quality soil is able to produce greater crops.

_____ 12. Pests and weed can affect the overall production and decrease the yields. And the use of pesticides may pollute the environment.

_____ 13. The initial cost for construction of this system is not high.

III. It is generally believed that soil, sunlight, water and oxygen are four essential ingredients (必要的构成要素) for growing healthy crops. If one says we can grow crops without soil, what do you think of him?

IV. The following four products are digital nutrient tester (营养物数码测试器), digital dissolved oxygen meter (溶解氧数码计量表), light tester, and nutrient solution (营养液) used in soilless cultivation. Work out their functions in view of their names.

> *Discussion assistant*
>
> be used for testing... (用于测试……); provide the plants with... (给植物提供了……); ensure (确保); levels of nutrient concentrations in solutions (溶液中的营养液浓度); dissolved oxygen (溶解的氧); monitor (监控); light intensity and levels (光照的强度和级别); consistent and repeated harvest (持续不断的收获); best crop yield (最佳农作物产量)

Reading

Soilless Agriculture Helps Save Planet

Question 1: What seems to be an alternative method that helps us save the future of our planet? (Para. 1)

1   With global warming, poor soil fertility and pesticides becoming bigger threats with every passing day, organic farming methods are becoming more and more popular. Among them, soilless agriculture is an alternative method that is likely to contribute to protecting the future of the planet.

Question 2: How did Gericke produce tall tomato plants? (Para. 2)

2   Soilless agriculture represents one of the most innovative practices in modern agricultural development. The first widely publicized soilless experiments were conducted during the 1930's. W.F. Gericke, a professor of the University of California at Berkeley, varied nutrient levels among samples suspended in a gravel substrate to demonstrate remarkable alterations in growth. Among the findings, what amazed his fellow horticulturalists most was the production of tomato plants over six meters high.

Question 3: What are the main types of soilless growing systems? (Para. 3)

3   Called hydroponics, soilless agriculture is the science of growing plants in water or inert media such as shavings, bark, compost, sand, pebbles and processed clay in organic and inorganic environments. It is a method for growing plants in nutrient-infused solutions that supply all the required elements needed for optimum plant growth. The crops can survive as

long as they are supplied with sufficient moisture, nutrients and oxygen. The main types of hydroponics growing systems are the reservoir method, the flood and drain method (Ebb and Flow), the drip system, the nutrient film technique (NFT), the wick system, the aeroponics method and so on.

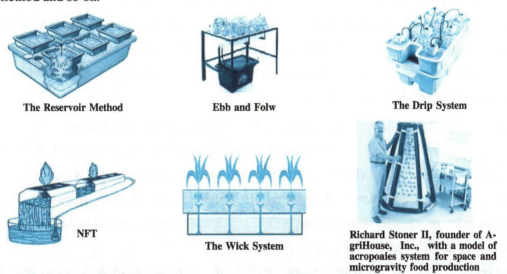

The Reservoir Method   Ebb and Folw   The Drip System

NFT   The Wick System   Richard Stoner II, founder of A-griHouse, Inc., with a model of acropoaies system for space and microgravity food production

> Question 4: Why has soilless agriculture caught attention around the world? (Para. 4—8)

4   Soilless agriculture is expanding throughout the world. There are many reasons why it is preferred. Loss of soil, the problem of chemicals, the excessive need for fertilizer and water, and low productivity can be listed as the leading reasons for switching to soilless agriculture.

5   Since the world's rapid population growth requires meeting increasing food needs, there is a risk that soil may not be efficient enough. Soilless agriculture is a good choice for some countries that do not have normal, adequate soil for agriculture, such as Arab countries and Israel, which have many desert areas. It's also appropriate for Japan, where the territory is small and stony. Some advocators even argue that it is a cultivation method that can be applied in every type of region that is not appropriate for cultivation.

6   The use of insecticides and herbicides in traditional soil farming is harmful for consumers' health and the environment. Besides, continuous cultivation of crops can result in poor soil fertility, which in turn leads to poor yield and quality. So a major benefit of soilless agriculture is the possibility of obtaining pesticide-free products and protecting people's health and environment.

7   Hydroponics uses as little as one tenth of the water that a conventionally grown crop would require. In a re-circulating hydroponics system, the plants use

all the nutrients put into the system. This results in a very efficient pollution-free method of growing that requires fewer nutrients than a conventional system. So efficient use of water and fertilizers is also its principal advantage.

8   Soilless agriculture is capable of producing greater yield. Hydroponic tomato, for example, has a higher production—up to ten times higher than field-grown one. It takes about four months for field-grown tomato to be harvested, but hydroponics can reduce that period of time significantly. With adequate care and regular nutrition the possibility for continuous year round production is entirely practical.

Question 5: What are some challenges to soilless agriculture? (Paras. 9—10)

9   However, there are some challenges to soilless farming. First and foremost, it requires higher initial capital for technological investment and modern equipment. It is generally more expensive than using fertile land. However, the system can pay for itself in just a few years because the revenue from these crops will be maximized. Some growers believe the key to success is growing high-value crops.

10   What's more, high degree of management skills is necessary for solution preparation, maintenance of pH, EC, nutrient deficiency judgment and correction, ensuring aeration, maintenance of favorable condition inside protected structures, etc. If the system malfunctions, environmental pollution may result.

Question 6: What is the most commonly cultivated crop through the soilless system? (Para. 11)

11   A variety of crops can be grown through soilless system. The crop most commonly cultivated through the system is tomato. Strawberry, lettuce, pepper, cucumber, melon, mushroom, and so on can be similarly cultivated. Of course, the method is not restricted to eatable crops. Flowers such as roses, tulips and orchids can also be grown in this way.

Question 7: What can be expected of soilless agriculture in the future? (Para. 12)

12   Soilless agriculture is now a growing industry. Marvin Brown, president of BBI Produce Inc. in Dover, Florida, the largest state grower and shipper of fresh strawberries, predicted soilless production—although still in its infancy—could be a part of our future. Brown said, "Advancements in technology and growing techniques will undoubtedly increase our desire and ability to use alternative production methods that are both economical and ecologically acceptable to all."

Vocabulary

adequate	/'ædikwit/	a.	适当的,足够的
advocator	/ædvəkeitə/	n.	拥护者,提倡者
aeration	/ˌeiə'reiʃən/	n.	通风
aeroponic	/ˌɛərəu'pɔnik/	a.	太空的
alteration	/ˌɔːltə'reiʃən/	n.	变更,改造
alternative	/ɔːl'tɜːnətiv/	a.&n.	二者可选其一的(事物)
appropriate	/ə'prəupriət/	a.	适当的
bark	/bɑːk/	n.	树皮
challenge	/'tʃælindʒ/	n.	挑战
cucumber	/'kjuːkʌmbə/	n.	黄瓜
compost	/'kɔmpɔst/	n.	混合肥料,堆肥
conduct	/kən'dʌkt/	vt.&vi.	进行
conventionally	/kən'venʃənəli/	ad.	按照惯例地,照常套地
deficiency	/di'fiʃənsi/	n.	缺乏,不足
drain	/drein/	vt.&vi.	排水,引流
ecological	/ˌiːkə'lɔdʒikəl/	a.	生态学的
economical	/ˌiːkə'nɔmikəl/	a.	节约的,经济的
fertility	/fɜː'tiliti/	n.	肥沃,丰产
horticulturalist	/'hɔːtikʌltʃərəlist/	n.	园艺家
hydroponics	/'haidrəu'pɔniks/	n.	水耕法,水栽培
insecticide	/in'sektisaid/	n.	杀虫剂
inert media	/i'nɜːt 'miːdiə/	n.	惰性的媒介
infancy	/'infənsi/	n.	幼年
innovative	/'inəuˌveitiv/	a.	创新的
lettuce	/'letis/	n.	莴苣,生菜
malfunction	/mæl'fʌŋkʃən/	vi.	运转不正常
maximize	/'mæksimaiz/	vt.	最佳化,最大化
optimum	/'ɔptiməm/	a.	最适宜的
orchid	/'ɔːkid/	n.	兰花

pebble	/ˈpebəl/	n.	小圆石，小鹅卵石
practice	/ˈpræktis/	n.	习惯做法
predict	/priˈdikt/	vt.	预知，预言
principal	/ˈprinsəpəl/	a.	主要的，首要的
remarkable	/riˈmɑːkəbəl/	a.	杰出的，非凡的
reservoir	/ˈrezəvwɑː/	n.	蓄水池
restrict	/risˈtrikt/	vt.	限制
sample	/ˈsɑːmpl/	n.	样本
shavings	/ˈʃeiviŋz/	n.	刨花
significantly	/sigˈnifikəntli/	ad.	显著地
strawberry	/ˈstrɔːbəri/	n.	草莓
suspend	/səsˈpend/	vt.	吊，悬挂
switch	/switʃ/	v.	转换，转变
territory	/ˈteritəri/	n.	领土，地域
tulip	/ˈtjuːlip/	n.	郁金香
vary	/ˈveəri/	vt.	改变
gravel substrate			沙砾培养基
initial capital			创办资本，启动资金
nutrient-infused solution			注入了营养液的溶液
pH			酸碱度
processed clay			加工过的黏土
wich system			毛细传送系统
EC: Electrical Conductivity			电导率
Ebb and flow			潮差无土栽培法
NTF			养分膜技术

BBI Produce Inc. in Dover（美国）多佛BBI农产品生产公司，创立于1990年，主要生产"Berry Boss"牌草莓，现为佛罗里达州最大的草莓生产和供应商。

Vocabulary exercises

I. Match each word with its explanation.

1. _____ circulate   a. new
2. _____ ecological   b. to increase or make as great as possible

3. _____ efficient   c. to prepare, treat
4. _____ innovative   d. all the income produced by a particular source
5. _____ maximize   e. showing a high ratio of output to input
6. _____ process   f. to move in or flow through a circle
7. _____ revenue   g. to remain alive or in existence
8. _____ survive   h. of the science of the relationships between organisms (有机体) and their environments

II. **Complete the following introduction of the aeroponics (太空无土栽培) with proper words and phrases from the box. Meanwhile, find out the disadvantages and advantages of this soilless growing system.**

| provided | crop yields | more growth | significantly | reduce |
| actually | less popular | protect | producers | soil-free |

Aeroponics is a (1)_____ growing method where plant roots are suspended in air within a 100 percent humidity (湿度), highly-oxygenated growing chamber (封闭的空间). This growing system was (2)_____ started by NASA (National Aeronautics and Space Administration (美国航空航天局) in 1997 when it sponsored (赞助) to study adzuki bean seeds and seedlings (赤豆种子和秧苗) in Mir space station(〈俄罗斯〉和平号太空站). The study found out that Mir-grown seeds and seedlings in aeroponic system showed (3)_____ than those grown on Earth.

For ordinary gardeners, aeroponics is (4)_____ for it is more expensive and harder to build than other hydroponic systems. Aeroponics is now being used by commercial growers and (5)_____ for clean, efficient, and rapid food production. Aeroponics can (6)_____ water usage by 98 percent, fertilizer usage by 60 percent, and pesticide usage by 100 percent, all while maximizing (最佳化) (7)_____. By conserving water and removing harmful pesticides and fertilizers used in soil, growers are doing their part to (8)_____ the Earth. Moreover, because aeroponic plants are (9)_____ with ideal levels of nutrients, water and oxygen, they grow (10)_____ faster, are healthier and more nutritious than plants grown in soil. (AeroGarden is a machine designed in the principle of aeroponics. The following two pictures show a comparison of lettuce plant growth using the AeroGarden system and traditional fertile soil.)

AeroGarden™ vs. Soil—Day 15   **AeroGarden™ vs. Soil—Day 33**

I. Listen to a lecture "Choose Hydroponics Gardening as a Hobby" given by Susan Slobacy as a guest of a horticulture program and then answer the following questions.

1. How does a person who loves gardening feel when winter comes?
2. According to Susan, what will happen if one chooses hydroponics gardening as a hobby?
3. What does one need to buy if he wants to start hydroponics gardening?
4. What kinds of advantages of hydroponics gardening does Susan mention in her lecture?
5. How does hydroponics gardening seem to be according to Susan?

II. Study the following two pictures and listen to a short passage entitled "Making a Homemade Nutrient Film Technique System (自制营养液膜水培系统)". Meanwhile, fill in the following blanks with the missing information.

To build a homemade hydroponics NFT system, you will need (1)_____ gutters (水槽), PVC pipe, or any flat container a few inches deep. You will need a cheap plastic tote (手提袋) for a (2)_____ reservoir, and an air pump to keep it oxygenated (充氧). You will also need a water pump (抽水机) to move the nutrient solution, and some capillary (毛状的, 毛细作用的) mat (垫子).

In this homemade hydroponics example, the gardener uses one line from the (3)_____ to feed the top PVC pipe. Gravity then pulls the water (4)_____ until it is back at the nutrient reservoir.

In this (5)_____, each row is being fed (6)_____ from a line off the pump. Each row drains back into a (7)_____ pipe, which drains back to the nutrient reservoir. This setup would use a much stronger water pump.

However you decide to (8)_____ your homemade hydroponics system, the key to this (9)_____ is the capillary mat in the bottom of every gutter, pipe, and tray. Also, (10)_____ to pitch (倾斜) your pipes a little to keep the water flowing in the right direction.

Speaking

I. Discuss all the possible advantages and disadvantages of soilless agriculture based on your previous (先前的) knowledge and understanding of the text. Please list them under the headings For and Against respectively.

For	Against
1) Land is not necessary. It can be practiced even in upstairs, open spaces and in protected structures. 2) 3) 4) 5) 6) ...	1) Higher initial capital expenditure. 2) 3) 4) 5) 6) ...

II. The pH can affect the availability (可用性) of nutrients and it can affect the absorption of nutrients by plant roots. The letters "pH" mean "potential hydrogen (氢)". The pH value of a nutrient solution is a measure of the acidity (酸性) or alkalinity (碱性) of a solution. The pH scale ranges from 0 (very acidic 强酸的) to 14 (highly alkaline 强碱的). A change of one unit in pH scale represents tenfold (十倍) change in acidity or alkalinity. That means a solution with a pH of 5.0 is 10 times more acidic than a solution with a pH of 6.0 and 100 times more acidic than a solution with a pH of 7.0. Please study the following two charts and work out the answers to the given questions with your partner.

1. What is the pH value of a neutral (中性的) solution?
2. What happens to a solution if its pH decreases?
3. What happens to a solution if its pH increases?
4. Above which value can pH cause iron, manganese, copper, zinc and boron ions to be less available to plants?
5. Below which value can pH cause the solubility of phosphoric acid, calcium and magnesium to drop?
6. With which range of pH values can a nutrient solution best suit most varieties of vegetables? What does this indicate?

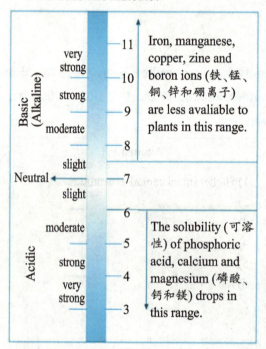

pH Values for Different Hydroponic Crops	
Plant	pH Range
Bean	6.0—6.5
Cabbage (卷心菜)	6.5—7.5
Carrot (胡萝卜)	5.8—6.4
Cucumber	5.8—6.0
Lettuce	6.0—6.5
Onion (洋葱)	6.5—7.0
Pineapple (菠萝)	5.0—5.5
Pumpkin (南瓜)	5.0—6.5
Strawberry (草莓)	5.5—6.5
Broccoli (球花甘蓝)	6.0—6.5
Radish (小萝卜)	6.0—7.0
Tomato	5.5—6.5

7. Which crop can be best cultivated in the nutrient solution with the pH between 5.5 and 6.5?
8. Which crop prefers a slightly alkaline solution?
9. Which crops like a moderate acidic solution?
10. Which crop can grow in a nutrient solution that is 10 times more acidic than that used for growing broccoli?

III. In conventional soil farming, pesticides are used to control weeds, pests and diseases in crops. At high dosages (剂量) they may not only kill insects, but also birds and mammals (哺乳动物). At lower levels they will probably cause a range of serious sublethal effects (潜在的致命效应). They are certainly a source of pollution.

1. Work with a partner to find out some other sources of pollution in agriculture and forestry.

2. Study the movement and cycle of pollutants shown in the following two diagrams and choose one to describe to your partner.

> *Discussion assistant*
>
> Once used, some of pesticides will be absorbed by..., leached below...or degraded by...
>
> Some of them will adhere to...
>
> Finally, they will run into...
>
> Pollutants like ... and so on will be partly absorbed by..., leached...by rain or irritation...
>
> leach (过滤); degrade (使有机化合物进行降解); adhere to (黏着); vaporize (使蒸发); bacteria oxidation (菌氧化物); particle (微粒); ultra violet light (紫外线); deposit (沉淀); pollutant (污染物); fertilizer (肥料); organic manure (有机肥料); slurry (泥浆); aquifer (蓄水层); permeable (可被渗透和穿透的); pore (小孔); zone (地域; 地带)

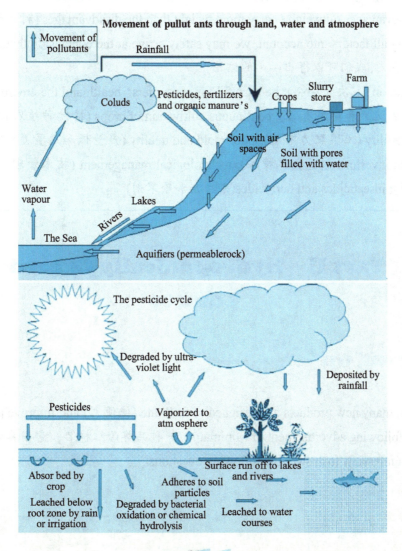

Writing

Now that you have learned a lot about soilless agriculture, please write a passage entitled "Why Sometimes People Prefer Soilless Agriculture to Soil Agriculture?"

Why Sometimes People Prefer Soilless Agriculture to Soil Agriculture?

> *Writing assistant*
>
> ...is playing an increasingly important role in...;
>
> With science and technology highly developed, ...
>
> Nowadays, more and more people come to realize the importance of...
>
> There are several advantages of...
>
> The first / the biggest advantage is...
>
> For all the disadvantages, it has its beneficial effects;
>
> However, ... just like anything else, has its negative (消极的) sides as well;
>
> The advantages outweigh / carry more weight than the disadvantages (利大于弊);
>
> Taking all factors into account, we may safely arrive at the conclusion that... (把……考虑在内,我们可以得出……的结论);
>
> depend on (取决于……); be harmful for consumers' health and the environment (对消费者健康和环境有害); continuous cultivation of crops (持续种植农作物); poor soil fertility (土壤肥力不足); poor yield and quality (产量低和质量差); high initial capital investment (高成本投入); technological management (技术管理); limitation (局限); insecticides and herbicides(杀虫剂和除草剂)

Part II Hydroponically Grown Tomato

Warming up

Listening

Nowadays, many new products are designed to facilitate (使便利) and improve people's life. Study the following advertisement of Minimato (一种品牌西红柿名,意指其小) and then listen to an interview to answer the following questions.

Words and phrases

antioxidant	/ˌænti'ɔksidənt/	n.	抗氧化剂
miniature	/'minətʃə/	a.	缩小的, 微型的
decorative	/'dekərətiv/	a.	装饰的

1 Place the **minimato** pot into a small dish

2 Feel the dish with 2 cm of water

3 Place in a well-lite area at room temperature

Now you are ready to grow and pick your own sweet cherry tomatoes

Easy to grow **minimato** gives your home that perfect touch of Mother Nature

Plant size (h):	28-33 cm	Fruit weight (Avg.):	11-13.5 gr.
Number of clusters:	8	Brix:	8-10
Number of fruits (Avg.):	50-70	Harvest period:	65 days
Fruit size (Avg.):	25-30 mm	Resistance/ Tolerance:	V, N

Questions

1. Which words does the manager use to describe Minimato?
2. What does the manager mean by saying "educational"?
3. Do you happen to know other hydroponic products?

Reading

Hydroponically Grown Tomato

Question 1: What can be inferred about hydroponically grown tomatoes? (Paras. 1—2)

1 Growing hydroponic tomatoes is one of the newest and hottest trends in gardening and it's well worth for both businessmen and home users alike. The quality of the hydroponically grown tomato is unsurpassed with a beautiful appearance, smooth skin, little or no blemishes, a deep red color when fully ripe, a real tomato smell, a meaty texture, and an excellent flavor. A comment often heard from people tasting a hydroponic tomato for the first time is, "this tomato really tastes like a tomato!"

2 A tomato's sweetness and flavor is largely dependent on light and temperature. Its nutritional value is dependent on the received

nutrition while growing and producing fruit. In the controlled environment, the exact requirements of hydroponic tomato can be met with artificial lighting, temperature control and supplemental nutrition. This enables growers to enjoy a continuous harvest all year long without sacrificing taste and nutrition.

Question 2: If growers want to harvest tomatoes all year round, what type of tomato should they grow? (Para. 3)

3   All tomatoes are divided into one of two growing types—determinate and indeterminate. The determinate varieties will grow in an upright position, reach full height, and then not grow much larger. Determinate varieties bear fruit all at one time. Indeterminate varieties have a tendency to sprawl. Branches on indeterminate tomato plants grow long and will drop if not staked. They bear fruit over an extended period of time but it's still a good idea to plant several plants at intervals if you want to enjoy them year round.

Question 3: What will probably happen to the plants if tomato roots are exposed to light when seedlings begin to sprout? (Para. 4)

4   Growers can choose their desired variety and start the seeds in one-inch rockwool starter cubes in a standard nursery tray with a dome. Rockwool cubes should be pre-soaked in water adjusted to a pH of 4.5 before planting. Keep covered tray in a moist, warm (20—25℃) environment until seedlings begin to sprout. Once vegetation appears, immediately move the seedling into a light source for at least 12 hours per day and remove domes. Failure to provide light soon enough will cause seedlings to bend in search of a light source. Ensure roots are never exposed to light as this will cause damage or death to the roots and delay plant growth.

Question 4: When is the best time for tomato seedlings to be transplanted to their hydroponic garden? (Para. 5)

5   Once true leaves appear and roots are showing through the bottom of the starter cubes, usually around 10 to 14 days, seedlings are ready to be transplanted to their hydroponic garden. There are several different hydroponic methods used for cultivating tomatoes. Space

restrictions, type of tomato and plant size all have to be considered when choosing a system.

Question 5: Which is the most common method employed for large tomato plants? (Para. 6)

6   The most common method employed for large plants is the drip irrigation system. In this fully automated, re-circulating system nutrient solution is pumped from a reservoir, fed to the plants through drip emitters and allowed to drain back to the reservoir by gravity. In order to create gravity flow the grow unit must be placed higher than the nutrient reservoir. The nutrient is continuously circulated during light-on hours. Irrigation will need adjusting as the plants grow, allowing for four liters of nutrient solution per day for mature plants.

7   Ebb and flow or "flood and drain" tables are another excellent method used for cultivating tomatoes. Tables range in size from 1' × 2' to 4' × 8' and can accommodate many plants in a small area. For cherry tomatoes or smaller determinate varieties, deep water culture may be used.

Question 6: What is the most important factor that influences the growth of hydroponic tomato? (Para. 8)

8   No matter what technique growers choose, there are several growth influencing factors to consider: light, pH, temperature, etc. The most important one is light. At maturity, tomato plants require a 16—18 hour photoperiod to ensure maximum fruit production and an 8-hour respiration period of total darkness. pH is another very important factor. If pH levels are not maintained at the suitable level (pH 5.8—6.3 for tomatoes), nutrient deficiencies and toxicity will occur. Temperature is also an important factor. The ideal  daytime temperature for mature tomato plants bearing fruit is 18—25° C and nighttime is 12—18° C. An independent thermostat should be placed among your plants to ensure temperature regulation. An exhaust fan will help control temperature and provide air exchange.

9   Once hydroponics tomato begins to flower, growers will spend a few minutes every day gently shaking the leaves and branches. This activity will distribute pollen more thoroughly around the plant, ensuring more widespread fertilization, which means more tomatoes.

Question 7: Between commercially grown hydroponic tomatoes and home grown hydroponic tomatoes, which ones are probably tasty and nutritious? (Para. 10)

10   Commercially grown hydroponic tomatoes are picked green and not given the opportunity to develop flavor with a view to extending their shelf life and for ease of transport. Home hydroponic gardeners do not have these concerns and can let their tomatoes

ripen on the vine and develop their full flavor. But in any case, hydroponic tomatoes are superior in flavor and nutrition to their soil grown counterparts. It's no wonder that they are getting increasingly popular though the cost to produce them is comparatively high.

Vocabulary

accommodate	/ə'kɔmədeit/	vt.	容纳，使适应
artificial	/ˌɑːti'fiʃəl/	a.	人工的
automated	/'ɔːtəmeitid/	a.	自动化的
blemish	/'blemiʃ/	n.	缺点，瑕疵
commercially	/kə'məːʃəli/	ad.	商业上
determinate	/di'təːminit/	a.	确定的
drain	/drein/	vt.	排出
dome	/dəum/	n.	圆顶
fertilization	/ˌfəːtilai'zeiʃən/	n.	施肥，授精
indeterminate	/ˌindi'təːminit/	a.	不确定的
irrigation	/'irigeiʃən/	n.	灌溉
meaty	/'miːti/	a.	肉的
maximum	/'mæksiməm/	n.	最大量，最大限度
photoperiod	/ˌfəutəu'piəriəd/	n.	光周期（有机物每天暴露于阳光的时间）
pump	/pʌmp/	n.&vt.	泵；（用泵）抽
pollen	/'pɔlin/	n.	花粉
respiration	/ˌrespi'reiʃən/	n.	呼吸，呼吸作用
reservoir	/'rezəvwɑː/	n.	小池，水库；贮液器
ripe	/raip/	a.	成熟的
rockwool	/'rɔkwəːk/	n.	岩石棉；石棉
sacrifice	/'sækrifais/	vt.	牺牲
seedling	/'siːdliŋ/	n.	秧苗，树苗
soak	/səuk/	vt.	浸透
sprawl	/sprɔːl/	vi.	蔓生，蔓延

sprout	/spraut/	vi.	萌芽
stake	/steik/	n.&vt.	木桩；用木桩系住
starter	/'stɑːtə/	n.	起动器
superior	/sjuː'pɪərɪə/	a.	质量或品种较高级的
supplemental	/ˌsʌplɪ'mentl/	a.	补足的，补充的
tendency	/'tendənsɪ/	n.	趋向，倾向
thermostat	/'θɜːməstæt/	n.	自动调温器
toxicity	/'tɒksɪsətɪ/	n.	毒性
tray	/treɪ/	n.	浅盘
unsurpassed	/ˌʌnsə'pɑːst/	a.	非常卓越的
variety	/və'raɪətɪ/	n.	品种，种类，变种
at interval			间隔
be exposed to			遭受，使曝露于……，使接触……
be superior to			优越于……
drip emitter			滴灌发射器
drip irrigation			滴灌
exhaust fan			排气风扇，抽风机
nursery tray			苗圃浅盘
with a view to			着眼于，考虑到

Vocabulary exercises

I. List the antonyms (反义词) of the following words with the prefixes like "in-, dis-, mal-, mis-, un-, il-, non-".

1. surpassed _____
2. determinate _____
3. happy _____
4. interesting _____
5. advantage _____
6. satisfy _____
7. dependent _____
8. adequate _____
9. place _____
10. smoker _____
11. lucky _____
12. function _____

II. Plant nutrition is the basis for hydroponics and holds the key to the nutritional quality of tomatoes. Fill in the blanks with the words from the box. Meanwhile, understand some changes in the growth of hydroponic tomatoes.

| deficiency | down | curling | fruit | nutritional | indicate |

1. Early diagnosis (诊断) and adjustment of _____ disorders is very important as they may rapidly increase in severity and spread quickly.

2. Check the color of the leaves. Yellow leaves may _____ that the nutrient solution isn't strong enough or the pH is too high, locking out nitrogen (氮) — leach and change the solution.

3. Leaf tips _____ up or red stem may indicate a magnesium deficiency (镁不足) caused by too low a pH—leach and change solution.

4. Leaf tips curling _____ may mean the nutrient level is too high—add pH 6.0 water.

5. A potassium deficiency (钾不足) may cause flowers to fall off before setting _____ — leach and change solution.

6. Blossom-end-rot (花底部腐烂) caused by too much water accumulating in the root zone will create a calcium (钙) _____ — leach and spray with a calcium nitrate (硝酸盐) solution.

Speaking

I. Scan the following chart about soil types and complete the given sentences. Then brainstorm with your partner any words or phrases that make for (促成) an ideal soil for cultivation and put them into the diagram.

Soil Types	Components and Characteristics (成分和特性)
Sandy Soil (砂土)	This type has the biggest particles (微粒). It consists of rock and mineral particles that are very small. Therefore the texture is gritty (含砂的). Sandy soil is formed by the disintegration (分解) and weathering (侵蚀) of rocks such as limestone, granite, quartz and shale (石灰石, 花岗岩, 石英和页岩). The soil is easier to cultivate if it is rich in organic material but then it allows drainage (排水) more than what is needed, thus resulting in over-drainage and dehydration of the plants in summer. It warms very fast in the spring season.

Unit 2

Silty Soil (粉砂土)	It is considered to be one of the most fertile of soils. It consists of minerals like Quartz (石英) and fine organic particles (微小的有机颗粒). It has more nutrients than sandy soil and it also offers better drainage. In case silty soil is dry it has a smoother texture and looks like dark sand. It offers better drainage and is much easier to work with when it has moisture (湿气).
Clay Soil (黏质土)	Clay is a kind of material that occurs naturally and consists of very fine grained (微小的颗粒) material with very less air spaces, that is the reason it is difficult to work with since the drainage in this soil is low. Clay soil becomes very heavy when wet and if cultivation has to be done, organic fertilizers have to be added.
Loamy Soil (壤质土)	This soil consists of sand, silt and clay to some extent. It is considered to be the perfect soil. The texture is gritty (含砂的) and retains water very easily, yet the drainage is well. There are various kinds of loamy soil ranging from fertile to very muddy and thick sod (草地). Yet out of all the different kinds of soil loamy soil is the ideal for cultivation.
Peaty Soil (泥炭土)	This kind of soil is basically formed by the accumulation of dead and decayed organic matter, and it naturally contains much more organic matter than most of the soils. Now the decomposition of the organic matter in peaty soil is blocked by the acidity of the soil. Though the soil is rich in organic matter, nutrients present are fewer in this soil type than any other type. Peaty soil is prone to water logging (水浸) but if the soil is fertilized well and the drainage of the soil is looked after, it can be the ideal for growing plants.
Chalky Soil (白垩土)	Chalky soil is very alkaline in nature and consists of a large number of stones. The fertility of this kind of soil depends on the depth of the soil that is on the bed of chalk. This kind of soil is prone to dryness and in summer it is a poor choice for cultivation, as the plants would need much more watering and fertilizing than on any other type of soil.

The two soils that offer better drainage are (1)_____. The soil that offers worst drainage is (2)_____. The soil that is acidic and rich in organic matter is (3)_____. The soil that is very alkaline is (4)_____. And the ideal soil for cultivation is (5)_____.

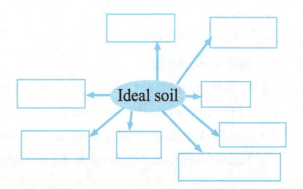

II. Soil conservation is very important for its productive potential. Discuss with your partner to divide the following phrases on some soil conservation methods under the headings "Dos" and "Don'ts".

1. abstract (抽取) underground water excessively (过分地);
2. cover the soil with organic matter like crop residues (残渣), grass and fallen leaves etc;
3. overgraze (过度放牧);
4. deforest (采伐森林);
5. use pesticides carelessly;
6. plant strips (带) of grass, trees or shrubs (灌木丛) between water and cropland;
7. fail to maintain soil organic matter levels;
8. practice over-cultivation;
9. water soil so as to keep it wet and make it settle down;
10. clear natural vegetation (植被);
11. cover the entire soil with plants;
12. practice rotational grazing (循环放牧);
13. cultivate soils on steep slopes;
14. construct wind barriers at the boundaries (边界) of the farm;
15. leave rainwater where it is;
16. consider the shape of the land when farming;
17. plant crops that improve the soil quality.

Dos	Don'ts
Do 2, 5,	Don't 1, 3, 4,

III. Scan the chart and work with a partner to answer the following questions.

Discussion assistant
K: potassium (钾); Ca: calcium (钙); P: phosphorus (磷); Mg: magnesium (镁); Se: Se (硒); Fe: iron (铁); Mn: manganese (锰); Cu: copper (铜); Na: Sodium (钠); Zn: zinc (锌); Folate (叶酸); pregnancy (怀孕); Pantothenic acid (泛酸, 维生素 B3); Niacin (烟酸); maximum (最大值); minimum (最小值)

Crops	Protein/ Fiber Contained	Minerals Contained (in descending order)	Vitamins Contained (in descending order)
Apple	One medium apple with skin contains almost 4 grams of dietary fiber.	K—158 mg; Ca—9.5 mg P—9.5 mg; Mg—7 mg Se—0.4 mg; Also contains small amounts of Fe, Mn, Cu and Zn.	Vitamin A—73 IU Vitamin C—9 mg Folate (important during pregnancy)—4 mcg Vitamin E—0.66 IU
Strawberry	A one-cup whole strawberry contains 3 grams of dietary fiber.	K—239 mg; P—27 mg Ca—20 mg; Mg—14 mg Se—1 mg; Fe—0.55 mg Mn—0.42 mg; Also contains trace amounts of Zn and Cu.	Vitamin A—39 IU Vitamin C—82 mg Folate—25.5 mcg
Tomato	One medium tomato contains 1.05 grams of protein and 1.35 grams of fiber.	K—396.7 mg; P—62.7 mg Mg—22.8 mg; Ca—31.9 mg Na—11.4 mg; Fe—0.51 mg Se—0.8 mg; Also contains small amounts of Mn, Cu and Zn.	Vitamin A—2364 IU Vitamin C—25 mg Folate—46 mcg Niacin—0.94 mg Vitamin B6—0.1 mg
Watermelon	One medium slice of watermelon contains 1 gram of protein and 1 gram of dietary fiber.	K—332 mg; Mg—31.5 mg P—26 mg; Ca—23 mg Fe—0.5 mg; Se—0.3 mg Also contains small amounts of Mn, Cu and Zn.	Vitamin A—1050 IU Vitamin C—27 mg Niacin—0.57 mg Vitamin B1—0.23 mg Vitamin B6—0.4 mg Folate—6.33 mcg
Mushroom	Half a cup of raw mushrooms contains 1.0 grams of protein and 0.42 grams of fiber.	K—129.5 mg; P—36.4 mg Mg—3.5 mg; Se—3 mg Ca—1.8 mg; Na—1.4 mg Fe—0.36 mg; Also contains small amounts of Mn, Cu and Zn.	Vitamin D—26.6 IU Niacin—1.4 mg Vitamin C—0.8 mg Pantothenic Acid—0.5 mg Contains some other vitamins in small amounts.
Carrot	Half cup cooked with no added salt contains 0.85 grams protein and 2.6 grams fiber.	K—177 mg; Na—51.5 mg Ca—24 mg; P—23.4 mg Mg—10 mg; Fe—0.48 mg Also contains small amounts of Se, Mn, Cu and Zn.	Vitamin A—19,152 IU Vitamin C—1.8 mg Niacin—0.4 mg Folate—11 mcg Pantothenic Acid—0.2 mg Vitamin B6—0.2 mg

Cucumber	Half a cup of sliced cucumber with skins contains 0.36 grams protein and 0.42 grams fiber.	K—74.9 mg; P—1.4 mg Mg—5.7 mg; Na—1 mg Ca—7.3 mg; Also contains small amounts of Se, Fe, Mn, Cu and Zn.	Contains some other vitamins in small amounts. Vitamin A—111.8 IU Vitamin C—2.6 mg; Contains some other vitamins in small amounts.
Green Pepper	One small raw pepper contains 0.66 grams protein and 1.3 grams fiber.	K—131 mg; P—14 mg Mg—7.4mg; Ca—6.7 mg Na—1.48 mg Also contains small amounts of Se, Fe, Mn, Cu and Zn.	Vitamin A—467.7 IU Vitamin C—66 mg Niacin—0.4 mg Folate—6.8 mcg Contains some other vitamins in small amounts.

Questions

1. Which fruits cannot be a source of folate?
2. If one is in badly need of Vitamin A for his vision, which fruit will be his best choice? Why?
3. If one wants to prevent common cold with the help of Vitamin C, which fruit in the chart will be his best choice? Why?
4. Among the fruits listed in the chart, which one contains maximum K? Which one contains minimum K?
5. Among the fruits listed in the chart, which one contains maximum Ca? Which one contains minimum Ca?
6. How to keep a healthy diet as far as you are concerned?

Background Reading

A Brief Introduction of Soilless Agriculture
Nutrient Controllers

Please refer to the attached disk.

Unit 3

Gene Technology in Agriculture

农业中的转基因技术

Part I The Application of Transgenic Technology in Agriculture

Warming up

I. Some purposes of using gene technology are listed below. Please decide whether they are generally suitable for animals or plants.

Animals: _____

Plants: _____

    a. To rid and destroy pests, diseases and weeds

    b. To diagnose, prevent and treat diseases

    c. To serve as a gene therapy

    d. To improve the nutritional traits

    e. To increase the efficiency of livestock production

    f. To serve as genetic bases leading to the design and testing of strategies for therapy

    g. To improve the performance in hostile environments

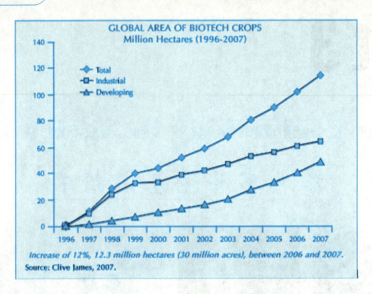

II. Study the following graph and briefly report to the class how the global area of biotech crops developed.

> *Discussion assistant*
>
> As is shown in the graph...
>
> The graph shows that...
>
> The number soared to a record high of...
>
> Remarkably, the growth continued at a growth rate of ...
>
> concentrate (集中); continue (继续); expand (扩大); soar (迅速上升); decade (十年); GM agriculture (转基因农业); non-existent (不存在的); in terms of (依据,按照……); industrial and developing countries (发达和发展中国家); industrialized (工业化的); export-oriented (以出口为主的); dozen (一打,十二个); consecutive (连续的)

Reading

The Application of Transgenic Technology in Agriculture

1   Recombinant DNA technology has contributed to exciting developments in agricultural biotechnology. There has been much improvement in the last few years about the ability to genetically engineered plants using the new techniques of gene isolation and insertion.

Question 1: What are the three techniques of transferring DNA and which one is an improved method? (Para. 2)

2   Several techniques can introduce genes into plant cells. The most successful method involves Agrobacterium tumefaciens. In nature, this transfer results in formation of plant

tumors at the infection site. Molecular biologists, however, have disarmed this bacterium and constructed domesticated strains that no longer cause tumors but transfer any DNA of interest to plant cells. Such a transfer produces organisms referred to as genetically modified (GM) or transgenic. Other techniques use physical or chemical agents to transfer DNA into plant cells. DNA can also be microinjected into target plant cells using very thin glass needles.

Question 2: What are the advantages of transgenic crops? Complete the diagram with information from the following paragraph. (Para. 3)

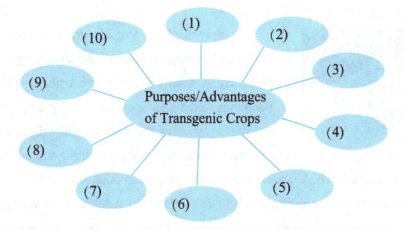

3   To improve crop production and soil management, research is now exploring how to increase the variety of transgenic characteristics to include resistance to drought, heat, disease, insecticide, cold, acid soils, and heavy metals. These characteristics will increase the range of soils and climates that are able to support agriculture. In this way, foods that are more nutritious and stable in storage can be produced through the use of GM technology. For example, genes to increase the content of amino acids in seed will increase nutritional value. One of the first agricultural products of biotechnology was the rot-resistant tomato. It can ripen longer on the vine by stopping the tomato from producing the enzyme that encourages rotting. Transgenic Bt crops can greatly reduce amounts of chemical pesticides entering the environment. Scientists also have obtained the genes for nitrogen fixation and have incorporated those genes into plant cells. Commercially produced transgenic crops such as soybean, cotton, tobacco, potato and maize have been grown annually in a number of both industrialized and developing countries.

Question 3: What methods are used in genetically engineered fish? (Para. 4)

4   Just when people have begun to digest the idea of custom-built crops, along comes another major advance: genetically engineered fish. In this technology, various methods, including direct microinjection and particle gun bombardment, have been used to transfer foreign DNA into fish embryos.

Question 4: What genetic traits are introduced into fish? (Para. 5)

5   By the introduction of desirable genetic traits into fish, superior transgenic strains can be produced for aquaculture. These traits may include elevated growth, improved food conservation efficiency, resistance to some diseases, tolerance to sub-zero temperature and thus reduce the burden on natural resources. Up to now, about 35 different fish species have been subjects of genetic modifications.

6   Transgenic farm animals are just another class of products developed through biotechnology. They are produced by inserting genes into embryos prior to birth. Each transferred gene is assimilated by the genetic material or chromosomes of the embryo and subsequently can be expressed in all tissues of the resulting animal. The objective is to produce animals which possess the transferred gene in their germ cells (sperm or ova). Such animals are able to produce many offspring that carry a desirable gene or genes.

Question 5: What are the targets that scientists have from transgenic animals? (Paras. 7—8)

7   Transgenic animals have been widely and successfully produced by microinjection of

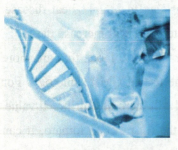

cloned gene(s) into a fertilized ovum. Scientists are now able to trace characteristics in animals that make these breeds more resistant to diseases and parasites. Recombinant growth hormones are now available for farm animals, resulting in leaner meat, improved milk yield and more efficient feed use.

8   Moreover, researchers now seek ways to genetically modify the organs of animals, such as pigs, for possible transplantation into humans. Potential applications for transgenic animals include manipulation of milk composition, growth, disease resistance, reproductive performance, and production of pharmaceutical proteins by livestock.

Question 6: What are the benefits and challenges of employing transgenic technology? (Paras. 9—10)

9   Transgenic technology promises more and better crops and food animals. In future, it

may serve the potential to solve many of the world's problems such as hunger, malnutrition, and to help protect and preserve the environment by increasing yield and reducing reliance upon chemical pesticides and herbicides, and even provide the production of medicinal or protein pharmaceuticals. Genetic engineering is the inevitable wave of the future and we cannot afford to ignore a technology that has brought such enormous potential benefits to agriculture.

10   However, there are many uncertainties over long-term ecological consequences of using genetic engineering techniques in agriculture, and many challenges are ahead for governments, especially in the areas of safety testing, regulation, international policy and food labeling. We must proceed with caution to avoid causing unintended harm to human health and the environment as a result of our enthusiasm for this powerful technology.

Vocabulary

agent	/'eidʒənt/	n.	制剂
amino	/ə'miːnəu/	a.	氨基的
aquaculture	/'ækwə,kʌltʃə/	n.	水产业
assimilate	/ə'simileit/	vt.	同化;吸收
bacterium	/bæk'tiəriəm/	n.	细菌(复数 bacteria)
breed	/briːd/	n.&vt.	物种;繁殖
chromosome	/'krəuməsəum/	n.	染色体
clone	/kləun/	vt.	克隆
composition	/kɔmpə'ziʃən/	n.	组成,合成物,成份
contribute	/kən'tribjuːt/	vi.	有助于,促成
custom-built	/'kʌstəm'bilt/	a.	定制的, 定做的
desirable	/di'zaiərəbəl/	a.	令人想要的,希望的
disarm	/dis'ɑːm/	vt.	解除,摘除
domesticate	/də'mestikeit/	vt.	驯养,驯化
drought	/draut/	n.	干旱
elevate	/'eliveit/	vt.	增加;举高
embryo	/'embriəu/	n.	胚胎
engineer	/ˌendʒi'niə/	vt.&n.	操纵,设计;工程师
enzyme	/'enzaim/	n.	酶

feed	/fiːd/	n.	饲料
herbicide	/'həːbisaid/	n.	除草剂
hormone	/'hɔːməun/	n.	激素
incorporate	/in'kɔːpəreit/	vi.&a.	合并;合并的
infection	/in'fekʃən/	n.	传染,影响,传染病
insertion	/in'səːʃən/	n.	(基因)嵌入
isolation	/ˌaisə'leiʃən/	n.	分离,隔离
label	/'leibəl/	n.&vt.	标签,签条;贴标签于,分类
livestock	/'laivstɔk/	n.	家畜,牲畜
maize	/meiz/	n.	玉米
malnutrition	/ˌmælnjuː'triʃən/	n.	营养不良
manipulation	/məˌnipju'leit/	n.	控制
medicinal	/me'disənəl/	a.	医学的
microinject	/ˌmaikrəuin'dʒekt/	vt.	显微注射
molecular	/məu'lekjulə/	a.	分子的
nitrogen	/'naitrədʒən/	n.	氮
nutritious	/njuː'triʃəs/	a.	有营养成份的,营养的
offspring	/'ɔfspriŋ/	n.	后代(复数不变)
ova	/'əuvə/	n.	卵子(ovum 的复数)
parasite	/'pærəsait/	n.	寄生虫
pharmaceutical	/ˌfɑːmə'sjuːtikəl/	a.	药用的
potential	/pə'tenʃəl/	n.& a.	潜力,潜能;可能的,潜在的
protein	/'prəutiːn/	n.	蛋白
range	/reindʒ/	n.&vt.	范围,行列;排列,归类于
recombinant	/ri'kɔmbinənt/	n.	重组体
reproductive	/ˌriːprə'dʌktiv/	a.	生殖的
resistance	/ri'zistəns/	n.	抵抗力,反抗
ripen	/'raipən/	vi.	成熟
rot	/rɔt/	vi.&n.	腐烂
soybean	/'sɔibiːn/	n.	大豆,黄豆
species	/'spiːʃiz/	n.	物种,种类(复数不变)
sperm	/spəːm/	n.	精子
strain	/strein/	n.	(动植物的)系,品系,类型

tissue	/'tisjuː/	n.	(动、植物的)组织
trait	/treit/	n.	特征,特点,特性
transgenic	/trænz'dʒenik/	a.	转基因的
transplantation	/trænsplɑːn'teiʃən/	n.	移植
tumor	/'tjuːmə/	n.	肿瘤
vine	/vain/	n.	藤,蔓
agrobacterium tumefaciens			根癌土壤杆菌
Bt			抗虫基因
DNA (deoxyribonucleic acid)			脱氧核糖核酸
fertilized ovum			受精卵
genetically modified (GM)			转基因的
germ cells			生殖细胞
particle gun bombardment			基因枪轰击技术
sub-zero			低于零度

Vocabulary exercises

I. Fill in each blank with the right word from the following box.

| domesticate | assimilate | characteristic | drought | utilization |
| composition | incorporate | offspring | species | isolate |

1. We humans _____ some kinds of food more easily than other animals.
2. The challenge for geneticists (遗传学家) is to _____ individual genes and determine their function—a painstaking (辛苦的) process often requiring years of laboratory trial and error.
3. A more important _____ of the experiment is that encouragement has been given to scientific and technological development.
4. The study shows that a stimulating (刺激性的) environment improved the memory of young mice with a memory-impairing (损害的) genetic defect (缺陷) and also improved the memory of their eventual _____.
5. The more unrelated (无亲缘关系的) cats you combine, the more outcrossed (异型杂交的) your _____ will be.
6. Some aspects of your body _____ are genetic (where you store fat), but most fat increase is related to lifestyle.
7. Do farmers reduce genetic diversity (多样性) when they _____ wild animals?
8. Monsanto (孟山都公司〈美国〉,全球第一家生物科技种子商业化企业) will accelerate

(加速) the selection process, which allows researchers to find and track genetic material associated with _____ tolerance.

9. Clinicians (临床医生) are reluctant to _____ genetic information into the medical record, as long as it is not clear whether health insurance companies might discriminate (歧视) against patients at high genetic risk for adverse (不利的) health events.

10. A _____ that has a large degree of genetic diversity among its population will have more variations from which to choose the most fit genes.

II. List words with the following prefixes and suffixes as many as possible.

1. dis- (not, the opposite of):
2. trans- (change; across; through; beyond):
3. micro- (small):
4. aqua- (water):
5. mal- (bad, evil):
6. -cide (cut, kill):

Listening

I. Learn the following words and phrases and then listen to the record of a radio program to fill in the blanks with the missing information.

Words and phrases

approve	/əˈpruːv/	vt.	赞同,核准,证实
commercialization	/kə,məːʃəlaiˈzeiʃn/	n.	商品化
consumer	/kənˈsjuːmə/	n.	消费者,用户
contaminate	/kənˈtæmineit/	n.	弄脏,污染
forum	/ˈfɔːrəm/	n.	论坛
modify	/ˈmɔdifai/	vt.	更正,修饰
mutate	/mjuːˈteit/	vt.	(使)变异,(使)突变
threaten	/ˈθretn/	vt.	威胁
variety	/vəˈraiəti/	n.	多样,种类
high-yielding	/haiˈjiːldiŋ/	a.	高产的

At the Forum of Genetic Technology in Agriculture 2008, John Smith, a scientist well known for his work developing high-yielding rice varieties, met Pang Chen, the Greenpeace

GM campaign manager, and they had a debate on the concerning issue.

1. What is the topic discussed in this dialogue?

    It is reported that China (1)_____.

2. The different attitudes of these two persons toward the topic:

    John Smith: (2)_____.

    Pang Chen: We have been calling on the government to (3)_____ about it.

3. List some specific reasons to support their view:

    Pang Chen: Transgenic crops threaten (4)_____.

    John Smith: The modified rice could (5)_____.

    Pang Chen: I admit (6)_____ rice could have (7)_____ benefits as you said, but the greater risks far (8)_____ the advantages. For example, the crops could mutate and become (9)_____, requiring extra strong (10)_____ to control, kill other insects and birds and contaminate different rice (11)_____.

    John Smith: But I believe the opposition to genetically modified (GMO) rice in Asia is likely to disappear in the next 5 to 7 years as the region (12)_____.

II. Read the notes in the two tables about a GM project. Then listen to a report carefully and fill in the tables with the information you hear.

Words and phrases

greenhouse	/ˈgriːnhaus/	n.	温室
interfere	/ˌintəˈfiə/	vi.	妨碍，冲突
minor	/ˈmainə/	a.	次要的，较小的
project	/ˈprɔdʒekt/	n.	项目，计划
survive	/səˈvaiv/	vi.	生存，生还
tobacco	/təˈbækəu/	n.	烟草

Reasons of going into this research:

1. The amount of land affected by (1)_____ has (2)_____ in the past (3)_____ years.
2. A lot of research is going into efforts to develop (4)_____ crops. One project involves tobacco plants (5)_____ to keep their leaves during water shortages.

Comparison	Normal tobacco plants	Transgenic tobacco plants
After growing fifteen days under the normal condition, the two kinds of plants did not receive any water.	Results: (6) _____	Results: (7) _____
After the fifteen dry days, all the plants were watered again for a week.	Results: (8) _____	Results: (9) _____ (10) seed production: _____ (11) water level: _____ (12) _____ energy (13) survive on _____ (14) yield loss: _____

Speaking

I. Study the following pictures carefully and explain the steps that transgenic plants and animals are created.

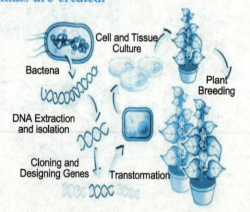
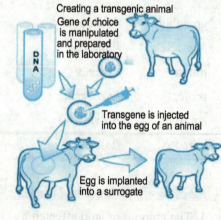

Discussion assistant

insert (插入); extract DNA (提取DNA); implant (移入); breed (繁殖); manipulate (操作); inject (注射); clone a gene (克隆基因); bacteria (细菌); extraction (提取); isolation (分离; *vt.* isolate); transformation (转化); tissue culture (组织培养); egg (卵); surrogate (代孕者)

II. Pair Work: Please read the following dialogue to learn the information about commercialization of transgenic crop and role it out with a partner.

(*Steven is a student majoring in Agricultural Engineering. He is asked to introduce the transgenic crop commercialization to a new student named Bill.*)

Bill: Would you please introduce the distribution of the transgenic crop area in the world?

Steven: Sure. The United States plants almost two-thirds of the transgenic crops grown worldwide. Although transgenic crop area in US continues to expand, its share of global transgenic area has fallen rapidly as Argentina, Brazil, Canada, China and South Africa have increased their plantings.

Bill: What are the most widely grown transgenic crops?

Steven: Well, they are soybeans, maize, cotton and canola (蓖麻).

Bill: What are their advantages?

Steven: Herbicide tolerance and insect resistance. Herbicide-tolerant soybeans now make up 55 percent of the global soybean production area, and herbicide-tolerant canola 16 percent. The transgenic cotton and maize varieties which are grown commercially are insect resistant, or herbicide tolerant or both. They now make up 21 percent and 11 percent, respectively, of the total area sown (播种) to those crops. Other commercially planted transgenic crops include very small quantities of virus-resistant papaya (木瓜) and squash (南瓜).

Bill: Are varieties of wheat and rice commercialized?

Steven: Neither of them has transgenic varieties commercially planted anywhere in the world.

Bill: Thank you very much for your introduction.

Steven: You are welcome.

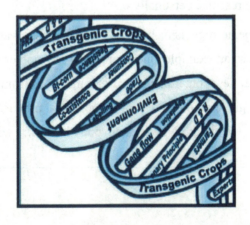

III. Biotech crops have been grown worldwide for more than a decade. Around the world, many agricultural biotechnology corporations are producers of genetically engineered (GE) seeds for various crops. They claim GE seeds would greatly increase yields and in turn, farmers' income. They want to feed all starving people of the world in this way. Look at this picture carefully and discuss with your partner on whether these companies will bring benefits to the farmers as they claim.

Discussion assistant

patent (专利, 取得……的专利权); sow (播种); afford to (买得起); increase the yield; end up lowering prices; reduce net gain (减少净产); test (测试); fulfill the promise (实现诺言); charge of biopiracy (生物剽窃的指控); marketing (市场营销); controversial (有争议的); anti-globalization (反对全球化), activist (活动分子)

Writing

Write a passage on My View on Transgenic Technology in Agriculture. Refer to the useful expressions in the following box.

My View on Transgenic Technology in Agriculture

Writing assistant

Transgenic technology has brought a lot of benefits to agriculture.

But many people think it is a risky business.

Considering all these reasons, personally, ...

GE organism; transgenic organism; bacteria; viruses; salty water; resist disease; For instance (To take ... as an example/One example is...; Another example is...); change the bacterial communities; contamination of organic crops from genetic drift (遗传漂变) of genetically engineered pollen (花粉); boost food production; some researchers question whether...; GE food; Nor does anybody know...; wipe out some diseases; feed the world

Part II Genetic Engineering of Rice: *Bt* Rice

Warming up

I. Discussion

Why is rice very important to human beings?

> *Discussion assistant*
> consume (消费); account for (占……比例); staple food (主食); production; population; caloric intake (热量摄取); fuel (燃料); thatching (用茅草盖屋顶); industrial starch (工业淀粉)

II. Listening

Listen to a news report and fill in the following blanks with the given words.

adoption	consuming	continent's	cross-breeding	derived
droughts	fertile	flooding	global	option
plots	predictions	prime	prodecctivety	supply

Every hectare of rice fields in Asia provides enough rice to feed 27 people. Fifty years from now, according to some (1)_____, each hectare will have to cater (满足……需要) for 43. Converting (转变) more land to rice field is not an (2)_____, since suitable (3)_____ are already in short (4)_____. In fact, in many of the (5)_____ most (6)_____ river basins (盆地), urban sprawl (扩张) is (7)_____ growing quantities of (8)_____ rice-farming land. Moreover, (9)_____ warming is likely to make farmers' lives increasingly difficult, by causing more frequent (10)_____ in some places and worse (11)_____ in others. Scientists at the International Rice Research Institute (IRRI) doubt it is possible to improve (12)_____ as much as is needed through better farming practices or the (13)_____ of new strains (14)_____ from conventional (15)_____. Instead, they aim to improve rice yields by 50% using modern genetic techniques.

Reading

Genetic Engineering of Rice: *Bt* Rice

1　Rice feeds more than two billion people worldwide and is the number one staple food in Asia. Today's global population of six billion is expected to reach eight billion by 2020. We must therefore produce 25—40% more rice with less land and water and with a reduced use of fertilizers. Genetic engineering provides an efficient breeding tool in which genes of interest have been incorporated in rice.

Question 1: What is Bt rice? (Para. 2)

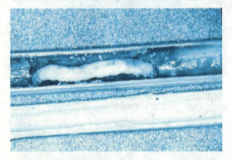

A stem borer feeding inside a rice stem. The damaged stem will not produce any grain. Bt rice will be resistant to stem borer.

2　"Bt rice" is rice that has been modified, by means of biotechnology, with genes from Bacillus thuringiensis to produce toxins for resistance to insects. Bt is a species of bacteria found in soil throughout much of the world. Maize, potato, and cotton plants containing Bt genes are now being grown by farmers in several countries. It is possible that additional Bt crops, including Bt rice, will become available to farmers in the next few years.

Question 2: What are the two potential benefits of Bt rice? (Paras. 3—4)

3　Bt rice will reduce yield losses caused by caterpillar pests in tropical Asia and temperate areas. Resistance to stem borers has been a goal of conventional plant breeding for many years, but only partial levels of resistance have been achieved. Average yield losses to stem borers in Asia are often estimated at 5%, and vary from region to region. Bt rice has now been field evaluated for several years and has shown resistance against several insect pests and excellent performance (28% higher yield than the natural plants).

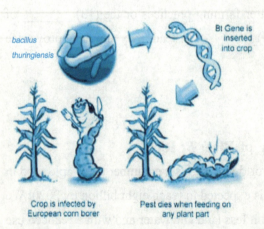

4　A second potential benefit of Bt rice is to reduce farmers' use of chemical insecticides. Surveys indicate that rice farmers typically use 50% of their insecticide sprays for control of caterpillars. The insecticide use in rice has negative effects on the health of farmers, the environment, and the natural control of pests by spiders and helpful insects.

Question 3: In what way is Bt rice produced by genetic engineering? (Paras. 5—6)

5   Over the past 30 years, the tools of biotechnology have made it possible to manipulate genes and even to transfer them between species. The manipulation of genes is sometimes referred to as "genetic engineering," and organisms "transformed" with genes from other sources are referred to as being "transgenic." Because a single gene encodes each Bt toxin, it is relatively straightforward to genetically engineer a plant to produce the toxin.

6   The toxin gene is isolated from Bt cells, modified for use in plants, and inserted into plant cells. The most frequently used transformation technique in this process is particle bombardment. Whole plants are then regenerated from the transformed cells. Additional work is required to ensure that the toxin is produced in enough quantities and desired locations within the plant.

Question 4: Under what condition will Bt rice be released and distributed? (Para. 7)

7   The first rice plants containing Bt genes are now available for scientists to study. However, some improvements need to be made before Bt rice varieties will be ready for evaluation and release by national seed boards. For example, the best toxin levels must be achieved and then verified to be consistent from generation to generation. In addition, in most countries many biosafety regulations concerning the field use of transgenic crops remain to be developed.

Question 5: What is the prospect of the sustainable use of Bt rice? (Para. 8)

8   As in the case with all insecticides, insect pests will develop resistance to Bt toxins. It is not possible to predict how long Bt rice will remain effective, but the development of pest resistance to Bt toxins can be slowed down by careful design of Bt rice plants and use of proper strategies. The second generation of Bt rice is now in progress; this may delay pest evolution even longer.

Question 6: What are the most important potential benefits of Bt rice? (Para. 9)

9   Cooperation among scientists, governments, and farmers is essential to realize the two most important potential benefits of Bt rice: sustainable control of stem borers and reduced use of chemical insecticides.

10   These goals can best be achieved if Bt rice is grown only in areas where it is needed. In addition, Bt rice should not be released to farmers until researchers have developed satisfactory Bt varieties and a plan for their sustainable use. More research on the environmental impact of Bt rice also remains to be done.

Vocabulary

bacteria	/bæk'tiəriə/	n.	细菌
biosafety	/ˌbaiəu'seifti/	n.	生物安全
caterpillar	/'kætəˌpilə/	n.	毛虫
consistent	/kən'sistənt/	a.	一贯的,一致的
encode	/in'kəud/	vt.	编码
evaluate	/i'væljueit/	vt.	评估,估价 (n. evaluation)
evolution	/ˌi:və'lu:ʃən/	n.	进化,发展,进展
regenerate	/ri'dʒenəreit/	vt.	再生,更新
spray	/sprei/	n.&vt.	喷雾器;喷雾
staple	/'steipəl/	n.&a.	主要产物,副食;主要的
stem borer	/stem'bɔ:rə/	n.	螟虫
straightforward	/streit'fɔ:wəd/	a.	直接的,率直的
sustainable	/sə'steinəbəl/	a.	可持续的
temperate	/'tempərit/	a.	温带的
toxin	/'tɔksin/	n.	毒素
tropical	/'trɔpikəl/	a.	热带的
verify	/'verifai/	vt.	查证,核实
Bacillus thuringiensis			(Bt)昆虫病原细菌苏云金杆菌
national seed boards			国家种子委员会
particle bombardment			基因枪法;粒子轰击法

Vocabulary exercises

I. Match each word with its explanation.

1. ____ vary   a. place or set apart
2. ____ refer   b. obtainable or accessible and ready for use or service
3. ____ isolate   c. absolutely necessary; vitally necessary
4. ____ available   e. make or become different in some particular way
5. ____ essential   f. any substance added to soil to make it more fertile

6. ___ sustainable   g. mention, cite
7. ___ fertilizer   h. (of weather or climate) free from extremes; mild
8. ___ temperate   i. (of economic development, energy sources, etc) capable of being maintained at a steady level without exhausting natural resources or causing severe ecological damage

II. Fill in each blank with the right word from the following box.

| evolution | tropical | variety | verified | evaluate |
| modification | consistent | breed | adequate | staple |

1. The growth rate of new branches and leaf area of three species were the fastest under ____ soil water conditions, and were the lowest under severe drought.
2. Scientists discovered stem cell model (干细胞模型) for _____ gene expression (基因表达) after years of hard work.
3. It is observed that many animals do not _____ when in captivity (笼养).
4. The training set was derived using twenty-eight compounds and six were used as test sets to _____ external predictability (预见性) of the model (型号).
5. The Hainan Island has abundant natural resources, such as rich oil and natural gas as well as rubber and other _____ crops.
6. _____ crops in eastern Africa are subject to (易受……的) serious pre-and-post-harvest pest damage (虫害).
7. Charles Darwin and Alfred Russell Wallace discovered _____ independently.
8. The computer _____ whether the data was loaded correctly.
9. It is clear that a wide _____ of different experimental techniques will be necessary, ranging (范围包括) from genetic analysis (基因分析), right through to cell biology (分子生物学) and biochemistry (生物化学).
10. "Green genetic engineering" describes all those science and application fields in which vegetable organisms (forest tree species as well) are the objective of genetic _____.

Speaking

I. The following pictures explain how Bt rice is produced by the particle bombardment (particle gun) method, one of several methods that can be used to transfer novel (新颖的) genes to rice by genetic engineering. Rearrange them correctly according to the application process of this method and report to the class:

___ → ___ → ___ → ___ → ___

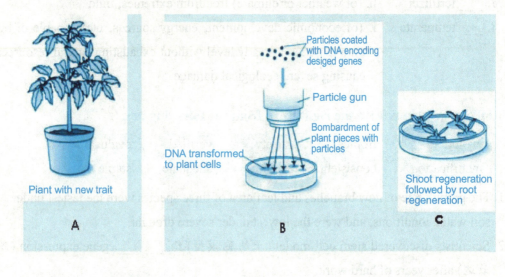

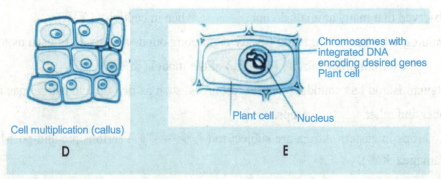

Words for reference
trait (特性); particle (粒子); encode (编码); shoot regeneration (发芽); root regeneration (生根); multiplication (增殖); callus (愈合组织); chromosome (染色体); nucleus (原子核)

II. Genetically modified crops now are grown so widely around the world. Look at the following chart and answer questions:

1. What major crops are involved?
2. How is the area planted with GM crops distributed in the world?

Discussion assistant
the Americas (美洲); Asia (亚洲); the top producer (最大生产者); hectare (公顷); agricultural land (农田); agricultural yield (农业产量); chemicals (化学物质); herbicide-tolerant GM crop (转基因抗除草剂作物); withstand (抵抗); apply to (应用); insecticide (杀虫剂); minimize (最小化); GM acreage (转基因作物面积); the

European Union (欧盟); GM agriculture (转基因农业); environmental hazards (环境风险); human health risks (人类健康风险); economic concerns (经济方面的原因)

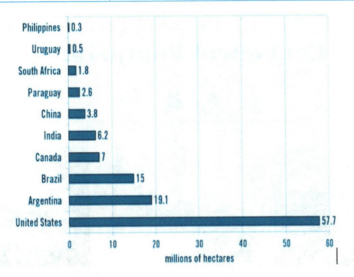

Background Reading

Plant Breeding Versus Plant Genetics

Transgenic Technology for Forestry

Scientists manipulate genes to create new breeds of grass.

Please refer to the attached disk.

Unit 4

Ecological Footprint

生 态 脚 印

Part I Ecological Footprint

Warming up

I. What resources are consumed to sustain a human's daily survival on the earth? What wastes are produced by human beings every day and how are they disposed of?

II. Have you ever heard of the Ecological Footprint (Eco-footprint)? If yes, do you know what it is?

III. The following chart shows the amount and development of the earth's biological capacity (地球生物容积量), human's total Ecological Footprint and man's CO_2 Eco-footprint from 1961 to 2006. Please first study the chart to finish the following three sentences briefly describing their changes, and then further describe some key changes in the process based on the models.

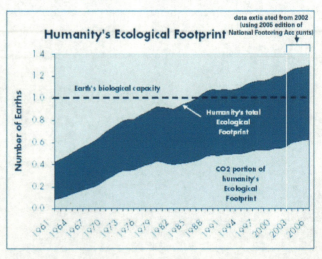

1. The chart *shows* that _____ remained the same from 1961 to 2006.
2. *It can be observed* from the chart that _____ continued to increase steadily from 1961 to 2006 and *tends to rise* in the future. In _____, it took only 40% of the earth's biological capacity, but it had been climbing so fast that in _____, it took more than 120% of that, which means it takes 1.2 earths or one and another 2 months to reproduce enough resources to satisfy human's survival and dispose of his rubbish.
3. The chart also *reveals* that man's CO_2 Eco-footprint had been _____ from 1961 to 2006.

> *Useful expressions for chart description*
> For rising: rise, increase, climb, go up, grow, improve
> For dropping: fall, decrease, decline, drop, go down
> For no changing: remain the same, remain steady, unchanged
> For changing: minimal, maximal, small, slow, slight, gradual, fast, obvious, clear, huge, tremendous, sharp, dramatic, sudden, steep, abrupt, an upward trend, an downward trend
> Verbs for chart description: show, indicate, reveal, observe (观察), imply, suggest, go on ..., continue to..., get to, reach, come up to, summit / peak (最高点, 顶峰), average, take up / account for (占据), tend to, be likely to, there is a tendency to..., at this rate / speed

Reading

Ecological Footprint

Question 1: What's the Ecological Footprint and who first advanced the idea? (Para. 1)

1   The Ecological Footprint is a resource management tool that measures how much land and water area a human population requires to produce the resources it consumes and to absorb its wastes under prevailing technology. This concept was first advanced by William Rees from University of British Columbia in Vancouver, Canada, in 1992. It was later developed by Mathis Wackernagel and Rees. The term is generally capitalized and can be abbreviated to Eco-foorprint.

Ecological footprint

2　　In order to live, we consume what nature offers. Every action impacts the planet's ecosystems. This is not serious as long as our use of resources does not exceed what the earth can renew. But are we taking more?

Question 2: What threat is man facing now? What does the italic word "overshoot" mean? (Para. 3)

3　　Today, humanity's Ecological Footprint is over 23% larger than what the planet can regenerate and it still continues to rise. Most countries, and the world as a whole, are running ecological deficits. The world's ecological deficit is equal to its ecological *overshoot*. In other words, it now takes more than one year and two months for the earth to regenerate what we use in a single year. We maintain this overshoot by liquidating the planet's ecological resources. This is a vastly underestimated threat and one that is not properly dealt with.

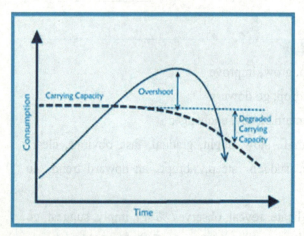

Question 3: What's the significance of measuring one's Ecological Footprint? (Para. 4)

4　　By measuring the Ecological Footprint of a population (an individual, a city, a nation, or all of humanity) we can assess our overshoot, which helps us manage our ecological assets more carefully. Ecological Footprints enable people to take personal and collective actions in support of a world where humanity lives within the means of one planet.

Question 4: How to keep a sustainable world? (Para. 5)

5　　Sustainability is a simple idea. It is based on the recognition that when resources are consumed faster than they are produced or renewed, the resource is depleted and eventually used up. In a sustainable world, society's demand on nature is in balance with nature's capacity to meet that demand.

Question 5: What may ecological overshoot result in? (Paras. 6—7)

6　　When humanity's ecological resource demands exceed what nature can continually supply, we move into what is termed ecological overshoot. With the growing depletion of non-renewable resources such as minerals, ores and petroleum, it is increasingly evident that renewable resources and the ecological services they provide are at even greater risk.

Examples include collapsing fisheries, carbon-induced climate change, species extinction, deforestation, and the loss of groundwater in much of the world.

7   We depend on these ecological assets to survive. Their depletion systematically undermines the well being of people. Livelihoods disappear, resource conflicts emerge, land becomes barren, and resources become increasingly costly or unavailable. This depletion is exacerbated by the growth in human population as well as by changing lifestyles that are placing more demand on natural resources.

Question 6: What can the Ecological Footprint help human beings do? (Paras. 8—12)

8   Keeping track of the compound effect of humanity's consumption of natural resources and generation of waste is one key to achieving sustainability.

9   As long as our governments and business leaders do not know how much of nature's capacity we use or how resource use compares to existing stocks, overshoot may go undetected—increasing the ecological deficit and reducing nature's capacity to meet society's needs.

10   The Ecological Footprint is a resource accounting tool used to address potential sustainability questions. It measures the extent to which humanity is using nature's resources faster than they can regenerate. It tells who uses how much of which ecological resources, with populations defined either geographically or socially. Moreover, it shows to what extent humans dominate the biosphere at the expense of wild species.

11   The Ecological Footprint clearly shows resource use by connecting individuals' and groups' activities with their ecological demands. It can be used to explore the sustainability of individual lifestyles, goods and services, organizations, industry sectors, neighborhoods, cities, regions and nations. It also helps decision makers more accurately and equitably measure and manage the use of resources throughout the economy, and shape policy in support of social and environmental justice.

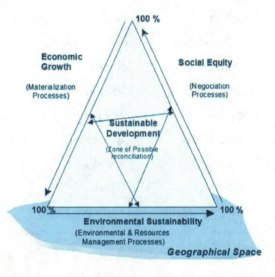

12   Continued overshoot is not inevitable. The Ecological Footprint provides a systematic resource accounting tool that can help us plan for a world in which we all live well, within the means of our one planet. So it is not only of great necessity to preserve

and improve agriculture and forestry for a better biocapability of nature, but also a must for humans to learn and decrease their Ecological Footprint. Only when a balance is kept between the reasonable use of natural resources and a harmony of economy, environment and society, can sustainable development be achieved.

Vocabulary

abbreviate	/əˈbriːvieit/	vt.	缩写
accounting	/əˈkauntiŋ/	n.	清算,核算;会计
achieve	/əˈtʃiːv/	vt.	获得,达到(目标)
advance	/ədˈvɑːns/	vt.	提出
assess	/əˈses/	vt.	估定(数量,价值等)
asset	/ˈæset/	n.	资源,资产
barren	/ˈbærən/	a.	贫瘠的
biosphere	/ˈbaiəsfiə/	n.	生物圈
capacity	/kəˈpæsiti/	n.	生产量;容载量
compare	/kəmˈpeə/	vt.	(with/to) 比较
capitalize	/kæˈpitlaiz/	vt.	用大写字母写
collapsing	/kəˈlæpsiŋ/	a.	崩溃的,倒塌的
collective	/kəˈlektiv/	a.	集体的
compound	/ˈkɔmpaund/	a.	综合的,复杂的
concept	/ˈkɔnsept/	n.	观念,概念
consume	/kənˈsjuːm/	vt.	消耗,消费
deficit	/ˈdefisit/	n.	赤字,亏损
deforestation	/diːˌfɔriˈsteiʃən/	n.	森林采伐
deplete	/diˈpliːt/	vt.	耗尽,使衰竭
dominate	/ˈdɔmineit/	vt.	支配,控制
equitably	/ˈekwitəbli/	ad.	公正地
exacerbate	/igˈzæsəbeit/	vt.	使恶化,使加剧
exceed	/ikˈsiːd/	vt.	超出,超越
fishery	/ˈfiʃəri/	n.	渔业,水产业
geographically	/ˌdʒiːəˈgræfikəli/	ad.	地理学地,地理地

harmony	/'hɑːməni/	n.	协调,和谐
humanity	/hjuː'mæniti/	n.	人类
justice	/'dʒʌstis/	n.	公平,公道
liquidate	/'likwideit/	vt.	清理,清算
livelihood	/'laivlihud/	n.	维持生命所需的东西
means	/miːnz/	n.	资源物力;财力;方法
mineral	/'minərəl/	n.	矿物,矿石
ore	/ɔː/	n.	矿石
overshoot	/ˌəuvə'ʃuːt/	n.	超出,超出量
petroleum	/pi'trəuliəm/	n.	石油
preserve	/pri'zəːv/	vt.	保护,保持
prevailing	/pri'veiliŋ/	a.	流行的,占优势的
renewable	/ri'njuːəbl/	a.	可更新的,可再生的
stock	/stɔk/	n.	储存,储存量
sustainability	/sə'steinəbiliti/	n.	可持续性
undermine	/ˌʌndə'main/	vt.	(暗中慢慢)破坏
carbon-induced		a.	由碳导致的
species extinction			物种灭绝

Vocabulary exercises

I. Match each word with its explanation.

1. ____ prevailing   a. to determine the value, significance, or extent of
2. ____ deficit   b. to decrease the fullness of; use up or empty out
3. ____ barren   c. to keep in existence; maintain
4. ____ sustain   d. lacking vegetation, especially useful vegetation; unproductive
5. ____ deplete   e. shortage or inadequacy or insufficiency
6. ____ assess   f. most frequent or common; predominant.
7. ____ clarify   g. idea
8. ____ concept   h. to make clear or easier to understand

II. Fill in each blank with the right word from the following box.

| consume | sustainable | fishery | extinction | deficit |
| undermine | underlying | address | liquidate | asset |

1. The field of _____ development conceptually (概念地) includes three parts: environmental sustainability, economic sustainability and sociopolitical (社会政治的) sustainability.

2. Starting about 100,000 years ago, species _____ has increased to a rate unprecedented (空前的) with an increase in the numbers and range of humans.

3. A barren desert is also a precious _____ as long as underground resources such as fossil fuel and water are detected.

4. The _____ can be saltwater or freshwater, wild or farmed. Most of it is marine (海洋中的) near the coast rather than freshwater, and wild rather than farmed.

5. With firm laws and more environment friendly technologies, more Chinese enterprises (企业) will successfully _____ their manufacturing-oriented (与生产有关的) pollution.

6. A new study shows that, compared with home meals, fast food and table service meals at restaurants have much more _____ threat against our health with more calories.

7. Paper mills within cities _____ local residents' health by polluting nearby water resources, air, land and crops.

8. Every year people _____ such a large quantity of food, water, timber, and other items from natural resources that they might be lack of raw materials now.

9. The dairy company makes every effort to _____ its debts by selling its stocks at a low price.

10. A serious drought (旱灾) broke out because of the continuous _____ in rainfall, which resulted in the sharp drop of local agricultural economy.

Listening

Learn the following words and phrases and have a glance at the following chart, the notes of a TV program named "Green Earth" whose topic is about Ecological Footprint. Then listen to it and fill in the blanks in the chart.

Words and phrases

average	/ˈævəridʒ/	a.	平均的
balanced	/ˈbælənst/	a.	平衡的
consumption	/kənˈsʌmpʃən/	n.	消费
curiosity	/ˌkjuəriˈɔsiti/	n.	好奇心
destination	/ˌdestiˈneiʃən/	n.	目的地
distribution	/ˌdistriˈbjuːʃən/	n.	分配
install	/inˈstɔːl/	vt.	安装
intentional	/inˈtenʃənəl/	a.	有意识的
mission	/ˈmiʃən/	n.	使命,任务
monitor	/ˈmɔnitə/	vt.	监控
poll	/pəul/	n.	民意测验
resident	/ˈrezidənt/	n.	居民

global hectare (gha) 全球公顷　　(1gha=2.47 acres< 英亩 >)
in direct proportion to　　与……成正比
per capita　　每人,人均
solar generator　　太阳能发电机

Distribution and Consumption of Global Resources	(1)_____ (Balanced/Unbalanced).	
Global Eco-footprint (2.2 global hectares per capita)	Unbalanced	About (2)_____ % of humanity's total eco-footprint is taken up by (3)_____ % of the population. The other (4)_____ % of the global human eco-footprint is taken by only (5)_____ % of the world population.
	Bigger in developed countries	Average American resident: (6)_____ global hectares.
	Smaller in developing countries	Average Chinese resident: (7)_____ global hectares.

Examples of How to Reduce Family's Eco-footprint	Drive (8)_____ (more / less). Walk (9)_____ (more / less). Take buses (10)_____ (more / less). Buy (11)_____ (more / less) heavily packed goods.
People's Awareness of Environmental Protection	Ages of 18-34: (12)_____ % Ages of 35-54: (13)_____ % Ages of 55-older: (14)_____ % Conclusion: It will be (15)_____ helping us develop new habits for the health of our planet.

Speaking

I. Look at the following chart and discuss.

1. What are the major components (组成成分) of human's Eco-footprint?
2. Which one takes the largest share or is the biggest part of the "Foot"?
3. How to cut down human's footprint in each area? Please give simple suggestions.

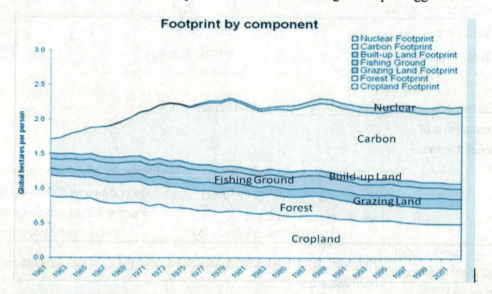

Discussion assistant

nuclear (原子核能的, 核的); radiation, leakage (泄漏); proliferation (扩散); nuclear weapons; nuclear power station; low-emission (低排量) cars; energy-saving; marine pollution (海洋污染); planned fishing; management; unplanned building; invade / take up cropland; preserve; planned grazing; deforestation (森林采伐); forestation (造林); crop rotation; no-tillage (免耕); vegetaion coverage (植被覆盖); high-yield (高产的); pestcide; fertilizer

Unit 4

II. Look at the following diagram and describe the classification of natural resources.

Natural resources (economically referred to as land or raw materials) are naturally forming substances that are considered valuable in their relatively unmodified (natural) form. They can be classified (分类) into different categories (种类) from different views. Here is a widely accepted classification.

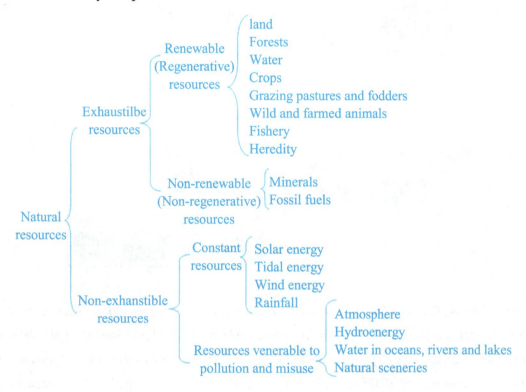

Discussion assistant

...can be divided into...groups

...include/cover...

...be made up of / be composed / consist of ... (由……组成)

...is further classified into...

The subgroups of...are...

The subcategories include...

The next level is...

exhaustible resources (耗竭性资源); renewable (可更新的); regenerative (再生的); constant resources (持久资源); vulnerable (易受影响或伤害的); misuse (滥用,误用); grazing pasture (牧场); fodder (饲料); heredity (遗传); mineral (矿物); fossil fuels (矿石燃料); tidal (潮汐的); hydroenergy (水能); component (组成部分)

III. Look at the following chart and learn the distribution of the limited global land and water resources for humans. Discuss with partners to figure out all possible ways to preserve and improve the earth's land and water resouces.

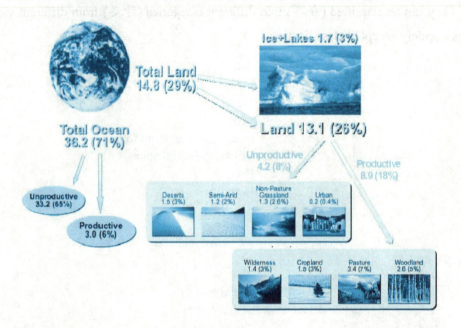

(Note: The earth is divided here into its various eco-systems <units=billion hectares>. The Fair Shares are based on the productive areas divided by world population: Fair Share = Productive areas/World Population. An individual's Fair Share is based on a world population: 1997: 5.8 billion, and 2047: 9.2 billion) (from FAO: Food and Agriculture Organization of the United Nations)

> *Discussion assistant*
> It is possible to do...
> We may do...
> It is a good idea to do...
> Immediate measures must be taken to...

IV. Read the following information to learn what sustainable development is and study the following diagram and table which cover all areas concerned in sustainable development listed by the United Nations. Please simply tell your own advice on how to achieve sustainable devleopment?

Sustainable development is a pattern of resource use that aims to meet human needs while preserving the environment so that these needs can be met not only in the present, but in the indefinite (无限的) future. The field of sustainable development conceptually includes three

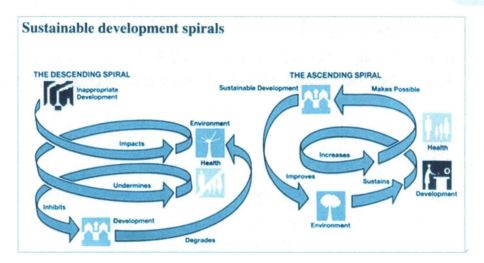

parts: *environmental sustainability,* economic sustainability and sociopolitical sustainability.

The increasing stress we put on resources and environmental systems such as water, land and air cannot go on forever. Especially as the world's population continues to increase and we already see a world where over a billion people live on less than a dollar a day. Globally we are not even meeting the needs of the present, let alone considering the needs of future generations. Unless we start to make real progress toward reconciling (和解，缓解) these contradictions, we face a future that is less certain and less secure. We need to make a decisive move toward more sustainable development. Not just because it is the right thing to do, but also because it is in our own long-term best interests. It offers the best hope for the future.

Nature	Fresh Water, Forests, Mountains, Oceans and Seas, Water Climate Change, Atmosphere, Energy, Biodiversity, Systems Ecology, Desertification and Drought
Human	Capacity-building, Human Settlements, Demographics, Major Groups, Health, Sanitation, SIDS, Poverty, Waste (Solid), Waste (Radioactive), Waste (Hazardous), Toxic Chemicals, Consumption and Production Patterns
Industries	Agriculture, Industry, Science, Transport, Biotechnology, Trade and Environment, Finance, Technology, Sustainable Tourism
Policies	International Law, Education and Awareness, Land Management, Information for Decision Making and Participation, National Sustainable Development Strategies, Disaster Reduction and Management, Integrated Decision Making, International Cooperation for Enabling Environment, Institutional Arrangements, Indicators

Discussion assistant

biodiversity（生物多样性）; pattern（模式）; demographic（人口统计学）; desertification（荒漠化，沙漠化）; systems ecology（系统生态学）; settlement（居住

地,社区); enabling environment (有利环境); strategy (策略); sanitation (卫生,卫生设施); SIDS (Sudden Infant Death Syndrome, 婴儿猝死综合征); institutional (制度的); toxic (有毒的); hazardous (危险的); radioactive (放射性的); integrated (综合的)

Writing

Write a passage to describe the relationship between human beings and nature based on the following diagram and with the helpful information in the Writing Assistant.

Man and Nature

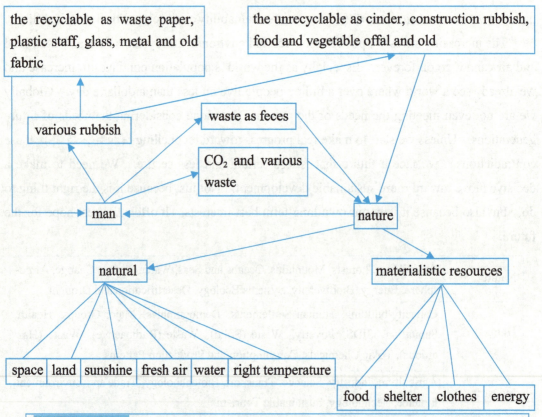

Writing assistant

　　man, nature, inseparable, integrated.

　　nature, provide, basic materials and conditions, man, survive on the earth; a nice natural environment as land, sunshine and water, basic materials like food, shelter and energy, vital for man. man, take from, nature.

　　meanwhile, man, return a lot to, nature. what, sent back? man, consume, materials, produce, wastes; a small part, the wastes, recycle, reuse, human. most, rubbish, return into, nature; some, absorb, nature, feces and urine, take by, the earth; certain amount of CO_2, waste gases, sequestrate, through photosynthesis; some, decompose; however, a big part, the rubbish, burn and landfill, take years, degrade, remain, the earth, forever; some, seriously pollute, the soil, underground water, the air; dispose wastes, take, many resources, like land, water and energy.

so, nature, provide, necessary land and materials, man's survival, serves as, a rubbish dump; more materials, take from, the nature, more waste, return back to, nature; as a result, nature, produce more, satisfy, needs. in fact, one earth, capacity, definite, deceasing, since, man, not, protect, the earth, but, harm, purposely, unconsciously; therefore, future, our offspring, high time, immediate measures, love, protect, nature, our homeland.

Part II   How Can We Reduce Our Ecological Footprint?

Warming up

I. Listening

Learn the following words and phrases and then listen to a news report to answer the following questions.

Words and phrases

asthma	/ˈæsmə/	n.	哮喘
conduct	/kənˈdʌkt/	vt.	指导,管理
efficiency	/iˈfiʃənsi/	n.	效率
emission	/iˈmiʃən/	n.	排放物
emit	/iˈmit/	vt.	发射出,排放出
premature	/ˌprɛməˈtjuə/	a.	早熟的,过早的
respiratory	/riˈspirətəri/	a.	呼吸的
rewarding	/riˈwɔːdiŋ/	a.	有利的,回报率高的
surpass	/səˈpɑːs/	vt.	超越,胜过
transboundary	/ˌtrænsˈbaundəri/	n.	超越国界
environmental governance			环境监管

Questions

1. What are the two major sources of air pollution in China?
2. Which country has the largest energy consumption and most greenhouse gases emission in the world?
3. What is the most polluted city in the world?
4. What are the reasons causing most of China's environmental problems?
5. What measures has China taken to solve its environmental problems? List at least two.

II. Discussion

List simple and workable strategies as many as possible on how to reduce Chinese Eco-footprint. The following pictures serve as good hints.

  The increasing big carbon footprint is only one component of the huge Eco-footprint of Chinese people. Having smaller land and water resources for each citizen and with a larger population, we now suffer from serious resource crisis. As global citizens and for the sake of our offspring, we still have a strong responsibility to reduce our Eco-footprint.

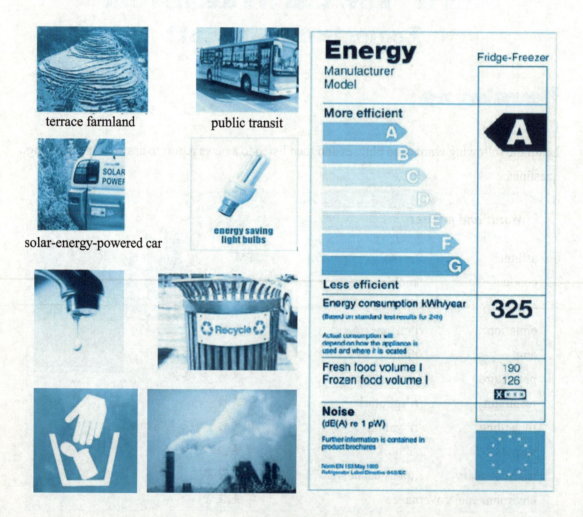

terrace farmland   public transit

solar-energy-powered car   energy saving light bulbs

local fruit and vegetable   waste of food   biomass water heater

Reading

How Can We Reduce Our Ecological Footprint?

1   Every now and then, an idea comes along that makes almost everybody pat his forehead and think "Hey, why didn't I think of that?" It was so simple—why didn't I think of it? Almost everyone who is interested in ecology and the wonderful and frightening interactions between people and the natural environment has the same reaction when he first reads a description of the concept of the Ecological Footprint.

Question 1: Why do individuals think nothing when consuming natural resources? (Para. 2)

2   We live in a society in which physical distance from resources to consumers has been largely obscured by an efficient global transportation network. It's perfectly common to walk into a store on any street corner and buy fresh bananas or fresh oranges, staples of our daily diet that a century ago were relative luxuries. As individuals we think nothing of flying to Florida or Europe or even Australia for business or for pleasure. We drive long distances in complex cars, burning fossil fuels and also making use of a huge network of paved and gravel roads.

3   Those of us who own property, mostly as our individual residential lots, tend to have a very good idea of how big the property is, who our neighbors are, and how we use the space within that property. Very few of us, however, earn our subsistence from the land that we own. By buying goods and services that are dependent on land that is somewhere else, we obtain our daily needs without an awareness of how much land must be dedicated to get those needs.

Question 2: What's the significance for individuals to reduce their Ecological Footprint? (Para. 4)

4　　Therefore, we, as individuals, have the responsibility to learn what the Ecological Footprint is and how big our footprints are. It is wise and responsible of you to do what you can to reduce your footprint, for the sake of yourself and your offspring as well as the whole human population and life on the earth.

Question 3: What does "disparity" mean in line 5? (Para. 5)

5　　An Ecological Footprint is a gauge of how many resources you use. Answering a short series of questions about your driving habits, source of food, garbage generation, and local area generates a rough estimate of how much land it takes to sustain you. 4.5 acres of usable land are available to every human being on Earth; in the United States, the average footprint is 24 acres. Clearly, there is a disparity between land usage and available resources. Many environmentalists believe that countries with more developed economies have an obligation to reduce their ecological footprints so that future generations will still have resources. Citizens can help by reducing their individual ecological footprints.

Question 4: Fill out the chart with information from the following paragraphs. (Paras. 6—9)

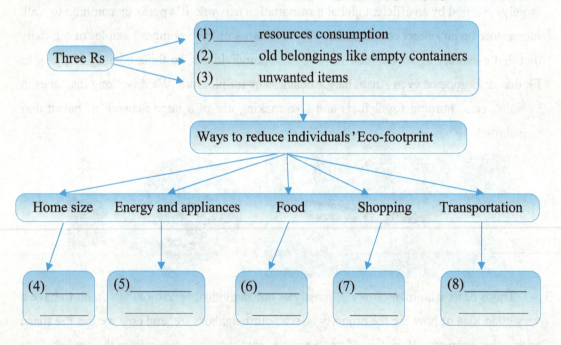

6　　In fact, it is relatively easy to make a few small changes that will drastically reduce your Ecological Footprint. One of the main ways to reduce your ecological footprint is to change the way you use energy. If you rent your home, try buying energy-efficient light bulbs, and remember to turn off electronic devices when you are not using them. If you own your

appliances, think about buying a gas stove, a more efficient fridge, or an on-demand hot water heater. High efficiency washers and dryers can also help to reduce the amount of energy you use, and make your utility bills cheaper. If you own your home and want to reduce your Ecological Footprint, find out alternative energy sources like solar panels and windmills.

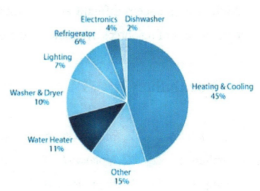

7   To reduce your Ecological Footprint away from home, think about how you get from here to there. Use public transit more, or ride a bicycle when the trip is short. Try walking instead of driving. Source your food locally to reduce the amount of energy wasted transporting your food from distant locations to the supermarket. In addition to being better for the environment, buying local food also supports the local economy.

8   Making your Ecological Footprint smaller can also be greatly assisted by the three R's: reduce, reuse, and recycle. Try to reduce the amount of resources you use by purchasing items with minimal packaging, and avoiding products you do not use. Reuse empty containers, take advantage of thrift stores, and find creative ways to bring new life to old belongings. Finally, recycle unwanted items, either in curbside recycling or in the form of donations to thrift stores.

9   To reduce your Ecological Footprint even further, think about more extreme lifestyle changes. Live in a smaller house, or share the space in your house with more people. Change your diet: animal products are far less efficient than plant products and require far more energy to produce. Fly less: commercial airplanes are a huge source of carbon emissions damaging our environment. Start growing a garden, and encourage others to do the same.

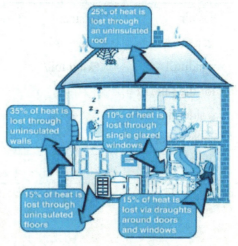

10   Whether you make small or large changes to reduce your Ecological Footprint, they will make a difference. Showing other citizens how easy it is will also encourage them to explore

ways to reduce their own ecological footprints, and lead to less consumption in general. While it might seem difficult at first, your changes will make a positive difference in the total amount of resources available on the earth, and will make human life more sustainable.

Vocabulary

alternative	/ɔːlˈtɜːnətiv/	n.	二中选一(的);可选择的办法、事物
appliance	/əˈplaiəns/	n.	用具,器具
complex	/ˈkɔmpleks/	a.	复杂的
curbside	/ˈkəːbsaid/	n.	路边,街头
dedicate	/ˈdedikeit/	vt.	(为某一特殊用途)奉献
disparity	/diˈspæriti/	n.	(数量、质量等)不一致,不等
donation	/dəuˈneiʃən/	n.	捐赠品
drastically	/ˈdræstikəli/	ad.	彻底地,激烈地
estimate	/ˈestimeit/	vt.&n.	估计,评估
gauge	/geʤ/	n.&vt.	尺度,标准;测量
generate	/ˈdʒenəreit/	vt.	使产生
gravel	/ˈgrævəl/	a.	碎石的,沙砾的
interaction	/ˌintəˈrækʃən/	n.	相互作用(v. interact)
luxury	/ˈlʌkʃəri/	n.	奢侈品
minimal	/ˈminiməl/	a.	最小的,最小限度的
obligation	/ˌɔbliˈgeiʃən/	n.	义务,责任
obscure	/əbˈskjuə/	vt.	使不明显
property	/ˈprɔpəti/	n.	财产
subsistence	/səbˈsistəns/	n.	生存,存活
sustain	/səˈstein/	vt.	支撑,维持
transit	/ˈtrænsit/	n.	运输(尤指公交系统)
windmill	/ˈwindˌmil/	n.	风车
for the sake of			为了……好处(利益)
residential lot			居住地
solar panel			太阳能电池板
thrift stores			廉价旧货店

Unit 4

Vocabulary exercises

I. Fill in each blank with the right word or phrase from the following box. Change the form when necessary.

concept	efficient	alternative	property	public transit
gauge	complex	minimal	available	thrift stores

1. IBM has expanded its Zodiac (黄道) consultancy (咨询) service with tools to _____ a firm's IT carbon footprint and it says energy consumption has become one of the biggest business overheads and companies must take it seriously.

2. To welcome the policy of environmental protection, each one should try to use _____ natural materials as far as possible.

3. Since it is regulated that private cars can only run on roads in fixed days, more and more people turn to _____.

4. Since traditional fuels such as petrol and coal will tremendously contribute to the worsening air quality, _____ energy must be developed.

5. _____ are ideal places for people to dispose of their old belongings so that they don't have to pay for extra money for their disposal but pick back some dollars.

6. All people in the world should hold the _____ that there is only one earth and they must treasure and love it.

7. Despite the fact that agriculture employs over one-third of the world's population, agricultural production accounts for (占有) less than five percent of the gross (总的) world product. So it is urgent to have more _____ agriculture.

8. The global land resources _____ are decreasing with intensive farming, soil degradation, growing desertification, and larger population.

9. Many people foolishly think the size of one's _____ is the only yardstick (标准) to measure his success.

10. Forestry is a subject studying the _____ system of forests management, tree plantations, and related natural resources.

II. The absorption of various wastes from humankind is a neck-breaking burden for nature. Learning human wastes will help us better know the influence of our daily production activities and life styles on nature. It will also guide us to reduce our Eco-footprint. Here are some common life wastes. Study and classify them by different categories of management. (Some wastes can be disposed of in several ways.)

Pop life waste: paper waste (newspaper, magazines), paper cups and plates, cardboard boxes, old cloth and fabrics, beverage cans (饮料罐), beer bottles, chemical bottles, beverage bottles, plastic bottles, styrofoam materials (泡沫塑料产品), used fluorescent light tubes (废旧荧光灯管), dry batteries (干电池), quasi-infectious wastes (拟似传染性废弃物) (injectors〈注射器〉, medical gloves, gauze〈纱布〉, paper towel with blood stains〈带血迹的纸巾〉), expired medicine (过期药品), solid plastic materials, plastic films (胶卷), bioplastics, animal corpses and tissues (尸体,组织), animal excreta (排泄物), food remainders (剩余物), fallen leaves and mowed grass (剪掉的草), glass and china wares (瓷器), metal waste, human waste (feces〈粪〉, urine〈便〉), brown waste (wood products, dry leaves, corn cobs〈玉米穗轴〉), construction waste (soil, rocks, concrete fragments〈混凝土块〉, broken brick), electric and electronic waste (used computers, refrigerators, wires), pesticide (杀虫剂).

Waste Management					
Purposes: recycle useful waste, reduce pollution and reduce land occupation					
Principles: Waste Classification ("3 Rs": reduce, reuse and recycle); Extended Producer Responsibility (EPR); Polluter Pays Principle					
Wastes to be recycled			Wastes to be disposed of		
physical processing	biological processing	energy recovery	landfill (填埋法)	incineration (焚烧法)	composting (堆肥法)

Speaking

I. Land and water resources are limited and energy crisis is threatening us. It is urgent that humans should try to cut down their Eco-footprint. Based on the chart on the right, discuss with partners how we can conserve energy and resources, how to improve their efficiency and what renewable alternatives can be found.

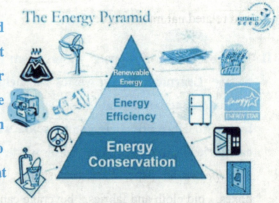

Unit 4

II. Learn the following popular signs for urban wastes, and then match them with their English terms from the following box.

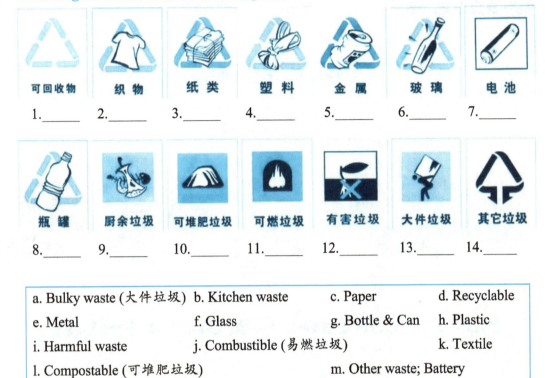

可回收物 织物 纸类 塑料 金属 玻璃 电池
1._____ 2._____ 3._____ 4._____ 5._____ 6._____ 7._____

瓶罐 厨余垃圾 可堆肥垃圾 可燃垃圾 有害垃圾 大件垃圾 其它垃圾
8._____ 9._____ 10._____ 11._____ 12._____ 13._____ 14._____

a. Bulky waste (大件垃圾)	b. Kitchen waste	c. Paper	d. Recyclable
e. Metal	f. Glass	g. Bottle & Can	h. Plastic
i. Harmful waste	j. Combustible (易燃垃圾)		k. Textile
l. Compostable (可堆肥垃圾)		m. Other waste; Battery	

Background Reading

What is biocapacity?

What is overshoot?

What is a global hectare?

How is an Ecological Footprint calculated?

What is the proper way to use the term Ecological Footprint?

Ways to Reduce Our Ecological Footprint

Differences Between Carbon Footprint and the Ecological Footprint

Water Footprint

Please refer to the attached disk.

Unit 5

Food Safety

食品安全

Part I Food Safety—A Global Problem

Warming up

I. Read the following statements and tick the ones that you think might be the sources of unsafe food.

1. _____ Pollution comes from farming.
2. _____ "Pollution-free food movement plan" is promoted (推进) in many countries.
3. _____ Industrial pollution makes agricultural environment worse.
4. _____ Illegal (非法的) food production and trade presents a big threat to food safety.
5. _____ Organic food has experienced steady (稳定的) development since 1990s.
6. _____ Some restaurants and other catering business (公共饮食业) have no necessary sanitations (卫生设施).
7. _____ Some foods can meet international standards.
8. _____ Some consumers are lack of common sense (常识) of food consumption.
9. _____ Food testing system is imperfect.
10. _____ Construction of market system and supervision (监督) of food circulation are being improved in most areas and countries.

Unit 5

II. The woman in the picture fears that the food she buys is not organically produced and some words related to unsafe food pop into her mind. Please work with your partner to figure out their Chinese equivalences (相应的汉语意思). Then try to tell your partner what you usually take into consideration (考虑) when buying foods.

hormones, pesticides, antibiotics, chemicals, bacterial contamination from food processing, genetically modified food, additives and preservatives, production date, expiration date, hygiene standard ...

Reading

Food Safety—A Global Problem

Question 1: Why is food safety a global problem? (Para. 1)

1 The scandals of contaminated milk powder and toxic rice, the outbreaks of mad cow disease (BSE), hand-foot-mouth disease, bird flu and so on make people worry about food safety time and again. Food safety is a global problem. Many problems happening in developing countries have been well documented in developed countries. The World Health Organization (WHO) estimates that each year, unsafe food makes 2 billion people ill, about one third of the world population. Jorgen Schlundt, director of the food safety department of the WHO says, "All countries need to improve their food safety systems. I said all countries, as food nowhere in the world is 100 percent safe".

Question 2: In what ways may pathogenic microbes and chemical contaminants enter the food chain? (Para. 2)

2 Food safety is a scientific discipline describing handling, preparation, and storage of food in ways that prevent foodborne illnesses caused by food contamination. Potential effects of food contamination, ranging from diarrhea to cancer, result from a number of sources. Pathogenic (human disease-causing) microbes and chemical contaminants may enter the

85

food chain naturally from the environment, through farm practices, such as using pesticides or animal drugs, or through food processing and handling. Some enter the food chain because they reduce the costs of producing food. Still others improve food quality in

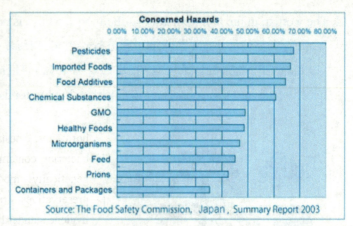

terms of taste, texture, visual appeal, or shelf life. The risks to human health depend on how toxic a substance is or how poisonous a microbe is, how much poison is in particular foods, and how much of those foods a person has. Even common and useful substances in food can be harmful if eaten too much. Other food safety concerns include the use of hormones, antibiotic resistance, genetic modification and so on.

Question 3: What can be expected about foodborn diseases in 21st century? (Para. 3)

3 During the early 21st century, more foodborn diseases can be expected to increase, especially in developing countries, in part because of environmental or demographic changes. These vary from climate changes, changes in microbial and other ecological systems. However, an even greater challenge to food safety will come from changes resulting directly in degradation of sanitation and human environment. These include the increase age of human populations, unplanned urbanization and migration and mass production of food due to population growth and changed food habits. Mass tourism and international trade in food are causing foodborn risks to spread transnationally, which makes the health and trade consequences of toxic chemicals in food have global implications.

Question 4: What kind of program is HACCP? (Para. 4)

4 Foodborne risks, if not controlled, can be major causes of disease and premature death as well as lost productivity and heavy economic burdens. To protect consumers from

foodborne diseases, efforts must focus on each point in the farm-to-table chain to better predict and prevent foodborne hazards, and to monitor and rapidly react to outbreaks of foodborne diseases. Both traditional and new technologies of assuring food safety should be improved and fully exploited. This needs to be done through legislative measures, and with much greater reliance on the voluntary compliance of education of customers and professional food handlers. This will be an important task for all the primary health care 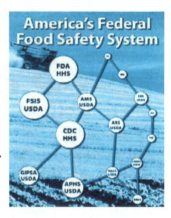 systems to aim at "health for all". And a food-service establishment should have an effective food safety program to prevent hazards before they occur. For example, the present internationally accepted program, the Hazard Analysis Critical Control Point (HACCP) is a preventative program started by the Food and Drug Administration (FDA) to ensure food safety for the astronauts in the space program.

Question 5: How do regulatory agencies at all levels of government in the United States do to be consistent with national food regulatory policy? (Para. 5)

5   To achieve food safety, most countries have established a strict network. In USA, FDA publishes the Food Code, a model set of guidelines and procedures that assists food control jurisdictions. The FDA Food Code provides a scientifically sound technical and legal basis for regulating the retail and food service industries. Regulatory agencies at all levels of government in the United States use it to develop or update food safety rules in their jurisdictions that are consistent with national food regulatory policy.

Question 6: What is High-level International Food Safety Forum? (Para. 6)

6   Food safety is a global problem. Not a country should be singled out for particular concern over food safety since it is an issue that poor and rich countries alike must cope with through better regulation and cooperation. For this reason, most countries are starting to carry out some suggestions of the World Health Organization (WHO) and Food and Agriculture Organization of the United Nations (FAO). They spare no efforts in improving law enforcement on product quality problems and updating the establishment of national standard food safety systems. And they also strengthen their cooperation with foreign countries in handling the issue. For example, High-level International Food Safety Forum is a high-level political commitment to enhance global food safety.

Vocabulary

antibiotic	/ˌæntibaiˈɔtik/	n.&a.	抗生素(的)
appeal	/əˈpiːl/	n.	吸引力
code	/kəud/	n.	法规
commitment	/kəˈmitmənt/	n.	许诺,承担义务
concern	/kənˈsəːn/	n.&v.	关注
compliance	/kəmˈplaiəns/	n.	依从,顺从
contaminant	/kənˈtæminənt/	n.	污染物
contamination	/kənˌtæmiˈneiʃən/	n.	污染
degradation	/ˌdegrəˈdeiʃən/	n.	降格,退化
demographic	/ˌdeməˈɡræfik/	a.	人口统计学的
diarrhea	/ˌdaiəˈriə/	n.	痢疾,腹泻
documented	/ˈdɔkjuməntid/	a.	备有证明文件的
enforcement	/inˈfɔːsmənt/	n.	执行,强制
enhance	/inˈhɑːns/	vt.	提高,增强
exploit	/iksˈplɔit/	vt.	剥削;利用;开发,开采
federal	/ˈfedərəl/	n.	联邦的,中央政府的
forum	/ˈfɔːrəm/	n.	论坛,讨论会
global	/ˈɡləubəl/	a.	全球的
hazard	/ˈhæzəd/	n.	危险
hormone	/ˈhɔːməun/	n.	荷尔蒙,激素
implication	/ˌimpliˈkeiʃən/	n.	含意,暗示
jurisdiction	/ˌdʒuərisˈdikʃən/	n.	权限
legislative	/ˈledʒislətiv/	n.&a.	立法(的),立法机关(的)
mass	/mæs/	n.&a.	大量;大规模的
microbe	/ˈmaikrəub/	n.	微生物,细菌
migration	/maiˈɡreiʃən/	n.	移民,迁移
pathogenic	/ˌpæθəˈdʒenik/	a.	致病的,病原的
pesticide	/ˈpestisaid/	n.	杀虫剂
preventative	/priˈventətiv/	a.	预防性的
reliance	/riˈlaiəns/	n.	依靠
sanitation	/ˌsæniˈteiʃən/	n.	卫生,卫生设施

strengthen	/ˈstreŋθən/	vt.	加强,巩固
toxic	/ˈtɔksik/	a.	有毒的,中毒的
transnationally	/trænzˈnætʃənəli/	ad.	跨国地
texture	/ˈtekstʃə/	n.	质地
visual	/ˈviʒuəl/	a.	视觉的,形象的
update	/ʌpˈdeit/	vt.	更新;使……跟上时代
urbanization	/ˈəːbənaiˈzeiʃən/	n.	都市化
voluntary	/ˈvɔləntəri/	a.	自愿的,主动的
be singled out			被挑选出
bird flu			禽流感
foodborne disease			食源性疾病
genetic modification			转基因
high-level			高阶层的
mad cow disease (BSE)			疯牛病
premature death			早夭
shelf life			保存限期
spare no efforts			不遗余力
Food and Drug Administration (FDA)			美国食品药品管理局
Food and Agriculture Organization of the United Nations (FAO)			联合国粮农组织
HACCP (Hazard Analysis Critical Control Point)			危害分析关键控制点
High-level International Food Safety Forum			国际食品安全高层论坛

Vocabulary exercises

I. Match each word with its explanation.

1. ____ potential   a. being in agreement with
2. ____ degradation   b. occurring or existing before the nutural or usual time
3. ____ transnational   c. intended or used to prevent
4. ____ premature   d. improve
5. ____ exploit   e. relating to or involving several nations
6. ____ preventive   f. capable of being but not yet in existence
7. ____ consistent   g. to use to the greatest possible advantage
8. ____ enhance   h. a decline to a lower condition, quality, or level

II. **Food Safety Crossword: Discuss and work out the solution with a partner in light of the given hints.**

Across	Down
1. A chemical compound that is added to protect against decay (腐烂).	2. To attack or infect (传染), as a disease.
6. A white substance used to inhibit (抑制) microbial growth for thousands of years, was especially important before refrigeration (制冷).	3. Any of various similar arthropod animals (节肢动物), such as flies, mosquitoes, and bees.
7. A food safety approach that focuses on preventative controls rather than monitoring and correction procedures.	4. Thin-shelled reproductive body of a hen, frequently causing Salmonella (沙门氏菌属) food poisoning cases.
8. Recently made, produced, or harvested; not stale (变味的) or spoiled.	5. Having a low temperature.
10. Parasitic (寄生的) plants lacking chlorophyll (叶绿素) and leaves and true stems and roots and reproducing by spores (长孢子).	7. Any of various similar substances found in plants and insects that control development.
11. (An illness) easily spreads.	9. A white liquid containing proteins, fats, lactose (乳糖), and various vitamins and minerals, usually heated to 161°F (72°C) for 15 seconds during processing.
14. The meat of a pig, host of trichina (旋毛虫的宿主).	12. Illness, a pathological (病理的) condition of a part of body, an organ, or a system of an organism resulting from different causes, such as infection, genetic defect, or environmental stress.
16. The possibility of suffering harm or loss; danger.	
17. Not available for public use, control, or participation, but very personally.	13. An umbrella-shaped vegetable.
19. To bring up to date.	15. To begin an activity or a movement.
20. The most dangerous bacterial breeding ground in the typical home.	18. Mad cow disease.

III. Choose the right word or phrase from the following box to finish each of the statements that are abstracted from "Beijing Declaration on Food Safety" in *2007 High-level International Food Safety Forum*. Meanwhile, try to understand these statements.

HACCP	the responsibility	consumers
food safety measures	the food industry	hazards (危险)
sound scientific evidence	food safety incidents (事件)	

1. Oversight (监督) of food safety is an essential (必须的) public health function that protects consumers from health risks presented by biological, chemical and physical _____ in food as well as by conditions of food.

2. Equal application (应用) of _____ between countries as well as within countries can improve global food safety.

3. Food safety measures should be based on _____ and risk analysis principles (风险分析原理).

4. Production of safe food is primarily _____ of the food industry.

5. Education of _____ is very important in promoting safe food practices.

6. All countries are urged (激励) to ensure effective enforcement (有效的实施) of food safety legislation using risk-based methods, such as the _____ system, where possible.

7. All countries are urged to establish procedures (程序), including tracing (追踪) and recalling (召回) systems in conjunction with (与……协力) industry, to rapidly identify (识别), investigate (调查) and control _____.

8. All countries are urged to communicate and consult effectively with consumers and _____ in developing, implementing (执行) and reviewing food safety policies and priorities (优先权), including education and other matters of concern.

Listening

Study the following chart to understand the rationale (理据) of food safety basics. Then listen to the passage and fill in the missing words.

Food contaminated with pathogenic micro-organisms (微生物), chemicals and foreign matters (异物) may present risks to (1)_____. Therefore, we should not accept food known or doubted to be contaminated with these substances.

Most pathogenic bacteria grow and multiply rapidly at temperatures between 4℃ and 60℃. This range of temperatures is therefore called the (2)_____. At temperatures lower than 4℃ and higher than 60℃, bacterial growth (3)_____. However, most bacteria can survive (幸存) cold temperatures and continue multiplication (繁殖) later when conditions become suitable again. (4)_____ hazardous food may be contaminated by pathogenic bacteria which can multiply to (5)_____ at ambient (周围的) temperatures. As such, potentially hazardous food should be kept at or (6)_____ 4℃, or at or (7)_____ 60℃ during delivery (运送), to prevent growth of these bacteria.

Freezing is a process in which the temperature of a food is reduced below (8)_____ and the majority of (9)_____ the food undergoes a change in a state to form ice crystals (晶体). Freezing preserves food for extended (延长的) period of time by preventing the growth of microorganisms (微生物) that cause food spoilage (腐坏) and foodborne illnesses. To maintain the quality of frozen food, a temperature of (10)_____ or less is preferred (首选的).

Speaking

I. Finish the following food safety interactive kitchen quiz. Check the answer with your partner and tell him or her about your usual practice (通常的做法) **related to each item and what you learn from the quiz.**

1. Hands should be washed in water for at least five seconds before preparing foods and after handling raw meats.

    A. True

    B. False

2. One way to prevent cross-contamination (交叉感染) is to use two cutting boards (切菜案板), one strictly for raw meats, poultry (家禽) and seafood and the other for ready-to-eat foods.

    A. True   B. False

3. After cutting meat on a cutting board, the best way to clean a cutting board is to _____.

   A. Wipe off with a clean sponge

   B. Wash in hot water with soap

   C. Wash in hot water with soap, then clean the board in chlorine bleach solution (氯漂白剂) and lastly wash with clean water.

   D. All of the above are acceptable

4. A meat/cooking thermometer is the only reliable way to check the doneness (煮熟的程度) of meats, poultry, egg dishes and leftovers (残羹剩菜).

   A. True   B. False

5. Leftover foods should be reheated to _____ ℃.

   A. 32   B. 60

   C. 74   D. Doesn't matter

6. Meat, fish and poultry should be defrosted (解冻) _____.

   A. on the counter   B. in the refrigerator

   C. in the microwave   D. in the refrigerator or the microwave

7. The proper (适当的) temperature for a home refrigerator should be below 4℃.

   A. True   B. False

8. As a rule, leftover foods should not stay out of refrigeration for more than _____ hours. In hot weather (32℃ or warmer), this time is reduced to _____ hour(s).

   A. four, three   B. three, one

   C. three, two   D. two, one

9. Four simple actions are suggested to take control of food safety in your kitchen. Which tip is most important?

   A. Wash hands often.

   B. Keep raw meat and ready to eat food separate.

   C. Cook to proper temperatures

   D. Refrigerate promptly below 4℃.

   E. All of the above.

II. There are altogether six incorrect practices about the placement of mayonnaise (蛋黄酱), backpack, cat, milk, sandwich and hot dogs in the picture. Please discuss with your partner to find out the six mistakes and tell where they shoule be.

III. The following picture contains different kinds of food. If you would like to enjoy better health and have a stronger body, you must have a healthy diet habit. Please choose the proper diet suggestions for the right food categories.

1. Choose a wide variety.
2. Choose low-fat alternatives whenever you can. Choose more fish than poultry.
3. Eat all types and choose high fiber kinds whenever you can.
4. Choose lower fat alternative whenever you can.
5. Try not to eat these too often, and when you do, try to have small amounts.

A. Fruit and vegetables: _____

B. Bread, other cereals and potatoes: _____

C. Meat, fish, poultry and alternatives: _____

D. Fatty and sugary foods: _____

E. Milk and dairy foods: _____

IV. Microbial food-borne illness, commonly called food poisoning (食物中毒), is monitored closely because the cases of food poisoning far outnumber any other type of food contamination. Many people have had first-hand experience of how unpleasant food poisoning can be, even for a fit and healthy person. And sometimes food poisoning can cause a serious illness. Study the following pictures and finish the following exercises.

1. What are some common symptoms of food poisoning?
2. When one has food poisoning, he has to consider three main things: rehydration, seeking medical assistance, and reporting. Please try to tell each of them in detail to your partner.
3. Why is it important to report food poisoning?

Discussion assistant

feel like throwing up (觉得反胃；想吐); vomit (呕吐，呕吐物); rehydration (补充体液); rehydration powder (生理补液盐); drugstore (药房); include (包括); contact 120 (联系120急救热线); ask doctors for advice (咨询大夫); seek medical assistance (寻求医疗帮助); have his vomit sample tested (将呕吐物送检); report to the local health service (向当地医疗卫生服务机构报告); investigate the business in question (调查有问题的企业); prevent other people suffering from food poisoning (防止他人食物中毒)

V. Study the following food pyramid and decide whether the following statements are true or false according to the picture and common wisdom. Write "T" for true and "F" for false. Then try to make a speech entitled "A Proper Diet and Good Health".

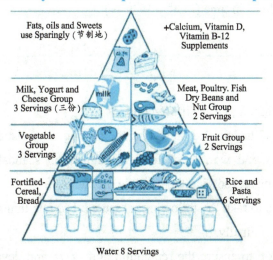

1. _____ If one wants to have a proper diet, he should not avoid fat and oil all together.
2. _____ What we eat will not actually increase the chances of a fuller, healthier, longer life.

3. _____ For good health, we should eat a variety of foods.
4. _____ We should eat the same foods day after day.
5. _____ Foods should be selected everyday from each of "basic four" according to their recommended servings (份额).
6. _____ The milk group, meat group, vegetable-fruit group, and bread-cereal group are the four essential groups of food that offer proper nutrition.
7. _____ Corn and tomato belong to the fruit group according to the picture.
8. _____ We are advised to drink 10 glasses of water every day.
9. _____ The common required nutrients are water, minerals, carbohydrate, fats and oils, proteins, and vitamins.
10. _____ A balanced diet will greatly do good to our physical health.

Writing

Some food businesses are faced with contaminated food scandals (有毒食品的丑闻). Suppose you work in a food corporation. Certainly you don't want your company to be involved in such kind of scandals. Please write a letter to the manger of your company. Your letter should include the following points:

1. Trying to produce foods that meet with international standards.
2. Establishing a strict network to realize effective supervision (监督) over processing, packaging, delivering (加工、包装和运输) and selling of the products.
3. Making periodic surveys and reports (定期调查和报告) on product information.
4. Recalling defective products in time (及时召回次品).
...

> **Writing assistant**
>
> Format of a letter
>
> *Addressing:* Dear Mr./Ms. ...; Dear Sir/Madame
>
> *Introduction* (purpose of the letter): I'm writing to...; I'm greatly disturbed by...
>
> *Body:* Tell your ideas and worries of food contamination scandal; present your suggestions of improving and solving the possible problems.
>
> It is advisable/desirable to take the following measures: For one thing, ... For another thing, ... Furthermore, ... Finally, ...
>
> take ...into consideration to ensure the reputation (名誉) and development of the company...

> *Conclusion:* Show your appreciation to your manager for his concern of the problems and adoption (采纳) of your suggestions.
> I would greatly appreciate ...
> I would be grateful if you could/would...
> It will be appreciated if you can/could...
> I am looking forward to hearing from you.

Part II   Pesticides and Food: How We Test for Safety

Warming up

I. Discussion

1. Why do people need pesticides?
2. What precautions should people take to minimize their exposure to pesticides?

II. Listening

Learn the following phrases and then listen to a VOA Special English Agriculture Report on food safety and decide whether the given statements are true (T) or false (F).

> **Words and phrases**
>
> a five-and-one-quarter percent chlorine solution 5.25%的氯溶液
> be disinfected with chemicals 用化学药品消毒
> chlorine, iodine or bromine 氯, 碘酒或溴
> deny pests a place to live 以防有害动植物的滋生
> enforce federal rules 执行联邦政府的规则
> food containers 贮存食物的容器
> make a list of pest control measures 列出有害动植物防治措施
> places where food is handled or stored 操作和贮存食品的空间
> rat and mouse 田鼠和家鼠
> storage areas 贮藏货物的地方
> supervisor 监督人
> the first line of defense against pests 预防有害动植物的第一道防线

> Vietnam 越南
>
> website 网页

1. _____ Experts say the first line of defense against pests is to clean places where food is handled or stored.
2. _____ Food containers should be stored about 19 meters off the ground. They should also be kept about one half a meter away from walls.
3. _____ We can infer from the report that a rat is generally bigger than a mouse.
4. _____ A list of pest control measures will help prepare for any inspections.
5. _____ Food services in US just need to follow federal laws.

Reading

Pesticides and Food: How We Test for Safety

Question 1: How do pesticides help crop production? (Para. 1)

1 As Americans, we enjoy a plentiful and affordable variety of fruits and vegetables, a key to a healthy food supply that is one of the world's safest. Pesticides have enabled farmers to produce crops in areas that otherwise would not be suitable, extend growing seasons, increase crop yields, maintain product quality, and extend shelf life. At the same time, pesticides can pose risks if used improperly or too frequently. All of us want to minimize our exposure to potentially dangerous chemicals, so we have questions about pesticides and food.

Question 2: Who makes sure that pesticides are used safely in California? (Para. 2)

2 Pesticides are among most regulated products in the country. Before a pesticide can be used in California, it must be evaluated and licensed by the US Environmental Protection Agency (EPA) and the California Department of Pesticide Regulation (DPR). The manufacturer must submit test data to show that the pesticide will not pose unacceptable risks to workers, consumers, or the environment. California has the nation's toughest pesticide restrictions and the country's largest and best-trained pesticide enforcement organization to make sure the rules are obeyed. Agricultural commissioners in all of California's 58 counties, assisted by 400 county biologists, are responsible for local enforcement, and—with their in-depth knowledge of local conditions—can make sure workers and residents are protected.

California was the first state to require pesticide reporting of all agricultural pesticide use. DPR also monitors air, soil, and water to check for possible contamination of the environment. As a final check, California has the largest state program to sample fresh produce and test it for pesticide residues.

Question 3: What will DPR do if a residue exceeds legal limit? (Para. 3)

3   Agricultural inspectors take samples from packing sheds, wholesale markets, chain store distribution centers, retail markets, and ports of entry. Within hours, samples are analyzed for more than 200 pesticides. This quick turnaround means DPR can immediately check produce with illegal residues. ("Illegal" means the produce has a residue that exceeds legal limit or a pesticide not licensed on that crop is used.) An illegal residue is uncommon but if it occurs, investigators track it to the source. If the crop is still in the field, DPR stops

the harvest and orders the produce destroyed. If the illegal crop is in the channels of trade, DPR bans it and can order it destroyed. Growers who violate the law may face the loss of a crop that can cost them an entire season and tens of thousands of dollars. They are also subject to civil and criminal prosecution, fines, and other penalties.

Question 4: Why does US EPA set legal residue limits with a margin of safety? (Para. 4)

4   About 1 percent of samples tested have illegal residues. No residues are detected in about 62 percent. Remaining samples have detectable pesticides, but most are residues, traces well below the legally allowable limit. US EPA sets these limits with a margin of safety in mind to protect infants, children, and other sensitive people.

Question 5: What is said about imported produce? (Para. 5)

5   All food sold in the US must meet the same safety standards. The result of the state and federal residue monitoring programs show that imported produce violates limits more frequently than domestically grown produce. However, since the tolerances are designed with a margin of safety, an illegal residue does not necessarily equate to a health risk, and the violation rates for both domestic and imported produce are very low. We know from the residue testing that some pesticides are detected more often in domestic produce, some only in imported produce, and some in both, sometimes at very different levels. Different chemicals have different health effects, so there is no simple way to make safety comparisons. Food safety experts agree that any small risk from trace residues found in produce should not keep you from eating a diet rich in fruits and vegetables.

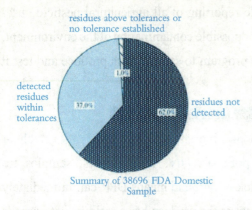
Summary of 38696 FDA Domestic Sample

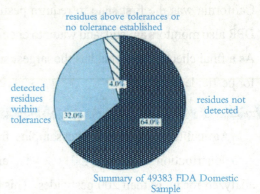
Summary of 49383 FDA Domestic Sample

Question 6: Should pesticide residues be a big food safety concern? (Para. 6)

6   Because residues are an inevitable byproduct of pesticide use, many regulations address the public health implications of pesticide use. Therefore, there are very strict restrictions on the amount of pesticide residues allowed in the food. For example, to give the residues time to break down, there are required waiting periods between a pesticide application and harvest. For this and other reasons, most fresh fruit and vegetables have little or no traceable residue by the time they reach market, and even less by the time they are washed and served.

Question 7: What is considered to be the key to good health? (Para. 7)

7   The National Institutes of Health has this advice about pesticide residues: "The fact they are found at all is only due to the significant advances in analytical chemistry. The tests are now so sensitive that the detection level that can be easily reached is equivalent to detecting one teaspoon of salt in one million gallons of water. Levels even lower than that can sometimes be detected. The mere presence of a trace amount of a pesticide does not mean the product is not unhealthy. On the countrary, eating a diet full of a variety of fruits, grains, and vegetables has been shown to significantly decrease your risk of a variety of health problems from high blood pressure to cancer. Variety is the key to good health."

Fruit and Vegetable Contamination List	
12 *Most* Contaminated *Buy Only Organic*	**12 *Least* Contaminated** *Organic Not Necessary*
Apples	Asparagus
Bell Peppers	Avocados
Celery	Bananas
Cherries	Broccoli
Imported Grapes	Cauliflower
Nectarines	Corn
Peaches	Kiwis
Pears	Mangos
Potatoes	Onions
Red Raspberries	Papaya
Spinach	Pineapples
Strawberries	Peas

Vocabulary

affordable	/ə'fɔːdəbl/	a.	能担负得起的;买得起的
allowable	/ə'lauəbəl/	a.	可准许的
analytical	/ˌænə'litikəl/	a.	分析的
byproduct	/'baiˌprɔdʌkt/	n.	副产品
commissioner	/kə'miʃənə/	n.	委员,专员
comparison	/kəm'pærisən/	n.	比较,对照
detectable	/di'tektəbəl/	a.	可发觉的
domestically	/də'mestikəli/	ad.	家庭式地,国内地
equate	/i'kweit/	vi.	等同
equivalent	/i'kwivələnt/	a.	相等的
exposure	/ik'spəuzə/	n.	受影响,暴露
extend	/ik'stend/	vt.&vi.	扩充,延伸
evaluate	/i'væljueit/	vt.	评价,估计
frequently	/'friːkwəntli/	a.	常常,频繁地
gallon	/'gælən/	n.	加仑
illegal	/i'liːgəl/	a.	违法的,不合规定的
imported	/'impɔːtid/	a.	进口的
improperly	/im'prɔpəli/	ad.	不适当地
infant	/'infənt/	n.	婴儿,幼儿
license	/'laisəns/	n.&vt.	许可(证),(发)执照
manufacturer	/ˌmænju'fæktʃərə/	n.	生产商
minimize	/'minimaiz/	vt.	最小化
otherwise	/'ʌðəwaiz/	ad.	否则
penalty	/'penlti/	n.	处罚,罚款
regulated	/regjuleitid/	a.	管制的
residue	/'rezidjuː/	n.	残留物
restriction	/ris'trikʃən/	n.	限制,约束
sensitive	/'sensitiv/	a.	易受影响的
significantly	/sig'nifikəntli/	ad.	值得注目地
submit	/səb'mit/	vt.	提交,递交

trace	/treis/	n.	痕迹,微量
traceable	/'treisəbl/	a.	可追踪的,起源于
tolerance	/'tɔlərəns/	n.	耐受性
tough	/tʌf/	a.	强硬的
turnaround	/'tə:nəraund/	n.	周转时间
variety	/və'raiəti/	n.	多样性
violate	/'vaiəleit/	vt.	违反或蔑视

break down	分解
chain store	连锁店
civil and criminal prosecution	民事和刑事诉讼
margin of safety	超过实际要求的安全系数
packing shed	包装棚
ports of entry	进口港,入境港
pose a risk	造成危险
retail market	零售市场
test data	测试数据
wholesale market	批发市场
US Environmental Protection Agency (EPA)	美国环境保护局
Department of Pesticide Regulation (DPR)	(美国)农药管理局
The National Institute of Health	(美国)卫生研究院

Vocabulary exercises

I. Write down words with the following prefixes and suffixes as many as possible.

1. un- (not, lacking, the opposite of)
2. pre- (before)
3. -able (added to verbs to form adjectives, meaning able to receive the action of the stated verb.)
4. -ous (added to nouns to form adjectives)
5. -en (added to adjectives to form verbs)
6. -tion (added to verbs to form nouns)
7. -ment (added to verbs to form nouns)

II. Match the following food safety terms in column A with their Chinese meanings in column B.

1. RfD (Reference Dose) 　　　　　　　　a. 风险分析
2. QA (Quality Assurance) 　　　　　　　b. 污染物一般标准
3. QC (Quality Control) 　　　　　　　　c. 最大残留限量
4. Risk analysis 　　　　　　　　　　　　d. 质量控制
5. Hazard identification 　　　　　　　　e. 质量保证
6. Dose-response assessment 　　　　　　f. 参考剂量
7. ADI (Acceptable daily intake) 　　　　g. 危害识别
8. CCPR (Codex Committee on Pesticide Residues) h. 剂量—反应评估
9. EMDI (Estimated maximum daily Intake) i. 评估最大日摄入量
10. GSC (General standard for contaminants) j. 每日允许摄入量
11. LOAEL (Lowest-observed-adverse-effect-level) k. 无可见不良作用剂量水平
12. MRL (Maximum residue limit) 　　　l. 最大耐受剂量
13. MTD (Maximum tolerated dose) 　　m. 最低可见不良作用剂量水平
14. NOAEL (No-observed-adverse-effect level) n. 农药残留法典委员会

III. Fill in each blank with the right word from the following box. Meanwhile, learn main types of pesticides, misuse of rodenticide and its consequences.

| the environment | poisoned | old | rodents | insects |
| animals | position | children | bacteria | ineffective |

Pesticides used on food mainly include: insecticides (杀虫剂) to control (1)_____, rodenticides (杀鼠剂) to control (2)_____, herbicides (除草剂) to control weeds (杂草), fungicides (杀菌剂) to control mold (霉菌) and fungus (真菌), and antimicrobials (抗菌剂) to control (3)_____.

Misuse of rodenticide	Consequence
Use of acute poisons (剧毒) in stores of foodstuffs.	Risk of poisoning customers and workers.
Unprotected poisoned baits (饵)	Risk to domestic (4)_____, (5)_____ and (6)_____ people.
No record of quantity and (7)_____ of bait.	Risk of forgetting the poisoned bait placed among the goods which could result in customers being (8)_____.

Bait made with poor quality products.	Treatment (9)_____.
Products poorly stored.	Risk of poisoning customers, workers, and (10)_____.

VI. The following diagram shows the role of the Food Safety Commission of Japan. Study it and change the forms of the given words to complete the summary of its role.

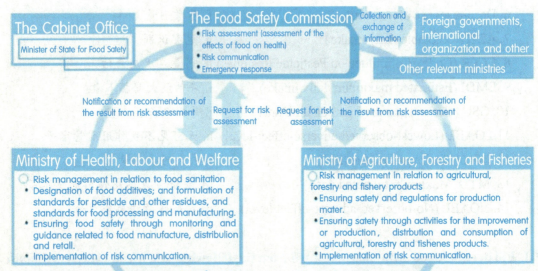

The Japanese Food Safety Commission（食品安全委员会）is an organization that undertakes risk assessment（风险评估）, risk (1)_____ (communicate) and emergency (2)_____ (respond). It is independent from risk (3)_____ (manage) organizations such as the Ministry of Agriculture, Forestry and Fisheries, and the Ministry of Health, Labor and Welfare（劳工和福利部）. By recognizing that protecting the health of the people is one of the country's most important issues, the Commission's primary goals can be (4)_____ (summary) into three main tasks:

1. Conducting risk assessment on food in a (5)_____ (science), independent, and fair manner, and making (6)_____ (recommend) to relevant ministries (7)_____ (base) upon the results from the risk assessment.

2. Implementing（执行）risk communication among consumers and food-related business operators.

3. Responding to food-borne accidents and (8)_____ (emergent).

Speaking

I. Bad eating habits may damage our health because they often cause foodborne illnesses. Look at the bad eating habits list according to an investigation, and then discuss the following questions.

1. What does the picture show?
2. What are some other bad eating habits that you often follow in your daily life?
3. What should you do with bad eating habits for the sake of good health?

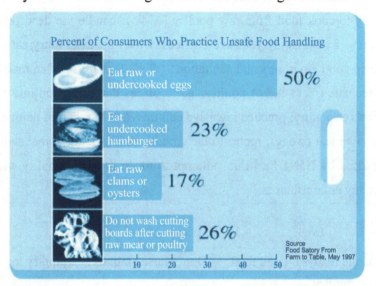

> *Discussion asistant*
>
> The picture illustrates/shows that... (此图表明……)
>
> We can tell from the picture that... (从图中我们可看到……)
>
> up to (多达); ignore (忽视); overcome bad eating habits (克服不良饮食习惯); form good eating habits (养成良好的饮食习惯)

II. What shall we do to get rid of our bad habits in dealing with food? How to reduce the risks of foodborne illnesses? "Clean, Check, Cook, Throw Away, Chill (冷藏), and Separate" are six WHO's recommended (推荐的) tips for food safety. Please study the following picture and write down each recommended tip.

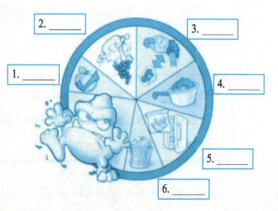

农林英语

III. Bird flu as the name suggests is a disease affecting birds. Bird flu can be of different types of virus. H5N1 flu (高致病性禽流感) infections among humans have now been recorded in many countries and the number of people being infected with this bird flu virus is increasing. Please study the following two pictures and finish the following exercises with your partner.

1. How does the H5N1 bird flu virus spread?
2. Choose the phrases and expressions from the following box to complete the chart about prevention measures against bird flu under Dos and Don'ts headings.

> separate ready-to-cook food from raw poultry (家禽); handle the dead poultry died of bird flu by yourself; wash hand if you have touched raw meat or dead poultry; eat disease-killed poultry; keep good environmental sanitation (环境卫生); raise animals and poultry together; vaccinate (预防接种) poultry; go to places that bring you into close contact with wild birds or poultry; practice intensive culture (集约化养殖) of poultry if you raise poultry; eat raw meat or eggs; report to the authorities if you doubt that sudden death of poultry is caused by H5N1 bird flu; attempt to touch the dead poultry with your bare hands under any circumstances.

Dos	Don'ts
Do seperate ready-to-cook food from raw poultry.	Don't raise animals and poultry together.

Background Reading

> Food Poisoning Warnings Go to Air
> China Asks NZ for Help over Food Safety
> Food Safety after A Flood

Please refer to the attached disk.

Unit 6

Ecotourism

生 态 旅 游

Part I Ecotourism

Warming up

I. Where do you prefer to travel if you have enough money? Why? What factors will you consider if you want to visit a foreign country?

II. The first chart shows the growth of the international tourist arrivals by region between 1950—2020. The second chart shows the forecasts of average annual growth rate worldwide and also by region covering a 25 years period, with 1995 as the base year. Please briefly describe the growth trends.

Chart 1

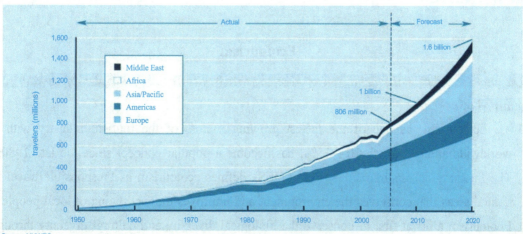

Source: UNWTO.

Chart 2

	Base Year 1995	Forecasts 2010	Forecasts 2020	Market share (%) 1995	Market share (%) 2020	Average annual growth rate (%) 1995-2020
		(Million)				
World	565	1006	1561	100	100	4.1
Africa	20	47	77	3.6	5.0	5.5
Americas	110	190	282	19.3	18.1	3.8
East Asia and the Pacific	81	195	397	14.4	25.4	6.5
Europe	336	527	717	59.8	45.9	3.1
Middle East	14	36	69	2.2	4.4	6.7
South Asia	4	11	19	0.7	1.2	6.2

Discussion assistant

be expected/anticipated/forecasted to reach ...

The top three receiving regions will be...

maintain the highest share of world arrivals...

tourist arrivals (入境旅游人数); forecast (预测,预报); base year (基准年,基年); market share (市场份额); average annual growth rate (平均年增长率); billion (十亿) inbound tourism (入境旅游); outbound travel (出境旅游); international tourism revenue(国际旅游收入); East Asia and the Pacific (东亚和太平洋地区); Middle East (中东) Americas (南北美洲,西半球); South Asia (南亚)

III. Have you heard of eco-travel or ecotourism? What is it? Do you have a frist-hand ecotourism experience that you'd like to share?

Ecotourism

Question 1: What's the definition of ecotourism? What are the principles of ecotourism? (Para. 1)

1 Ecotourism, as one of the fastest growing sectors of the tourism industry with a worldwide annual growth 10—15%, has become a popular concept since the late 1980s. The International Ecotourism Society (TIES) defines ecotourism as "responsible travel to natural areas that conserves the environment and improves the well-being of local people". Ecotourism aims at first to conserve the biological diversity and cultural diversity through

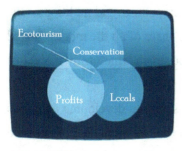

ecosystem protection and promote the sustainable use of biodiversity. It also intends to share socio-economic benefits with local communities. This means that those who implement and participate in ecotourism activities should follow the following principles:

(1) Minimize impact.

(2) Build environmental and cultural awareness and respect.

(3) Provide positive experiences for both visitors and hosts.

(4) Provide direct financial benefits for conservation.

(5) Provide financial benefits and empowerment for local people.

(6) Raise sensitivity to host countries' political, environmental, and social climate.

Question 2: What are the major activities of ecotourism? (Para. 2)

2   Practically speaking, ecotourism includes activities in which visitors enjoy hands-on experiences, such as bird-watching in the Brazilian rainforests, hiking in the mountains of Nepal, participating in a traditional village celebration, or taking a canoe trip down a river.

Local guides usually accompany small groups of tourists on expeditions, teaching them about the local flora, fauna, and culture of the region. Ecotourism is characterized by small-scale outfits in remote locations where commercialization and mass-tourism outfits have not yet penetrated. Tourists typically stay with local families, or at small, environment-friendly hotels called ecolodges. Prime locations where ecotourism has become popular include Latin America, Southeast Asia, and Australia.

Question 3: What are the major types of ecotourism? (Paras. 3—6)

3   There are actually different types of ecotourism that exist. The first type of ecotourism is known as agro-tourism, which encourages visitors to see the agricultural growth and

experience the agricultural life at first hand, such as learning about local plants and animals on a farm.

4   The second type is community-based tourism that will try to get the community to come together as one. Community-based tourism is a mode of tourism that is initiated, managed and owned by local communities. Sustainability is achieved by keeping the tourism

activity on a small scale, and in harmony with the environment, culture, and traditions. One of the most important features of this type is that a reasonable share of all the money gained is enjoyed by the community. This is one of the types of ecotourism which truly maintains and respects the local culture and heritage.

5   A third type of ecotourism is pro-poor tourism, which is set up in developing countries as a means to improve the local economy for local people. In this way it is able to enhance the linkages between tourism businesses and poor people, so that poverty is reduced and poor people are able to participate more effectively in tourism development. The aims of pro-poor range from increasing local employment to involving local people in the decision making process.

6   A forth type of ecotourism is nature-based tourism which concentrates more on enjoying and respecting the exotic wildlife and the environment.

Question 4: What are the potential benefits of ecotourism? (Paras. 7—9)

7   One of the benefits of ecotourism is the influx of money into the host country. In addition, since ecotourists often travel to remote areas, these tourists spend money in remote areas, helping with local economic development. Revenues from safari expeditions, for instance, may go to protecting the animals from poaching, while the entry fees from visiting a village may go to supporting education and health care for the local children. This type of tourism can also add economic diversity to a developing nation by helping create new jobs and businesses that are different from their traditional sources of income.

8   When ecotourism targets national parks, the parks directly benefit from the fees paid by tourists. It enables the parks to be managed and conserved more effectively. This can become a beneficial cycle as funds spent by travelers who are dedicated to leaving as few footprints as possible are used to maintain complex ecosystems. Furthermore, ecotourism may ultimately protect more ecosystems over time. If, for example, local people can sustain themselves through ecotourism-related ventures, they may not need to

cut down forests, mine or deplete local natural resources as much as they might otherwise have done.

9   Another advantage of ecotourism is that it can promote local crafts, events and traditions. This will not only bring additional cash into local communities, but also preserve traditional culture as visitors want to learn about and experience local practices as well as purchase locally-made arts and crafts.

Question 5: What is the prospect of ecotourism? (Para. 10)

10   As more people learn about the possibilities of ecotourism, these wonderful parts of the world will become more popular as holiday destinations. If pursued sincerely, as a new type of vacation travel, ecotourism can be beneficial to all involved. The local population can thrive while traditions and customs survive. Travelers can relax and enjoy, while learning about rather than exploiting the local resources. Most important of all, the environment remains intact, preserved for future generations.

Vocabulary

agro-tourism	/ˈægrətuəriəzəm/	n.	农业生态旅游
biodiversity	/ˌbaiəudaiˈvəːsiti/	n.	生物多样性
Brazilian	/brəˈziliən/	a. &n.	巴西的;巴西人
craft	/krɑːft/	n.	工艺(品);手艺
deplete	/diˈpliːt/	vt.	用尽;使减少;耗尽
ecolodge	/ˌiːkəuˈlɔdʒ/	n.	生态度假村,生态旅店
effectively	/iˈfektivli/	ad.	有效地
expedition	/ˌekspiˈdiʃən/	n.	远征(队),探险(队),考察(队)
exploit	/ikˈsplɔit/	vt.	剥削;利用;开发,开采
fauna	/ˈfɔːnə/	n.	动物群
feature	/ˈfiːtʃə/	n.	特征,特色
flora	/ˈflɔːrə/	n.	植物群(尤指某一地区或某一时期的植物群)
heritage	/ˈheritidʒ/	n.	遗产,继承物,传统

hiking	/ˈhaikiŋ/	n.	徒步旅行
influx	/ˈinflʌks/	n.	涌进,流入,注入
initiate	/iˈniʃieit/	vt.	开始,创始,开始实施
intact	/inˈtækt/	a.	完整无缺的,未受损伤的
mine	/main/	n.&vt.	矿,矿井;开矿
mode	/məud/	n.	方式,模式
Nepal	/niˈpɔːl/	n.	尼泊尔(南亚国家)
outfit	/ˈautfit/	n.	全套装备,全套用品
poach	/pəutʃ/	vt.&vi.	偷猎
pro-poor	/ˈprəu-puə/	n.	扶贫
revenue	/ˈrevənjuː/	n.	收入,收益
safari	/səˈfɑːri/	n.	狩猎旅行,狩猎的旅行队,野生动物园
sector	/ˈsektə/	n.	部分,部门
survive	/səˈvaiv/	vt.&vi.	活下来,幸存
target	/ˈtɑːgit/	vt.	把……作为目标(或对象)
thrive	/θraiv/	vi.	兴旺,繁荣

bird-watching	(在大自然中)观察研究野鸟
community-based tourism	乡村生态旅游
hands-on	亲自动手的,躬亲的
Latin America	拉丁美洲
mass tourism	大批游客旅游(游客同时涌入同一个旅游点)
small-scale	小规模的
socio-economic	社会经济的
Southeast Asia	东南亚
ecotourism-related ventures	生态旅游相关企业
in harmony with...	与……和谐共处
the host country	主办国,东道国
The International Eco-tourism Society	(TIES)国际生态旅游学会

Unit 6

Vocabulary exercises

I. Match each word with its explanation.

1. _____ eco-friendly
2. _____ ecological
3. _____ ecologist
4. _____ ecology
5. _____ ecosystem
6. _____ eco-warriors
7. _____ mass tourism
8. _____ ecotourist
9. _____ ecolodge
10. _____ intact

a. connected with the way plants, animals, and people are related to each other and to their environment
b. a scientist who studies ecology
c. large-scale tourism, typically associated with "sea, sand, sun" resorts and characteristics such as transnational ownership, minimal direct economic benefit to destination communities, seasonality, and package tours
d. a type of tourist accommodation with small, environment-friendly hotels designed to have the least possible impact on the natural environment in which it is situated
e. not broken, damaged, or spoiled
f. all the animals and plants in a particular area, and the way in which they are related to each other and to their environment
g. the way in which plants, animals, and people are related to each other and to their environment, or the scientific study of this
h. not harmful to the environment
i. a worker who is responsible to stop damage to the environment
j. a person who experiences the unspoiled natural world and leaves it that way when he returns home

II. Fill in each blank with the right word from the following box. Change the form when necessary.

| conserve | exploit | depleted | annual | exotic |
| heritage | thrive | diversity | sustain | influx |

1. This area's rich plant life has been severely _____ by the huge amount of irresponsible tourists in recent years.
2. Ecotourism is a growing component of the larger tourism industry, and several factors indicate that it is likely to _____ over time.
3. We have a firm conviction that man should not _____ the natural resources at the expense of other species.
4. The nomadic community-based tourism in Mongolia brings real benefit to local communities, and that honors their cultural _____.

5. Responsible tourism maximizes the benefits to local communities, but minimizes negative social or environmental impacts, and thus helps local people _____ their fragile cultures, habitats, and species.

6. According to the World Tourism Organization, China is one of the world's top 10 outbound tourism nations. From 1994 to 2003, the cumulative number of outbound Chinese travelers reached nearly 100 million, with an average _____ growth rate of 13.9 percent.

7. The large _____ of ecotourists disrupted the traditional economic practices of the community, as people left the indigenous subsistence farming for tourist-related businesses such as woodcarving and posing in traditional dress for tourist cameras.

8. Trees are a renewable resource that when managed properly can _____ our needs indefinitely.

9. The increase of wildlife trade will directly influence nature tourism as the number of _____ animals which draw tourists to the particular country slowly decrease.

10. The biological _____ crisis is often called the "Sixth Extinction" because an event of this magnitude (重要,严重) has occurred only five times in the history of life on Earth. The last was at the end of the Cretaceous period (白垩纪), when the dinosaurs (恐龙) disappeared.

Listening

Learn the following words and phrases and then listen to a passage to fill in the missing information.

Travel and holiday (1)_____ say ecotourism is the fastest growing part of the holiday vacation industry. It is possible to visit almost any country to learn about the (2)_____, history, food, plants, animals or anything else that might (3)_____ you.

You can visit a natural area in Costa Rica(哥斯达黎加,中美洲国名), one of the (4)_____ ecotourism countries in the world. You can travel to the huge national parks (国家公园) in several African countries to see and (5)_____ lions, elephants and other wild animals.

You can swim deep under water to (6)_____ this beautiful world if you learn how to use special breathing equipment. Companies (7)_____ underwater (8) trips in Australia, Mexico (墨西哥), several islands in the Caribbean (加勒比地区), the Mediterranean (地中海) and many other places.

Tourism, the travel and holiday industry, (9)_____. So ecotourism has become extremely important. And officials in the travel industry say ecotourism works to (10)_____.

Ecotourism also teaches the people who live in areas that tourists may want to visit and enjoy. Government agencies (11)_____.

Speaking

I. Each year, millions of travelers pack their bags and head for the usual destinations  (目的地): Paris, Bangkok (曼谷,泰国首都), San Francisco (旧金山) and Beijing. Such kind of mass tourism may focus only on the economic benefits, even at the cost of environment. While eco-travelers would like to see people step off the beaten path (踏出的路) and choose uncommercialized places as their holiday destinations. Please compare and contrast the traditional mass tourism and ecotourism.

> **Discussion assistant**
>
> similarly; the same as; equally; different from; in contrast; however
> Another negative effect is...; have an adverse effect (反作用) on...;
> A second problem is...
> ruin natural beauty; pollute beaches; destroy the habitats (栖息地) of wildlife; undermine (破坏); commercialize (使商业化,使商品化); agro-tourism; community-based tourism; pro-poor (扶贫) tourism; nature tourism; sustainability (持续性,永续性); observation and appreciation of nature; promote the economy (促进经济); protect the environment; relieve poverty (扶贫); poverty-stricken areas (贫困地区); minimum (最小的,最低的); negative impacts upon the natural and socio-cultural

environment; generate economic benefits; provide employment and income opportunities; increase awareness (提高意识); conservation of natural and cultural heritage (保护自然和文化遗产)

II. Look at the following chart to learn the main elements in tourism which can reduce poverty, and then discuss:

1. What is pro-poor (扶贫) tourism?
2. What are the major benefits of pro-poor tourism for reducing poverty?

Linkages between Tourism and Poverty Reduction

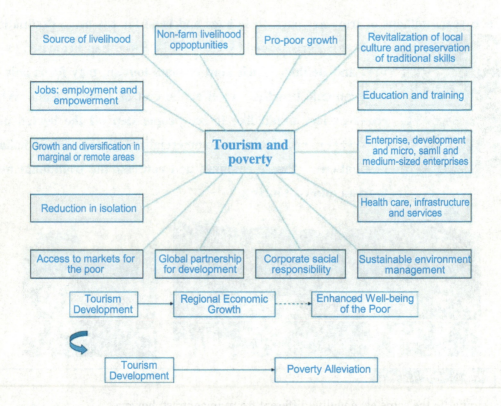

Discussion assistant

...would be beneficial for reducing poverty in developing countries.

...will expand business opportunities for the poor.

...will expand employment opportunities for the poor.

...will improve the local infrastructure.

...will enhance collective benefits.

livelihood (生活；生计); non-farm (非农的); employment (就业); empowerment (激励自主创业); growth and diversification (多元经济发展); marginal and remote areas (边远地区); isolation (隔离,孤立); access to markets (打开市场); partnership (合伙或合作的关系); corporate (公司的); revitalization (新生,复兴); micro-/ small-/ medium-sized enterprises (小／中企业); infrastructure (公共建设,基础建设); sustainable (可持续发展的); enhanced well-being of the poor (增强贫民的福利); benefit (有益于,有助于); relieve (缓解); beneficial (有益的,有利的); recreational facilities (娱乐设施)

III. According to the World Tourism Organization (WTO), China has overtaken Italy as the world's fourth most popular tourism destination since 2004. It is also forecasted by WTO that China's tourism industry will take up to 8.6% of world market share by 2020. Please describe the following chart briefly and then analyze the contributing reasons for the rapid growth of tourism in China.

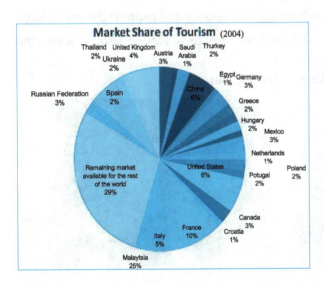
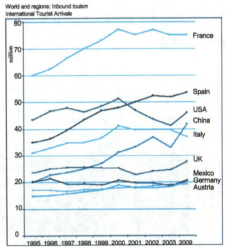

> **Discussion assistant**
>
> a leading international tourist destination （一个重要的国际旅游目的地）; natural beauty; economic reforms （经济改革）; the open-door policy （开放政策）; international visitors（国际游客）; account for （占……比例，份额）; the global market share （全球市场份额）; holiday economy（假日经济）; "Golden Week" holiday tourism（"黄金周"假日旅游）; National Day（国庆节）; International Labor Day（五一国际劳动节）; the Spring Festival（春节）

Writing

Jason is a 20-year-old college student from America and he just gets off the plane. He wants to have an eco-travel around Qinghai Lake in Qinghai Province this weekend. Please go to the library or surf the Internet for useful information and then help him write down a travel plan. Your plan should include the following parts: a. An introduction of Qinghai Lake; b. Itinerary （旅行路线） and major sights on Saturday; c. Itinerary and major sights on Sunday. Write down the special attraction of each sight and don't forget to remind Jason of loving the environment.

An Eco-travel Plan

> **Writing assistant**
>
> migrate（候鸟等定期迁徙）; breed（繁殖）; eat some Tibetan food（品尝藏族美食）; comprise of（包含，由……组成）; km.（公里）; mile（英里）; meter（米）; sq. km.（平方公里）; national nature reserve area（国家级自然保护区）; enjoy the sunrise; observe the water and the fish; the Bird Island（鸟岛）; watch the birds; crown（王冠）; plateau（高原）; birds of different species（不同品种的鸟）; geese（鹅）; gulls（鸥）; skylark（云雀）; swan（天鹅）; nest（筑巢）; paradise（天堂，乐园）; hundreds of thousands of migratory birds（候鸟）; Buddhist Monastery of Kumbum（塔尔寺）; hike（远足，徒步旅行）; Jinyintan Prairie（金银滩大草原）

Part II Can China Embrace Ecotourism?

Warming up

I. Listening

Learn the following words and phrases and then listen to a dialogue about ASTA's Ten Commandments on Ecotourism. Fill in the missing information according to what you hear.

Words and phrases			
designated	/'dezigneitid/	a.	指定的
dignity	/'digniti/	n.	尊严;尊贵
endangered	/in'deindʒəd/	a.	濒临灭绝的
frailty	/'freilti/	n.	脆弱,虚弱
patronize	/'peitrənaiz/	vt.	光顾,惠顾
privacy	/'praivəsi/	n.	隐私
subscribe	/səb'skraib/	vi.	赞成,赞许;订购(书籍等)
trail	/trei/	n.	路线,小路
toxic	/'tɔksik/	a.	毒(性)的,有毒的
utilize	/juː'tilaiz/	vt.	利用
conservation-oriented			节约(能)型的
The American Society of Travel Agents		(ASTA)	美国旅行社协会

ASTA's *Ten Commandments on Ecotourism*

1. Respect the frailty of the Earth.
2. Leave only (1)_____. Take only pictures.
3. To make your travels more meaningful, educate yourself about the geography, (2)_____, manners and (3)_____ of the region you visit.
4. Respect the (4)_____ and dignity of others.
5. Do not buy products made from endangered plants or animals.
6. Always follow designated trails.
7. Learn about and support conservation-oriented programs and organizations working to (5)_____ the environment.
8. Whenever possible, walk or utilize environmentally sound methods of (6)_____.
9. Patronize those members of the travel industry who (7)_____ energy and environmental

conservation; water and air (8)_____; recycling; safe management of waste and toxic materials; (9)_____ involvement; and which provide experienced, well-trained staff dedicated to strong principles of conservation.

10. Ask your ASTA travel agent to (10)_____ those organizations which subscribe to ASTA Environmental Guidelines for air, land, and sea travel.

II. Discussion

The China National Tourism Administration has issued a notice that the year 2009 has been declared Chinese Ecotourism Year with a slogan of "be a green traveler and experience eco-civilization (生态文明)". What does this notice indicate? Can China embrace (拥抱,大力发展) the ecotourism at present? Why or why not?

> *Discussion asisstant*
>
> The notice indicates that...
>
> This declaration urges... (迫切要求)
>
> ...enhance the promotion of ecotourism products and the environment-friendly concept (概念,观念).
>
> create a good social environment (创造良性社会环境); a green industry; the new trend (新趋势); sustainable development; tourism consumption (旅游消费); resource-saving (资源节约型的); market promotion (市场推广); operation and management (运作和管理); consumption guidance

Reading

Can China Embrace Ecotourism?

Feng Yongfeng

Southwest China's cultural heritage and natural environment make it an ideal destination for eco-tourists. But irresponsible attitudes to travel may threaten efforts to balance sightseeing with sustainability.

Question 1: What's the new option for the isolated Yushi to build a strong community? (Para. 1)

1   Yushi, over 90% of which is covered by forest, is proud of its cultural traditions, which have emphasized the protection of the local environment. The residents know that if they were connected to the road network, their forests could be cut down and their fragile culture could be threatened under the strain of powerful external influences. For many years they have chosen to remain isolated, hoping to build a strong and healthy community before opening to the outside world. But currently, to build a strong community, they can develop ecotourism.

Question 2: What are the current problems there? (Paras. 2—4)

2   However, the village does not yet have the facilities that tourists expect, such as clean  toilets, washing facilities or Internet access. Tourism experts have visited and were impressed by the unique local culture and environment. But if Yushi wants to benefit from eco-tourism, the village and its households must change to meet the demanding standards of today's tourists.

3   Tourism is a kind of technology that adds value to raw materials. Take a regular chicken, cook it in the local style and put it in front of a hungry tourist—and watch its value rocket. Similarly, Yushi's mountains, which were in the past seen as barriers to transport and thus economic development, would become priceless if the villagers could attract eco-tourists.

4   Many places in Yunnan are looking for ways to protect the environment and traditional culture while also raising income—and that almost always means ecotourism is the only choice. But if conditions in the villages are not improved, many tourists will simply not come, since most city-living Chinese lack confidence in rural living. A lack of cleanliness and orderliness, mosquitoes, poor-quality toilets and unclear pricing mean that many areas ideal for ecotourism cannot attract visitors.

5   Yunnan's first officially recognized organic farm lies on the outskirts of the provincial capital Kunming. It has been making a loss for years, since consumers fail to differentiate its products from those of farms which use chemicals and genetically modified plants. Similarly, tourists rarely consider the quality of their destinations; they simply look for ease of access and impressive scenery. For many, tourism is simply sightseeing—it's not about improving their life in any meaningful way.

Question 3: What are the major types of ecotourism? (Paras. 3—6)

6   The vast majority of people are not interested in watching nature, much less in paying for the privilege of doing so. Some are forced to in the course of government-funded research, but when the funding dries up very few continue. Enjoyment of the untamed environment is not something that comes naturally to Chinese people. We prefer to look at paintings of nature, rather than nature itself; to appreciate a wooden carving of the Buddha rather than the forest the wood grows in; and to let our children be educated about the wild in the classroom, rather than take them to experience it first-hand.

7   This attitude among tourists is responsible for the unusually slow growth of China's ecotourism sector. Faced with consumers' unwillingness to get too close to nature, the tourist industry ignores areas like Yushi. Since only a tiny minority of Chinese people are willing to appreciate the beauty of Yushi, people often turn to high-spending foreign tourists—but this is also a hope too far. Foreign tourists are also dropping, while the number of tourists who travel simply to indulge themselves is increasing. Travelers who go abroad to learn and share experiences are also being replaced by narrow-minded tourists who are only interested in consumption.

8   So when we complain about ecotourism operators failing to attract visitors, perhaps we should take some time to consider the visitors themselves—because if a tourist is unwilling to become an ecotourist, any amount of careful planning and good intentions will be wasted.

Vocabulary

access	/'ækses/	n.	接近,进入;接近的机会,进入的权利;使用;通道,入口
autonomous	/ɔː'tɔnəməs/	a.	自治的;自治权的;自主的
carving	/'kɑːvɪŋ/	n.	雕刻;雕刻品
chemical	/'kemɪkəl/	n.	化学制品;化学药品
currently	/'kʌrəntli/	ad.	目前,眼下

demanding	/dɪˈmɑːndɪŋ/	a.	苛求的;要求高的
differentiate	/ˌdɪfəˈrenʃieɪt/	vt.&vi.	区别,区分,鉴别
ethnic	/ˈeθnɪk/	a.&n.	种族,少数民族,异教的
facility	/fəˈsɪləti/	n.	设备,设施,(供特定用途的)场所
fragile	/ˈfrædʒaɪl/	a.	易碎的,脆的;易损坏的;脆弱的
fund	/fʌnd/	n.&vt.	资金,基金,专款提供(事业,活动等的)资金
household	/ˈhaʊshəʊld/	n.	一家人;家庭,户
indulge	/ɪnˈdʌldʒ/	vt.&vi.	沉迷于;放纵
isolated	/ˈaɪsəleɪtɪd/	a.	孤立的,(被)隔离的
majority	/məˈdʒɒrɪti/	n.	多数,大多数
minority	/maɪˈnɒrɪti/	n.	少数;少数派;少数民族
orderliness	/ˈɔːdəlɪnɪs/	n.	整洁;整齐,有条理
outskirt	/ˈaʊtskɜːt/	n.	市郊,郊区
price	/praɪs/	vt.	给……定价;给……标价
privilege	/ˈprɪvɪlɪdʒ/	n.	特权
provincial	/prəˈvɪnʃəl/	a.	省的;外省的
rocket	/ˈrɒkɪt/	vi.	迅速上升;猛涨
rural	/ˈrʊərəl/	a.	农村的;田园的;有乡村风味的
sightseeing	/ˈsaɪtˌsiːɪŋ/	n.	观光,游览
township	/ˈtaʊnʃɪp/	n.	小镇;镇区
unique	/juːˈniːk/	a.	唯一的,独一无二的;独特的
untamed	/ˌʌnˈteɪmd/	a.	未驯服的;未被抑制的;未开发的
raw materials			原材料
make a loss			亏损
dry up			干涸;用尽
the Buddha			佛祖;佛像
Yushi			玉狮(云南省兰坪县普米族居住区)

Vocabulary exercises

I. Match each word with its explanation.

1. ____ rocket   a. coming from or happening outside a particular place or organization
2. ____ indulge   b. probably not honest, true, right, etc.
3. ____ external   c. being still in its natural state and not developed by people
4. ____ unique   d. to let yourself do or have something that you enjoy, especially something that is considered bad for you

5. ____ rural   e. happening in or relating to the countryside, not the city
6. ____ dubious   f. to come to an end and no more is available
7. ____ ethnic   g. the amount of energy, oil, electricity etc that is used
8. ____ dry up   h. to increase quickly and suddenly
9. ____ untamed   i. completely different from anyone or anything else; unusually good and special.
10. ____ consumption j. relating to a particular race, nation, or tribe and their customs and traditions.

II. Fill in each blank with the right word from the following box.

| depleting | disrupted | sustainable | converted | indigenous |
| tourist-related | shortage | access | economic | addressed |

Among the most degrading effects of ecotourism is the marketing of indigenous heritage, cultural identity, and sacred (宗教的, 神圣的) rituals (仪式). The influx (流入) of ecotourists (1)_____ the traditional (2)_____ practices of the community, as people left the indigenous subsistence (维持生计, 自给自足) farming for (3)_____ businesses such as woodcarving and posing in traditional dress for tourist cameras. The woodcarving industry is (4)_____ local forest resources. And a water (5)_____ is occurring because the community has to share water with hotels and restaurants. Some have (6)_____ their rice paddies (稻田) into residential lots where lodges (旅舍) and shops are built. Others have left farming altogether in favor of tourism-related jobs.

Many (7)_____ groups are extremely concerned that the threats to their societies from ecotourism are not being (8)_____ by these international organizations. Some of the fundamental problems of the ecotourism industry, according to indigenous organizations, include: no adequate assessment (评价, 评估) of the nature of the ecotourism industry and its effects on the environment and people; disruption (分裂; 扰乱) of local economies by displacement of activities that have previously served to carry self-reliant (自力更生的) and (9)_____ community development; increasing damage to the environment and local communities as ecotourism grows; need to expand physical infrastructures (基础设施) to provide tourist (10)_____ to remote areas; increased encroachment,(侵占) illegal logging, and mining; and the plundering (掠夺, 侵掠) of biological resources.

Speaking

I. Describe the current problems existing in China's ecotourism market and then try to answer the following questions: What can the government and tourists do to develop and make use of new natural resources to achieve a win-win benefit, that is, good both to the local economic growth and environmental protection?

> *Discussion assistant*
>
> Although ecotourism can offer ..., there are also serious ...
>
> Only in this way can ...
>
> The government should draw up (制定) some regulations to ...
>
> environmental and cultural damage (环境和文化破坏); poor management (管理不善); irresponsible behavior of tourists (游客不负责的行为); killing of wildlife (滥杀野生动物); over-fishing (过度捕捞); destruction of geological features (地貌破坏); loss of habitats (栖息地消失); trash accumulation (垃圾积累); commercialization of cultures (文化商业化); ecological problems (生态问题)

II. Ecotourism is becoming increasingly popular. People long to come in contact with nature in an environment that is as fresh as possible. However, many argue that ecotourism does not offer enough environmental protection. In fact, some believe that ecotourism threats will actually damage the very environment that ecotourism strives to (努力) preserve. Do you agree? Why or why not?

Discussion assistant

Many argue that ...

Some believe that ...

One of the problems that ecotourism poses (造成) is ...

Another threat ecotourism poses is that ...

Another problem associated with ecotourism is ...

airplane fuel (飞机燃油); automobile fuel (汽车燃油); wasteful; in terms of energy consumption (在能源消耗方面); fragile (脆弱的) ecosystems; have a negative impact on... (对……产生负面影响); upset the local ecosystem (破坏生态系统); mismanage (管理不当); corruption (腐败); greed (贪婪)

Background Reading

About TIES

Fact Sheet: Global Ecotourism

Oslo Statement on Ecotourism

Ecotourism: Current Status and Challenges

Recommendations from GEC07

Please refer to the attached disk.

Unit 7

Vertical Farming

垂直农场

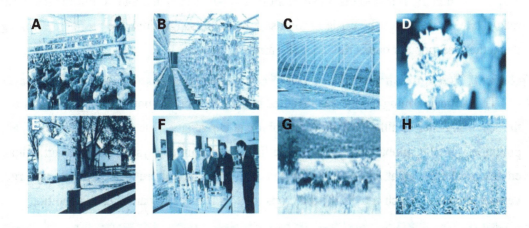

Part I Vertical Farming

Warming up

I. Match the following places with the proper pictures above.

1. bee farm/yard
2. wildlife refuge
3. experimental field
4. greenhouse
5. experimental lab
6. livestock shed
7. enclosed chicken coop
8. soilless cultivation house

II. Discuss the possible advantages of the eight places in Exercise I in agriculture and forestry.

Reading

Vertical Farming

Question 1: What is the purpose of the Vertical Farming? (Para. 1)

1   A biggest problem in modern agriculture is the conflict between the constantly increasing population and the continuously decreasing farmland. According to a BBC report, the soaring food prices in international market have made some African countries in Sub-Sahara hungry. It is said that the current food crisis results in about 30 million people at risk starvation. To solve the crisis in food supply, some suggestions are proposed. Among them, the most popular one is the Vertical Farming.

Question 2: Will plants in a Vertical Farm Tower be free from weather influence? (Para. 2)

2   The vertical farming theory was invented by Dr. Dickson Despommier, a professor from the environmental health department at Columbia University. Due to the influence of hail, pollution, drought, global warming and the like, Despommier says, the natural agriculture environment is not great. Therefore, people need to bring agriculture inside by building large, vertical structures which can ensure the crops to grow in a healthy and steady condition.

Question 3: What are the advantages of VFT compared with the traditional agriculture? (Para. 3)

3   As founder and director of the Vertical Farming (VF), Dr. Despommier believes the Vertical Farm Tower or VFT is promising. In his description, one day all the fresh products that we need will be grown in towers which will be only five blocks away. Thus, the fuel for long-distance transportation can be saved, and the pollution caused by the burning of fossil fuel can be reduced greatly. In addition, growing crops in a controlled environment has benefits: no animals to transfer diseases; no big influence from weather-related disasters; all food could be grown organically, without herbicides, pesticides, or fertilizers. Keeping away from weather influence, the farmland in a farm tower could be used more than 4 times every year.

Question 4: Why are solar panel and wind spire installed in the vertical building? (Para. 4)

4   To use space most efficiently and allow maximum light into the building, a VFT is designed in circular shape. A solar panel (see 1) as well as wind spires (see 2) are installed on the top of the building, both of which can supply clean energy for the building. In terms of the inner structure of the building, every floor is divided into many rooms. More than two crops are grown in each room and some crops like tomatoes are hanging on the ceiling to maximize the space. In every floor, a control room is designed. From the control room, farmers could watch the change of crops in time and cultivate them when necessary. The crop picker (see 3) is also widely used. It can monitor fruits and vegetables with an electronic eye which tests ripeness of crops by color. To use water effectively, black-water treatment system (see 4) is set up in the building. Through a series of filters, the wastewater from all the cities could be used for irrigation. Such an endeavor may benefit the environment by returning existing farmland to nature and restoring the natural functions and services of the ecosystem.

Question 5: Why is Mr. Stringer interested in vertical Farming? (Para. 5)

5   The idea has captured the attention of several scientists and architects in the United States and Europe in the past several years. As Mr. Stringer, the Manhattan borough president said he immediately pictured a "food farm" in the New York City skyline when he heard such a concept. "Obviously we don't have vast amounts of vacant land," he said in a phone interview. "But the sky is the limit in Manhattan." Stringer added.

Question 6: What are the difficulties mentioned by Dr. Despommier for building VFTs ? (Para. 6)

6   In connection with the implementation of such a design, Dr. Despommier believes that there are a great many difficulties, especially those in technical and economic. For example, he estimates that it would cost $20 million to $30 million to make a prototype of a vertical farm tower which could feed 50,000 people. "I'm a biologist swimming in very deep water right now," he added. In spite of some challenges, Dr. Despommier further points out that Vertical Farming could become a reality with enough input from multiple disciplines such

as industrial and soil microbiology, public health, policy making, urban planning, architecture, plant genetics and economy.

Vocabulary

architect	/'ɑːkitekt/	n.	建筑师
architecture	/'ɑːkitektʃə/	n.	建筑学
capture	/'kæptʃə/	vt.	捕获
challenge	/'tʃænlindʒ/	n.	挑战
circular	/'səːkjulə/	a.	圆形的
constantly	/'kɔnstəntli/	a.	持续地
crisis	/'kraisis/	n.	危机(复数 crises)
cultivate	/'kʌltiveit/	vt.	耕种,耕作
discipline	/'disiplin/	n.	学科
drought	/draut/	n.	干旱
endeavor	/in'devə/	n.	努力,尽力
ensure	/in'ʃuə/	vt.	确保
estimate	/'estimeit/	vt.	估计,评估
filter	/'filtə/	n.&vt.	过滤器;过滤
genetics	/dʒi'netiks/	n.	遗传学
hail	/heil/	n.	冰雹
herbicide	/'həːbisaid/	n.	除草剂
implementation	/ˌimplimen'teiʃən/	n.	实施,执行
irrigation	/ˌiri'geiʃən/	n.	灌溉
maximize	/'mæksimaiz/	vt.	使……至最大限度
microbiology	/ˌmaikrəubai'ɔlədʒi/	n.	微生物学
multiple	/'mʌltipl/	a.	多个的
panel	/'pænl/	n.	嵌板,镶板;壁板;镜板
pest	/pest/	n.	有害物
picture	/'piktʃə/	vt.	描绘
propose	/prə'pəuz/	vt.	提议
prototype	/'prəutətaip/	n.	原型
ripeness	/'raipnis/	n.	成熟
skyline	/'skailain/	n.	地平线

soaring	/ˈsɔːrɪŋ/	a.	剧增的
spire	/spaɪə/	n.	螺旋
starvation	/stɑːˈveɪʃən/	n.	饥饿
transportation	/ˌtrænspɔːˈteɪʃən/	n.	运输
urban	/ˈəːbən/	a.	城市的
vacant	/ˈveɪkənt/	a.	空白的
vertical	/ˈvəːtɪkəl/	a.	垂直的
crop picker			作物采摘机
in terms of			在……的方面
Sub-Sahara			撒哈拉以南
weather-related			与天气相关的

Vocabulary exercises

I. **Learn the models and translate the following Chinese phrases in the brackets into English.**

1. <u>increasing</u> population (增加的人口)　　　　_____ (飞涨的价格)
   _____ (领导人物)　　　　_____ (有前途的方法)
   _____ (艰巨的任务)　　　　_____ (进展的遗传学)
   _____ (惊人的速度)　　　　_____ (邻近的城市)

2. the tower <u>built in</u> circular shape (建造成圆形的塔)
   the crops _____ (在垂直农场种植的农作物)
   the plan _____ (由美国政府提出的计划)
   the wind spire _____ (安装在建筑物屋顶的风车叶片)
   the control room _____ (在垂直农场里使用的监控室)

3. the possibility <u>to create</u> an organism structure (制造有机结构的可能性)
   the potential to _____ (使用作物采摘机的可能性)
   the solar panel to _____ (吸收太阳光的光电板)
   the possibility to _____ in New York (在纽约建造垂直农场的可能性)
   the proposal to _____ (在室内种植农作物的提议)
   the hope to _____ all over the world (解决世界饥饿问题的愿望)

II. **Match each word with its explanation.**

1. ____ irrigation　　　a. to plant and take care of a particular crop
2. ____ herbicide　　　b. the branch of biology that deals with microorganisms and their effects on other living organisms

3. ____ cultivate   c. using fertilizers of animal or vegetable matter, rather than synthetic fertilizers or pesticides

4. ____ crisis   d. a substance used to kill unwanted plants

5. ____ organic   e. frozen rain drops falling as hard balls of ice

6. ____ pesticide   f. the branch of biology that deals with heredity

7. ____ prototype   g. an original type, form, or instance that serves as a model

8. ____ microbiology   h. a chemical substance used to kill insects and small animals that destroy crops

9. ____ hail   i. supplying with water by means of streams, reservoirs, channels, pipes, etc.

10. ____ genetics   j. a serious situation with lots of problems that must be dealt with quickly

Listening

Listen to a dialogue about the Vertical Farm Tower, and then answer the following questions.

Words and phrases

dome	/dəum/	n.	屋顶
expand	/iks'pænd/	vt.&vi.	扩展
original	/ə'ridʒinəl/	a.	最初的
rehabilitate	/ˌriː(h)ə'biliteit/	vt.	使复原
district	/'distrikt/	n.	区域
focus on			集中于

Questions

1. Who proposed the Vertical Farming theory?
2. When was the Vertical Farming theory proposed?
3. What is the original idea about?
4. What's the purpose to build multi-story indoor farming?
5. According to the dialogue, how many vertical farm buildings could supply food for the whole New York City?

Unit 7

Speaking

I. Please briefly describe what Vertical Farming is based on the reading passage.

Discussion assistant

Theory inventor: Dr. Despommier

Shape: blocks with multi-stories

Appliances: solar panels; wind spires; recycling systems; separated rooms and multi-layers; control rooms

Functions: to provide necessary water, sun, energy, fresh air and maximum space for plant growing and produce all kinds of vegetables and fruit year round

Advantages: to protect environment
　　　　　　to provide organic food
　　　　　　to avoid bad weather or disasters
　　　　　　to save farmland
　　　　　　to relieve food crisis all over the world

II. Suppose you are a designer of the VFT and is designing a tower. What do you think its outer appearance looks like and why? What kinds of fruit would you like to grow in it and why? The following three pictures may give you some clues.

Words for shapes

circular/round (圆形); triangle (三角形); cone (圆锥); dome (圆顶); mosque (清真寺); cube (正方体); diamond (菱形); base/foundation (底座); hexagon (六边形); octagon (八边形); quadrangle (四边形); polygon (多边形); right triangle (直角); balcony (露台); observation (观景台); column (圆柱).

Words for fruit:

lemon (柠檬); cherry (樱桃); orange (橙子); pear (梨); avocado (牛油果); dragon fruit (火龙果); nectarine (柚桃); peach (桃); kiwi (猕猴桃); tangerine (橘子); apricot (杏); watermelon (西瓜); pineapple (菠萝)

Sample: For me, the vertical tower should look like a pyramid and there are two reasons for my design. First, exterior walls of pyramid-shaped buildings can receive more sunlight. Second, the design of a pyramid-shaped building may be creative and interesting.

With respect to the kinds of food, I prefer growing more tropical food such as bananas and mangoes. With my hometown located in the Northeast of China, it is difficult for the local people to eat fresh tropical food.

III. Finish the following exercises according to what you have learned from the reading.

1. Match different parts of the following VFT numbered from 1 to 6 with their proper functions from A to F.

   1) the solar panel   2) the wind spire
   3) the glass panel   4) the control room
   5) the building shape   6) individual room with multi-layers

   A. built as a column which uses growing space most efficiently and receives maximum light into the center in accordance with designers.

   B. rotating to follow the sun and transforming the received sunlight into energy.

   C. a substitute of solar panels, which can transform wind into energy by using small blades to turn air upward, like a screw.

   D. growing various plants living in similar environment together and dividing the growing space in the same room.

   E. observing crop change and pick them up at proper time.

   F. collecting and cleaning pollutants, preventing rain from beading (起泡剂), and maximizing light.

2. Look at the following picture and match the following places and devices within a VFT with their functions. Then describe how crops and fruits are grown in it and how they are irrigated and fueled with nutrients.

   1) the crop picker   2) the field
   3) the pool   4) the feeder

   A. collecting runoff from irrigation and piping it to a filtration system

B. directing the amounts of water and light to individual crop

C. using color detection to test ripeness

D. rendering two layers of crops at least

IV. **The following chart lists and categorizes some wastes produced in a VFT. Learn the following wastes and then look at the picture on the right showing a system called Pellet Power system used in the VFT. Based on your knowledge and imagination, please tell what wastes may be produced in it and how they can be recycled for other usages within it.**

> *Discussion assistant*
>
> *Sewage/runoff:* most of sewage will be gray water through black-water recycling system; for irrigation.
>
> *Biomass (生物量):* something like straws (麦秆), rotten leafs, etc; for green manure (绿色肥料), fodder (饲料) and methane (沼气)
>
> *Animal Manure:* for organic manure or methane
>
> *Carbon Dioxide (二氧化碳) and Oxygen (氧气):* through photosynthesis (光合作用), CO_2, O_2.
>
> *Fertilizer Residues:* reused, like nuts, grass; some, like shells, corpses (尸体), dropped off
>
> be used for/as; work as; be turned into; be fermented into (使发酵成); filter (过滤); condense (压缩); smash (粉碎); stir (搅拌); transmission machine (传输器); blowing machine (增压器); heater (加热器); pellet (小团, 小体积的材料); powder (粉末); steam (气体)

V. **Here are some widely used agricultural appliances. Match them with their proper English names provided below.**

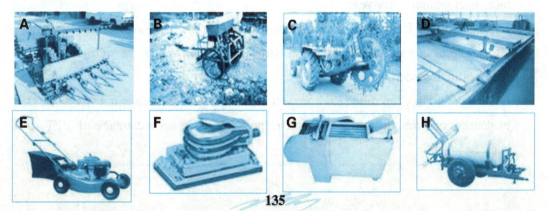

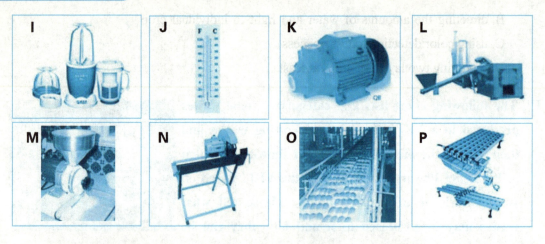

1. lawn mover (草坪修剪机)
2. thermometer (温度计)
3. food processor (食品加工机)
4. sprayer (喷雾机)
5. polisher (磨光机)
6. weed mover (除草机)
7. water pump (水泵)
8. sewage equipment (污水处理设备)
9. harvester (收割机)
10. forage drier (饲料干燥机)
11. planter/seeder (播种机)
12. furrow drill (沟播机)
13. grain mill (磨面机)
14. breeding facility (育种器皿)
15. food conveyer belt (食品传输带)
16. sawmill (锯木机)

Based on what you have learned from the reading, write a passage to introduce advantages of VF.

Advantages of Vertical Farming

Writing assistant

All food could be grown organically, without herbicides, pesticides, or fertilizers.

Keeping away from weather influence, the farmland in a farm tower could be used more than 4 times every year.

Vertical Farming is proposed for the purpose to relieve the pressure from food supply.

VF is helpful in reducing the potential harm to our environment as well as securing food health in modern age.

Growing crops in a controlled environment has benefits; no animals to transfer diseases; in connection with, in terms of, with respect to, the main advantage of VFT, in addition

Advantages

1. to avoid long-distance transportation
2. to be free from fertilizers, pesticides, herbicides and weather-related influences.
3. to reduce fossil fuel.
4. to create a living organism structure where both plants and animals can survive without the influence of the natural environment around them

Part II   Top Issues of the Vertical Farm Tower

Warming up

Despite advantages of VF, do you think it has some problems actually? Can you list some of them?

Discussion assistant

1. How much money would it cost in the whole process to construct a VFT? For example, the land cost in the city is very expensive.
2. It is doubtful if a vertical farm could actually save both energy and protect our environment, for concrete and steel involve in energy waste and pollution.
3. The respites (休憩之所) in cities will be reduced a lot.
4. Security is a big concern (顾虑, 关注的事).

Reading

Top Issues of the Vertical Farm Tower

1 Due to the increasingly growth of population, the theory of the Vertical Farm Tower has received a wide attention all over the world. However, the dispute about its possibility has never stopped since it was proposed.

Question 1: According to the opponents, what is the toughest problem in the application of VFTs? What does the last sentence imply? (Para. 2)

2   Based on the opponents, their biggest concern is how much money it would cost in the whole process. Even Dr. Despommier believes that hundreds of millions of dollars are needed in the project to build a 30-story tower which could feed 50,000 people. Such an idea is further explained by Armando Carbonell, chairman of planning and urban farm department at the Lincoln Institute of Land Policy in Cambridge, Mass. He says even though the idea of the VFT was very progressive, the demanding requirement for money should be considered seriously. Carbonell  further points out that the vertical farm tower will be built in lower Manhattan in accordance with Despommier's design, where the real estate is one of the most expensive places in America. The land cost in the city would still outweigh any savings from not having to transport food from a long distance or the total cost spent on herbicides, pesticides, and fertilizers. In addition, solar panels, wind spires and water recycling system need to be installed to sustain the regular operation of the vertical farm tower. Therefore, it seems that the traditional model in agriculture is going to survive. As Carbonell said "Would a tomato in lower Manhattan be able to outbid an investment banker for space in a highrise? My bet is that the investment banker will pay more."

Question 2: Why do the opponents think that the VFT could not save energy as well as our environment? (Para. 3)

3   Another question from Mr. Carbonell is whether a vertical farm could actually save both energy and environment. He points out that concrete and steel will be used in the construction, both of which are involved in energy waste and pollution. To produce year-round food supply, fresh air, water and light are used to keep the ideal condition for plant growing. In addition, a lot of soil must be removed from other places to keep plants growing. With the appearance of more and more vertical farm towers, the land in cities will become increasingly limited. More and more people have to live far away from cities. Lots of fossil fuel will be consumed on the way to work. There will be less gardens, grasslands, trees and respites in a city. To some extent, ecosystem may be destroyed. Thus, it is doubtful that whether such a design will really benefit our nature.

Question 3: What is the problem that Dr. Despommier concerns? (Para. 4)

4　　The security is another problem related to VFTs. Even Dr. Despommier said "If I were to set myself as a certifier of vertical farms, I would begin with security." He further said "How do you keep insects and bacteria from invading your crops without pesticides; how do you keep plants constantly getting the nutrients they need without chemical fertilizers; how do you keep the crops in the building gaining enough sunlight compared with direct sunshine?"

Question 4: Why is the VFT called ivory tower? How many people will probably face the risk of starvation within the following 50 years? (Para. 5)

5　　Although described as ivory tower, the idea of bringing food closer to the city is gaining attention among pragmatists and dreamers alike. When Dr. Despommier appeared on "The Colbert Report," a visit program on TV, he said that nearly 80% of the Earth's population would reside in urban centers by the year 2050. The human population is projected to increase by about 3 billion people by 2050. If successfully applied, the theory of verticality will offer the promise of urban renewal, constant production of a safe and varied food supply (year-round crop production), and the eventual repair of ecosystems. Otherwise, the next 3 billion people will surely go hungry in just another 50 years.

Vocabulary

bacteria	/bæk'tiəriə/	n.	细菌
certifier	/'sɜːtifiə/	n.	见证者
concern	/kən'sɜːn/	n.&v.	关注
concrete	/'kɔnkriːt/	n.	混凝土
demanding	/di'mɑːndiŋ/	a.	苛求的
dispute	/di'spjuːt/	n.	争论
invade	/in'veid/	vt.	侵略
investment	/in'vestmənt/	n.	投资
nutrient	/'njuːtriənt/	a.	有营养的
opponent	/ə'pəunənt/	n.	反对者
outbid	/aut'bid/	vt.	出高于……的价钱
outweigh	/aut'wei/	vt.	在……上超过
pragmatist	/'prægmətist/	n.	实用主义者
project	/'prɔdʒekt/	vt.	计划
renewal	/ri'njuːəl/	n.	更新,恢复

reside	/rɪˈzaɪd/	vi.	居住
respite	/ˈrespɪt/	n.	休憩场所
security	/sɪˈkjʊərɪti/	n.	安全
skyscraper	/ˈskaɪˌskreɪpə/	n.	摩天大厦
verticality	/ˌvɜːtɪˈkælətɪ/	n.	垂直,垂直状态
be involved in			涉及
in accordance with			依照
real estate			房地产

Vocabulary exercises

I. Fill in each blank with the right word or phrase from the following box. Change the form when necessary.

| renewal | outbid | be involved in | to some extent | project |
| nutrient | concern | according to | dispute | consume |

1. Although a series of successes were achieved, the feasibility of soilless cultivation is widely being _____.

2. According to Dr. Despommier, his biggest _____ for the Vertical Farm Tower rests on its security.

3. The _____ called Vertical Farm Tower may save more than 1 billion people from the edge of hunger.

4. As fish can not live without water, the plant can not live without absorbing(吸收) _____ from the soil.

5. Exhaust Gas Recirculation, a new technique about reducing exhaust fume from vehicles, will purify the current environment _____.

6. The Ministry of Agriculture claims that an adult generally _____ staple food (主食) up to 235 kilos per year.

7. Spring is time for _____.

8. _____ crop cultivation, some new techniques like solar panels, wind spires and recycling tube systems are introduced.

9. Carbonell believes that the cost on VFT construction will greatly _____ that on the traditional agriculture.

10. _____ scientists, VF is helpful in relieving the potential harm to our environment as well as securing food health in modern age.

Unit 7

II. Study the components of trees and flowers, and then get to learn some popular plants of the major plant categories.

Components of a tree

1. truck (树干) 2. leaf (树叶)
3. bark (树皮) 4. root (树根)
5. nerve (叶脉) 6. branch (树枝)

Components of flowers

1. pistil /stamen (雌雄蕊); ovary (花房); style (花柱); stigma (柱头)
2. scape (花茎) 3. corolla (花冠)
4. calyx (花萼) 5. receptacle (花托)

 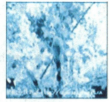 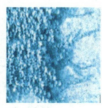  

Locust　　　Chinese Wisteria　　　Creeper Woodbine　　　Cape Jasmine　　　Water Lily

Woody plant (木本植物)：pine (松树); fir (杉树); maple (枫树); poplar (杨树); camphor tree (樟树); cypress (柏树); locust (洋槐); elm (榆树); willow (柳树); oak (橡树); camellia (茶花); Chinese rose (月季); peony (牡丹); shrubatchea (木槿)

Vine/Liana (藤本植物)：grape; Chinese wisteria (紫藤); morning glory (牵牛花)

Climber (攀缘植物)：creeper woodbine (爬山虎); honeysuckle (金银花); polygonum multiflorum (何首乌); passion flower (西番莲); Chinese wisteria (紫藤)

Ground cover (地被植物)：azalea (杜鹃花); cape jasmine (栀子花); matrimony vine (枸杞); shamrock (三叶草)

Perennial flowers (宿根花卉)：water lily (睡莲); lotus (荷花); Chinese herbaceous peony (芍药)

III. **Learn some useful vocabulary in plant classification.**

1. Match the English categories with their Chinese terms.

   (1) plant kingdom   a. 门
   (2) family   b. 种
   (3) order   c. 目
   (4) genus   d. 植物界
   (5) class   e. 属
   (6) species   f. 纲
   (7) phylum   g. 科

2. Fill in the diagram of a general way of plant classification with the given terms.

plants	
lower plants	(1) _____
algae, fungusa (2) _____	mosses, (3) _____, seed plants

   a. lichen (地衣)   b. ferns (蕨类)   c. higher plants (高等植物)

3. Pair the following plant classes.

   (1) angiosperm (被子植物)   (2) spore-producing plant (孢子植物)
   (3) monocotyledone (单子叶植物)   (4) bush (灌木)
   (5) terrestrial (陆生植物)   (6) gymnosperm (裸子植物)
   (7) arbor/tree (乔木)   (8) dicotyledon (双子叶植物)
   (9) hydrophyte/water plant (水生植物)   (10) spermatophyte (种子植物)

4. We know from the exercise that a plant category can have two or more terms, of which one is more scientific. The academic one always contains a prefix (前缀), or a suffix (后缀), or a root (词根) or a word. Learn the follows:

   di- (二)   mono- (一个)   hydro- (水)   gymno- (裸)
   phyll- (叶)   phyllo- (叶)   phylon- (种系)   sperm(a)- (精子,种子)
   terra- (土地)   -ial (具有特性)   -phyll (叶)   -phyte (植物)
   -sperm (精子,种子)   -cotyledon (子叶)

Listening

Learn the following words and phrases and then listen to the introduction of a small vertical tower design in Seattle, America, to fill in the missing information.

Unit 7

Words and phrases

acre	/'eikə/	n.	英亩
backup	/'bækʌp/	n.	备用
consummation	/ˌkɔnsə'meiʃən/	n.	消费
hydrogen	/'haidrədʒən/	n.	氢气
victorious	/vik'tɔ:riəs/	a.	获胜的

  To spread the idea of vertical urban agriculture, a regional green building contest was held in America in (1)_____. A smaller-scale farm tower, named Center for Urban Agriculture or CUA, won the contest. The main feature of the victorious work should be fully self-efficient offer in energy and water. If successfully applied, this work would supply about (2)_____ of the food needed for (3)_____ people. Though taking up less than (4)_____ acres, there are greenhouses, gardens, (5)_____ studios and even a chicken farm in the building. Vegetables, grains and fruits are planted here. On the top of the building, some advanced technologies are used. For example, a (6)_____ square feet tank for water collection; a (7)_____ square feet of solar PV cells with hydrogen gas backup for light and a recycling system for dealing with waste water up to (8)_____ times of its own consummation.

Speaking

I. Supporters of Vertical Farming have advanced many good designs and models of VFTs and try to put them into practice. However, opponents have been doubting its feasibility(可行性). Do you think Vertical Farming will work in Chinese cities? And is it necessary for China to build VFTs? With the topic, "The Feasibility of the Vertical Farm Tower" to organize a debate within class.

For	Against
1. It is feasible to build a VFT near big cities, such as Hebei, where the land cost is cheap. 2. All the problems in the application will be solved eventually. 3. National and local governments may invest much money.	1. Nobody can guarantee the satefy of plants produced in a VFT. 2. Some potential problems may exist. 3. With technical progress, the traditional agriculture will surely be improved a lot.

4. The VFT will relieve environmental problems and provide healthy food for us. 5. 3 billion people will be hungry in future if we don't change and improve the traditional farming.	4. Concrete and steel are wildly used in a VFT construction. 5. Some respites in cities will be replaced by VFTs.

> **Discussion assistant:** *(for debate)*
>
> *How to present one's argument(s)*
>
> It is said by some people that...
>
> I agree/disagree with...
>
> My points are as follows: First... Second... Third...To conclude, ...
>
> Some people believe/consider...
>
> As far as I am concerned (在我看来)...
>
> I will support the former ones/latter ones. The main reason is ... What's more... To sum up, ...
>
> It is advisable to believe that...
>
> *How to disagree*
>
> That's correct. But ...
>
> That's true. But...
>
> There is no doubt that... However,
>
> It is clear that..., but ...
>
> It is hard to say.
>
> I doubt that...
>
> Well, maybe, but...
>
> Have you thought about ...
>
> There is no sense in your point.
>
> I guess what you said just now is too far from our topic to catch it. We've no interest in it.

II. Here are two examples on how to improve the efficiency of vertical towers. Please specify and perfect them to an ideal state, and then give some more suggestions for the same purpose.

Example 1: In some places like the Northeast of China, both solar energy and wind energy are not adequate all year-round. Therefore, a tank connected with solar panels and wind spires should be set up. It can save extra energy in one season and give it out in another.

Example 2: In my design, an Evaporation Recovery System could be installed in the ceiling in each floor. As we know, the hot air should be slightly heavier compared with the cool one. Therefore, the Evaporation Recovery System should be with temperature much lower than the air around it. Through physical movement, it will absorb the hot air and change it into water. The water can be used to raise fish, oyster, etc, for it is clean and healthy.

Background Reading

> What is solar panel?
> Who is Dr. Despommier?
> What is black-water treatment system?
> What is Pellet Power system?

Please refer to the attached disk.

Unit 8

Bioenergy

生 物 能 源

Part I An Overview of Biomass Energy

Warming up

I. Briefly describe the graph below, and discuss which shows the growth of energy consumption in China.

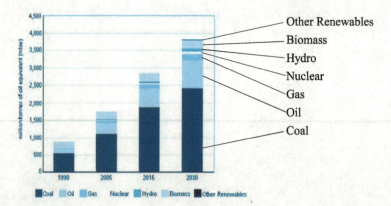

> *Discussion assistant*
> *Energies:* geothermal energy (地热能); hydro energy (水能); nuclear energy (核能); solar energy (太阳能); tidal energy (潮汐能); wave energy (波浪能); wind energy; fossil fuel (矿物燃料); renewables (可再生能源); biomass (生物量); energy mix (能源结构)

Unit 8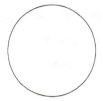

II. Have you ever thought that one day the world may face energy crisis? What do you think we can do to avoid that?

III. Can you predict your energy use in 2050 and draw your own energy pie chart in the circle. The chart may concern energies as fossil fuel energy (such as petroleum and coal), bioenergy, solar energy, wind energy, nuclear energy (核能), thermal energy (热能), etc.

IV. Do you think forestry and agriculture will contribute tremendously to the energy sector? And how?

> *Discussion assistant*
> have easy access to (容易获得); make use of; arouse extensive attention (引起广泛的注意); energy security (能源安全); residue (剩余废物); solutions to energy problem; technologies to be matured (有待成熟的技术)

Reading

An Overview of Biomass Energy

1 Biomass is the name for the material of which living things, animals and plants, are made. Biomass contains energy that living plants capture by the process of photosynthesis. Biomass energy provides about 5% of energy for home use and 17% of energy used by industry.

2 We use coal, oil, and natural gas, major sources of energy in most industrialized countries, far faster than nature produces them. These are non-renewable sources of energy; once pumped dry, an oil well stays dry.

3 But as long as nutrients are replaced in the soil, a woodlot can provide wood for heating a home year after year. Biomass, in other words, is a renewable source of energy.

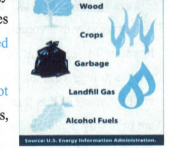

Question 1: What are the three stages of developing forest biomass? And how residues can be made use of ? (Paras. 4—5)

Forest Biomass

4 Some countries in the world have advocated a staged program of developing forest

biomass to increase the role of bioenergy in primary energy mix. The first stage would use all logging and mill wastes created by existing forest industries. This material is being increasingly used as a substitute for fossil fuels. Because the material is concentrated and the costs of handling and transport are carried by the primary forest product, economics of using wastes are favorable. The second stage would be the use of residues and residuals not currently used in conventional forest-harvesting operations.

5   Residues are tree components left behind when merchantable material (e.g., sawtimber, pulpwood) has been removed. Residuals are unmerchantable species of trees as well as defective, dying and dead trees currently unusable. The forest industry might use this material for producing steam or steam-generated electricity for on-site consumption; or, for sale to the power grid. A final stage would be to give serious consideration towards the establishment of energy plantations of fast-growing hybrid species and grasses.

6   Harvesting energy from forest biomass could be an economic boon for new industries: all cellulosic material now thrown away (e.g., branches, bark, boles and stumps, and

crooked, diseased, insect-infested, fire-damaged, dying and dead trees) could become valuable energy products. Use of forest biomass for energy also affords the opportunity to liquidate low-grade stands and replace them with productive stands of the more valuable species. In some areas, it has been estimated that forest-industry wastes alone could provide enough solid and liquid fuels to replace much of the current oil consumption, once the energy conversion technologies are proven to be economic.

Question 2: What does the italic word "rotation" in line 4 mean? (Para. 7)

7   In areas with favorable conditions, energy plantations would be needed to provide enough biomass for significant oil displacement. Marginal and sub-marginal agricultural land, as well as nonagricultural land (e.g., wetlands), could be used for high-yield "forest farming" with *rotations* of less than 10 years between harvests. The tree species under trial in Canada are primarily poplar and willow hybrids, and include larch, willow, alder and soft maples.

Agricultural Biomass

8   Agricultural Biomass includes animal manure, cellulosic crop residues, fruit and vegetable culls and food-processing effluent. Potential energy crops include high-yielding, high-carbohydrate crops such as switchgrass, vegetable-oil crops such as canola and sunflower, and carbonhydro plants such as milkweed and gumweed. The potential for

agriculture biomass derived energy is less than that of forest derived biomass. Most agricultural residues have alternative uses as animal fodder or soil conditioners and typically have a much lower energy intensity than wood (i.e. 1 m³ of wood contains as much energy as 5-10 m³ of baled field residues).

Question 3: Compared with forest biomass, what are the advantages of agricultural biomass? (Para. 9)

9 Also, agricultural biomass is usually only available at one time of year, while forests can be harvested year-round. The average inventory of biomass on forested land is about 20 times bigger than the annual yield from cropland. However, agricultural biomass does have a place in farm-scale or localized operations. Biogas from animal manures can be used to heat farm buildings or, if scrubbed and compressed, to power farm vehicles. The use of animal and food-processing wastes can abate pollution and reduce disposal problems as well as produce energy. Straw can be burned in a specially designed furnace to dry grain and heat farm buildings, or converted into ethanol for transportation fuel. The development of vegetable oils as fuels in farm diesel engines is undergoing continual development.

The Future

10 International Energy Agency Bioenergy Agreement, signed by 16 countries, promotes cooperation and collaboration among all members. Information is exchanged; new and promising technologies are tested and reported on, and advice is given to policymakers on the potential of increasing the proportion of energy generated by using biomass.

Question 4: What are the major concerns about expanding bioenergy? (Para. 11)

11 The main problems facing expansion of biomass energy are the relatively high costs of new facilities and the need to make the industry truly renewable. The cost barrier may be overcome by government policies and rising prices of conventional energy sources. However, careful attention is also needed for problems of reforestation, land use, water use, soil quality, erosion and pollution. Producing energy, in addition to lumber and paper, could put new stress on the sustainability of a forest resource base, which is already endangered by past practices of the forest industries. Biomass energy must be farmed, not mined; otherwise it will merely join coal, oil and natural gas as yet another non-renewable energy source.

Vocabulary

abate	/ə'beit/	vi.&vt.	使(数量,程度等)减少
advocate	/'ædvəkit/	vt.	提倡,鼓吹
alder	/'ɔːldə(r)/	n.	桤木
baled	/beild/	a.	打包的
bark	/bɑːk/	n.	树皮
barrier	/'bæriə/	n.	障碍物,屏障
biomass	/'baiəumæs/	n.	(单位面积或体积内)生物的数量
bole	/bəul/	n.	树干,树身
boon	/buːn/	n.	恩惠,实惠
carbonhydrate	/ˌkɑːbəu'haidreit/	n.&a.	碳水化合物(的)
cellulosic	/ˌselju'ləusik/	a.	有纤维质的
collaboration	/kəˌlæbə'reiʃən/	n.	合作
compress	/kəm'pres/	n.	压缩
conversion	/kən'vəːʃən/	n.	变换,转化
crooked	/'krukid/	a.	弯曲的
cull	/kʌl/	n.	杂质
defective	/di'fektiv/	a.	有缺陷的,有欠缺的
deregulation	/ˌdiː'regjuleitʃən/	n.	违反规定,反常
diesel	/'diːzəl/	n.	柴油
displacement	/dis'pleismənt/	n.	转移,移植
disposal	/dis'pəuzəl/	n.	处理,处置
economics	/ˌekə'nɔmiks/	n.	经济情况,财务情况
effluent	/'efluənt/	n.	废物,废水
endanger	/in'deindʒə/	vt.	危及
erosion	/i'rəuʒən/	n.	腐蚀,侵蚀
ethanol	/'eθənɔːl/	n.	乙醇,酒精
fodder	/'fɔdə/	n.	饲料,草料
fossil	/'fɔsəl/	n.	化石
furnace	/'fəːnis/	n.	炉子,熔炉
gumweed	/'gʌmwud/	n.	胶草
hybrid	/'haibrid/	n.	杂种,混合物
intensity	/in'tensiti/	n.	强烈,强度

inventory	/'invəntəri/	n.	存货,存量
larch	/lɑːtʃ/	n.	落叶松属植物
logging	/'lɔgiŋ/	n.	伐木,采伐
lumber	/'lʌmbə/	n.	木材
manure	/mə'njuə/	n.	肥料
maple	/'meipəl/	n.	枫,枫树
marginal	/'mɑːdʒinəl/	a.	边缘的
milkweed	/'milkwiːd/	n.	乳草属植物
mill	/mil/	n.	(木材)碾磨加工
photosynthesis	/ˌfəutəu'sinθəsis/	n.	光合作用
poplar	/'pɔplə/	n.	白杨
proportion	/prə'pɔːʃən/	n.	比例,均衡
pulpwood	/pʌlpwud/	n.	纸浆用木材
pump	/pʌmp/	vt.	(用泵)抽(水),抽吸
residue	/'rezidjuː/	n.	残渣,剩余物
residual	/ri'zidʒuəl/	n.	剩余部分
sawtimber	/'sɔːˌtimbə(r)/	n.	锯材,锯材原木
scrub	/skrʌb/	n.	洗擦,擦净,净化
stand	/stænd/	n.	林分,(一块地上的)林木
stump	/stʌmp/	n.	树桩
substitute	/'sʌbstitjuːt/	vt.&n.	替代,替代物
switchgrass	/'switʃgrɑːs; -græs/	n.	柳枝稷
trial	/'traiəl/	n.	试验
willow	/'wiləu/	n.	柳树
woodlot	/'wudlɔt/	n.	植林地
energy mix			能源构成
energy plantation			能源林
fossil fuel			化石燃料
high-yielding			产量高的
on-site			现场的
power grid			电网
put stress on			施加压力
soft maple			软枫
soil conditioner			土壤改良剂
International Energy Agency Bioenergy Agreement			国际能源机构《生物能源协定》

Vocabulary exercises

I. Match each phrase with its Chinese meaning.

1. ___ renewable sources　　　　a. 能源转化
2. ___ forest biomass　　　　　　b. 年产量
3. ___ agricultural biomass　　　c. 能源结构
4. ___ energy mix　　　　　　　　d. 可销售材料
5. ___ energy conversion　　　　e. 再生能源,可更新能源
6. ___ merchantable material　　f. 农业生物量
7. ___ alternative uses　　　　　g. 可选择的用途
8. ___ annual yield　　　　　　　h. 林业生物量

II. Fill in each blank with the right word or phrase from the following box. Change the form when necessary.

| fossil fuel | advocate | biomass | sustainability | abate |
| collaboration | residue | inventory | replace | mine |

1. Their methods do not attempt to estimate the actual _____ of fish species in particular parts of the ocean.
2. We _____ a diversified (多样化的) and sensible approach (方法) in transitioning (转变) from petroleum to biofuels.
3. Coal is one kind of _____.
4. Field _____ are materials left in an agricultural field or orchard (果园) after the crop has been harvested.
5. A tree _____ is the gathering of accurate information on the health and diversity of the community forest.
6. We must _____ the water contamination (污染) in our city.
7. Is it possible that new energies will _____ all unrenewable energy?
8. The two countries have agreed to strengthen their power _____.
9. We need to carefully study the impact of urbanization on environmental _____.
10. There was a man in town last week from a coal _____ down there.

Unit 8

 **Listening**

Listen to a passage and then fill in the blanks in the following paragraph as well as those in the table.

One of the main arguments to encourage biofuel production is that biofuels will be a reliable (可靠的) source of energy and will decrease dependence on fossil fuels. However, a preliminary (初步的) assessment (评估) of the extent to which the potential ethanol or biodiesel supply meets those fuel needs is (1)_____. Global production is still too small and the need for (2)_____ materials is still too high for biofuels to have a significant (3)_____ on the fuel market and be able to compete with fossil fuels.

US	Canada
Using (4)_____ of its total corn production in 2006, (5)_____ 3% of its annual fuel consumption with biofuels.	The biofuel target of fuel consumption by the year 2010 is 5%. AAFC (7)_____ 4.6 million tonnes (公吨) of corn, 2.3 million tonnes of (8)_____ and 0.56 million tonnes of canola will be required.
If 100% of the total corn production was used, that (6)_____ would rise to 20%.	If all feedstocks (给料) were grown (9)_____, they would (10)_____ 48-52% of the total corn seeded area... 8% of the total canola (菜子油) seeded area in Canada.

Speaking

I. This is a diagram of the components of biomass. Please work out all kinds of materials that can be converted into (转化,转变) biomass for each branch.

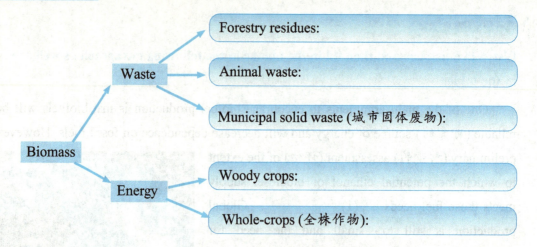

II. Study the following graph which shows conversions (转化) between biomass and energy, and briefly describe the process.

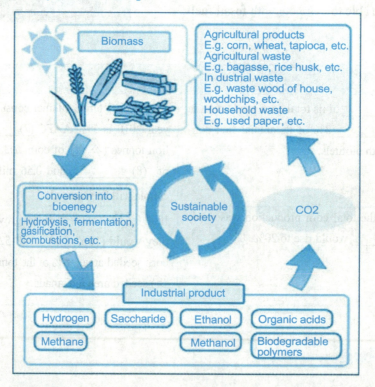

Discussion assistant

convert into; transform into; change into; produce energy; apply technologies (运用技术); consume (消耗); emit into the air (释放到空气中); a cycle of energy; renewable; bagasse (甘薯渣); combustion (燃烧); fermentation (发酵); gasification (气化); husk (谷物或果类的壳); hydrolysis (水解); hydrogen (氢); methane (甲烷, 沼气); methanol (甲醇); saccharide (糖类); tapioca (木薯); woodchips (木屑); biodegradable polymer (生物降解材料); organic acid (有机酸)

Writing

In the future, bioenergy is said to be able to replace large amount of our fossil fuels consumption. More and more countries are resorting to bioenergy to meet the needs of their growing economy, while experts express their concerns about developing bioenergy for issues like food security, environmental protection, and so on. Write a passage on bioenergy development.

Development of Bioenergy

> *Writing assistant*
> You may follow these clues: energy security problem→seek for solutions (bioenergy) →bring additional problems (grain-based, increase of food prices)→more balanced and sustainable development of bioenergy.
> turn to (转向……的帮助); make up (占); every coin has two sides (事物都有两面性); as a result of; take... into consideration

Part II Biofuels

Warming up

Look at the two pictures and describe what energy use will be like in the New Energy Age.

Reading

Biofuels

1 Also known as agrofuels, biofuels mainly came from biomass or bio-waste. These fuels can be used for any purposes, but the main use is in the transportation sector. Most of the

vehicles require fuels which provide high power and are dense, so that storage is easier. Ethanol, biodiesel and methane are three main biofuels meeting these vehicle requirements.

2   The most common biofuel used today is ethonal, which is alcohol produced through fermentation of sugar sources, such as plants. Brazil and the United States produce about 70% of the world's ethanol. It can be used as it is, or blended with regular gasoline. Fuel blends containing 5—10% ethanol require no changes to the engine and are the most widely available at present.

Question 1: Why are some companies developing biobutanol? (Para. 3)

3   Because it tends to absorb water molecules, ethanol is difficult to transport, especially by pipeline. In addition, it is relatively corrosive and evaporates easily. For these reasons, some companies, such as British Petroleum (BP) and DuPont, are looking into converting their ethanol plants to biobutanol production. Butanol is an alcohol that can be produced by fermentation of the same types of sugar sources that are used for ethanol. Butanol has various advantages over ethanol: it delivers more energy, evaporates more slowly, and can be transported by pipeline.

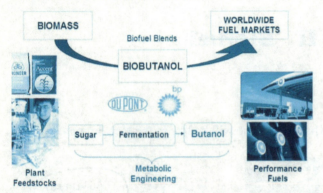

Question 2: What does the italic word retrofits" in line 6 "mean? (Para. 4)

4   Biodiesel is also an important biofuel. It is a safe alternative fuel to take the place of traditional petroleum diesel. With high-lubricity, it is a clean-burning fuel and a fuel component for use in existing unmodified diesel engines. This means that no *retrofits* are necessary when using biodiesel fuel in any diesel-powered combustion engine. It is the only alternative fuel that offers such convenience.

Any diesel vehicle can be powered by biodiesel from 10% to 100% blend with regular petroleum diesel. Performance is usually not affected.

Question 3: What are the similarities and differences between biodiesel and petroleum diesel? (Para. 5)

5   Similar to ethanol, biodiesel is rarely used in neat form but is most commonly blended with diesel fuel. The majority of the 91 million gallons of biodiesel produced in 2005 came from soybean oil, but it can also be made from other oilseed crops, animal fats, and grease. Biodiesel acts like petroleum diesel but produces less air pollution. It comes from renewable sources, being biodegradable and safer for the environment. Biodiesel can extend diesel fuel supply, but it too is limited compared to total petroleum diesel demand. A much larger quantity of energy feedstock is needed to allow biofuels production to reach a larger scale.

Question 4: What are the benefits when methane is used as a fuel? (Paras. 6—7)

6   In the nature, natural gas or biogas is made up mainly of methane (CH_4), which is another biofuel with a bright future. One important difference of bio-methane from other bio-fuels is that it can be produced very efficiently from almost any biogenic sources (green waste, wood, liquid manure, etc.) and it does not compete with food production. The process that creates biogas is called anaerobic digestion. In its simplest form, an anaerobic digester biologically breaks down animal waste and captures the methane gas that is a natural by-product of the process. Methane is a colorless and odorless fuel and very well suited to be used in spark ignited internal combustion engines. It is generally a very safe fuel. The worst accident case is where the piping is cut off. In this case, a flame would burn very locally in contrast to a gasoline accident where the fuel tank can leak which can lead to a much more serious incident. In addition, methane, a potent greenhouse gas, is not emitted into the atmosphere when animal wastes are converted into energy.

7   Biofuels can be looked upon as a way of energy security, which stand as an alternative of fossil fuels that are limited in availability. Today, the use of biofuels has expanded throughout the globe. Some of the major producers and users of biogases are Asia, Europe and America. Theoretically, biofuel can be easily produced through any carbon source, making the photosynthetic plants the most commonly used material for production. Almost all types of materials derived from the plants are used for manufacturing biogas. One of the greatest problems that is being faced by the researchers in the field is how to convert the biomass energy into the fuel. One long-run vision is the development of a biorefinery industry. Biorefineries have the potential to replace nearly all petroleum-based products, including transportation fuels, electricity, natural gas, and petrochemicals.

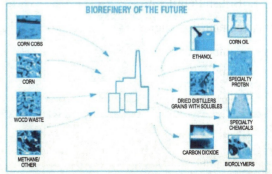

Vocabulary

availability	/əˈveiləˈbiliti/	n.	可用性
biodegradable	/ˌbaiəudiˈgreidəbəl/	a.	可生物降解的
biorefinery	/ˌbaiəriˈfainəri/	n.	生物炼油厂
butanol	/ˈbjutənəul/	n.	丁醇
dense	/dens/	a.	密集的,浓厚的
derive	/diˈraiv/	vi.	(from) 得自,由……来
convert	/kənˈvəːt/	vt.	(使) 转变
corrosive	/kəˈrəusiv/	a.	腐蚀的
efficiently	/iˈfiʃəntli/	ad.	有效率的,高效的
evaporate	/iˈvæpəreit/	v.	(使)蒸发,消失
feedstock	/ˈfiːdstɔk/	n.	给料(供送入机器或加工厂的原料)
fermentation	/fəːmenˈteiʃən/	n.	发酵
grease	/griːs/	n.	油脂
lubricity	/ljuːˈbrisiti/	n.	光滑,润滑
manufacture	/ˌmænjuˈfæktʃə/	vt.	制造,加工
methane(CH_4)	/ˈmiːθein/	n.	甲烷,沼气
molecule	/ˈmɔlikjuːl/	n.	分子
odorless	/ˈəudəlis/	a.	无嗅的
photosynthetic	/ˌfəutəusinˈθetik/	a.	光合作用的
potent	/ˈpəutənt/	a.	有力的,有效的
retrofit	/ˈretrəufit/	n.	改造,改装
theoretically	/θiəˈretikli/	ad.	理论上,理论地
unmodified	/ʌnˈmɔdifaid/	a.	未更改的
vision	/ˈviʒən/	n.	先见之明,幻想
anaerobic digestion			厌氧消化
British Petroleum			英国石油公司
combustion engine			内燃机
compete with			和……竞争
DuPont			杜邦公司
spark ignited			火花点火

Unit 8

Vocabulary exercises

I. Match each word with its explanation.

1. ___ fermentation
2. ___ evaporate
3. ___ alternative
4. ___ replace
5. ___ unmodified
6. ___ combustion
7. ___ neat
8. ___ feedstock
9. ___ by-product
10. ___ biorefinery

a. to take or fill the place of
b. the process of energy production in a cell under anaerobic conditions (without oxygen)
c. not changed in form or character
d. the process of burning.
e. to change into vapor
f. allowing or necessitating a choice between two or more things.
g. raw material required for an industrial process
h. a facility that integrates biomass conversion processes and equipment to produce fuels, power, and value-added chemicals from biomass
i. not diluted (冲淡的) or mixed with other substances
j. something produced in the making of something else

II. Read the accounts about renewable energy utilization and meanwhile translate the given Chinese in the brackets to fill in the blanks.

Renewable energy is energy generated from (1)_____ (自然资源)—such as sunlight, wind, rain, tides and (2)_____ (地热的) heat—which are renewable (naturally replenished (补充). In 2006, about 18% of global final (3)_____ (能量消耗) came from renewables, with 13% coming from traditional biomass, such as wood-burning. (4)_____ (水电) was the next largest renewable source, providing 3% (15% of global electricity generation), followed by solar hot water/heating, which contributed 1.3%. Modern technologies, such as geothermal energy, wind power, solar power, and ocean energy together provided some 0.8% of final energy consumption. Present renewable energy sources supply about 18% of current world energy use and there is much (5)_____ (潜力) that could be exploited in the future. The technical potential of renewable energy sources is 18 times more than current global primary energy use.

In China, at the end of 2006, annual (6)_____ (利用) quantity of China renewable energy is totally 200 million tons standard coal, (excluding biomass traditionally utilized), which occupies about 8% of total consumption of China primary energy, increasing by 0.5 percentage point than that in 2005. This is a firm step toward target for renewable energy occupying 10% of national (7)_____ (一次能源) in 2010. According to China mid-long-term energy planning, China could meet the needs of national economy development and people's living standard improvement for energy basically relying on (8)_____ (常规能源) before 2020. With the increasingly outstanding strategy position of renewable energy, several hundred million tons even over billion tons of standard coal energy will be provided by renewable energy till 2020. So the strategy target of Chinese renewable energy will be improving the energy supply capacity furthest, perfecting (9)_____ (能源结构), realizing energy variety and guaranteeing the security of energy supply feasibly.

🎧 Listening

Learn these words and phrases and then listen to a BBC world news to answer the following questions.

Words and phrases			
accelerate	/əkˈseləreit/	vt.&vi.	加速
alarmingly	/əˈlɑːmiŋli/	ad.	令人担忧地
boom	/buːm/	n.	繁荣
clear	/kliə/	vi.	扫除,清除
deteriorate	/diˈtiəriəreit/	v.	(使)恶化
environmentalist	/inˌvairənˈmentəlist/	n.	环境保护者
gasoline	/ˈgæsəliːn/	n.	汽油
plantation	/plænˈteiʃən/	n.	种植园,大农场
tropical	/ˈtrɔpikəl/	a.	热带的
Amazon rainforest			亚马逊热带雨林
make way for			为……让路
pour into			川流不息地涌入

Unit 8

Questions

1. What is the environmentalists' concern about Amazon rainforest?

2. Which countries are the largest and second largest ethanol producers in the world?

3. How many out of ten new cars run on ethanol in Brazil?

4. What is the price of ethanol in Brazil?

5. According to the passage, why is the Amazon rainforest deteriorating?

Speaking

I. The automotive refueling business has become more competitive as gasoline prices have shot up. Can you find out the economical benefits (节省的好处) of using biofuels from the picture below.

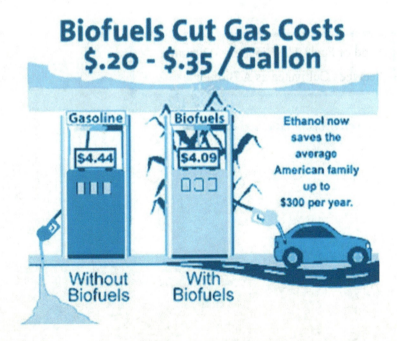

II. Study the following cartoon *First Biofuel Commercial Airline Flight*. Please further list other benefits of developing biofuels to find out the connotations (隐含意义) it conveys.

> **Discussion assistant**
> Brazilian babassu (一种巴西棕榈树); coconut (椰子); propel (推进, 驱使); virgin (首次); green bullet (绿子弹, 发射后不会污染环境的环保子弹)

Background Reading

> Food or Fuel? The Bioenergy Dilemma
> Seaweed Cultivated as A Biofuel

Please refer to the attached disk.

Unit 9

Remote Sensing

Part I Remote Sensing in Agriculture

Warming up

Remote sensing systems offer four basic components (组成部分) to measure and record data about an area from a distance. These components include the energy source, the transmission (传输) path, the target and the satellite sensor. The energy source, electromagnetic energy (电磁能), is very important. It is the crucial medium (媒介) required to transmit information from the target to the sensor.

Remote sensing provides important coverage (覆盖率), mapping (制图) and classification (分类) of land-cover (土地覆盖) features, such as vegetation (植被), soil, water and forests.

1. Please find out the energy source, the transmission path, the target and the satellite sensor in the picture. And then describe the remote sensing process.
2. Based on your knowledge of remote sensing, please list more applications of remote sensing in your own field such as agriculture, forestry, fishery (渔业) or meteorology (气象学).

> **Discussion assistant**
>
> find wide application in...; erupt (爆发); monitor; detect; prevent; provide; apply fertilizers; irrigate; obtain; analyze, sense; control; save; reach; reflect; transmit; at the earliest; properly; agriculture; forestry; oceanology (海洋资源研究); cycle; insect infestations (虫害); frost; gale (7—10级的大风); natural disaster; loss in yield; precise information; soil conditions; water conditions; crops; areas inaccessible (难以接近的区域); forest fire; conservation of forest; ocean bottom; distribution; activities of lava (熔岩); desert; volcano (火山); environment; pest; flood; frost; reclamation (改造, 开垦); resource; coverage (覆盖范围); satellite; productivity; ecosystem; radar; vegetation; structure; density; tide

Reading

Remote Sensing in Agriculture

1 When farmers or ranchers observe their fields or pastures to assess their condition without physically touching them, it is a form of remote sensing. Observing the colors of leaves or the overall appearances of plants can determine the plants' condition. Remotely sensed images taken from satellites and aircraft provide a means to assess field conditions without physically touching them from a point of view high above the field.

Question 1: Is there any difference between the view of human eyes and that of a remote sensor? (Para. 2)

2 Most remote sensors see the same visible wavelengths of light that are seen by the human eye, although in most cases remote sensors can also detect energy from wavelengths that are undetectable to the human eye. The remote view of the sensor and the ability to store, analyze, and display the sensed data on field maps are what make remote sensing a potentially important tool for agricultural producers. Agricultural remote sensing is not new and dates back to the 1950s, but recent technological advances have made the benefits of remote sensing accessible to most agricultural producers.

The Use of Remote Sensing on a Farm

3 Remotely sensed images can be used to identify nutrient deficiencies, diseases, water deficiency or surplus, weed infestations, insect damage, hail damage, wind damage, herbicide damage, and plant populations.

The *Electromagnetic Spectrum*

4   The basic principles of remote sensing with satellites and aircraft are similar to visual observations. Energy in the form of light waves travels from the sun to Earth. Light waves travel similarly to waves traveling across a lake. The distance from the peak of one wave to the peak of the next wave is the wavelength. Energy from sunlight is called the electromagnetic spectrum.

Question 2: What is the visible region for human eyes in the electromagnetic spectrum? (Para. 5)

5   The wavelengths used in most agricultural remote sensing applications cover only a small region of the electromagnetic spectrum. Wavelengths are measured in micrometers (μm) or nanometers (nm). One μm is about .00003937 inch and 1 μm equals 1,000 nm. The visible region of the electromagnetic spectrum is from about 400 nm to about 700 nm. The green color associated with plant vigor has a wavelength that centers near 500 nm.

Question 3: Which one do you think has longer wavelength, blue lights or red lights? (Para. 6)

6   Wavelengths longer than those in the visible region and up to about 25 μm are in the infrared region. The infrared region nearest to that of the visible region is the near infrared region (NIR). Both the visible and infrared regions are used in agricultural remote sensing.

Question 4: What will happen to electromagnetic energy from the sun when it strikes the plants? Complete the diagram in Para. 7.

Electromagnetic Energy and Plants

7   When electromagnetic energy from the sun strikes plants, three things can happen. Depending upon the wavelength of the energy and characteristics of individual plants, the energy will be reflected, absorbed, or transmitted. Reflected energy bounces off leaves and is readily identified by human eyes as the green color of plants. A plant looks green because the chlorophyll in the leaves absorbs much of the energy in the visible wavelengths and the green color is reflected. Sunlight that is not reflected or absorbed is transmitted through the leaves to the ground.

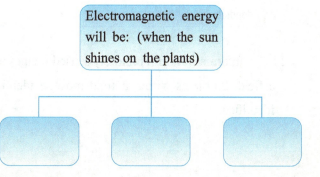

8   Interactions between reflected, absorbed, and transmitted energy can be detected by remote sensing. The differences in leaf colors, textures, shapes or even how the leaves are attached to plants, determine how much energy will be reflected, absorbed or transmitted. The relationship between reflected, absorbed and transmitted energy is used to determine spectral signatures of individual plants. Spectral signatures are unique to plant species.

Question 5: Why can remote sensing identify a stressed area? (Paras. 9—10)

9   Remote sensing is used to identify stressed areas in fields by first establishing the spectral signatures of healthy plants. The spectral signatures of stressed plants appear altered from those of healthy plants.

10   Stressed sugarbeets have a higher reflectance value in the visible region of the spectrum from 400—700 nm. This pattern is reversed for stressed sugarbeets in the non-visible range from about 750—1200 nm. The visible pattern is repeated in the higher reflectance range from about 1300—2400 nm. Interpreting the reflectance values at various wavelengths of energy can be used to assess crop health.

Area of agricultural phenomena	Wavelength employed
1. Plant diseases and insect infestation	0.4—0.9 mm and 6—10 mm
2. Natural vegetation, types of crop and fresh inventories (储存)	0.4—0.9 mm and 6—10 mm
3. Soil moisture content (radar)	04—0.8 mm and 3—100 mm
4. Study of arable (可耕种的) and non-arable land	0.4—0.9 mm
5. Assessment of plant growth and rigor (严重困难) for forecasting crop yield	0.4—0.9 mm
6. Soil type and characteristics	0.4—1.0 mm
7. Flood control and water management	0.4—1.0 mm and 6—12 mm
8. Surface water inventories, water quality	0.4—1.0 mm and 6—12 mm
9. Soil and rock type and conditions favorable for hidden mineral deposits (沉积物).	0.4—1.0 mm and 7—12 mm

11   Information from remotely sensed images allows farmers to treat only affected areas of a field. Problems within a field may be identified remotely before they can be visually identified.

Vocabulary

accessible	/ək'sesəbl/	a.	容易取得的,容易达到的
bounce	/bauns/	vi.&vt.	弹回
center	/'sentə/	vi.&vt.	居中,使……聚在一点,以……为中心
chlorophyll	/'klɔrəfil/	n.	叶绿素
deficiency	/di'fiʃənsi/	n.	缺乏,不足
detect	/di'tekt/	vt.	(a. detectable)探测,查明,发现
hail	/heil/	n.	雹子
herbicide	/'həːbisaid/	n.	除草剂
identify	/ai'dentifai/	vt.	认出,识别
infrared	/ˌinfrə'red/	a.	红外(线)的
infestation	/in'festeiʃən/	n.	(v. infest)(害虫/盗贼等)群袭出没
interaction	/ˌintər'ækʃən/	n.	(v. interact)相互作用,合作
micrometer	/mai'krɔmitə/	n.	微米,测微计
nanometer	/'nænəˌmiːtə/	n.	纳米,1/1,000,000,000 米
overall	/'əuvərɔːl/	a.	总体的
pasture	/'pɑːstʃə/	n.	牧场,牧草
potentially	/pə'tenʃəli/	ad.	潜在地
rancher	/'rɔːntʃə/	n.	大农场主
reverse	/ri'vəːs/	vt.	颠倒,逆转
stress	/stres/	v.&n.	强调,压力,施压力于……
sugarbeet	/'ʃugəbiːt/	n.	甜菜
surplus	/'səːpləs/	n.&a.	过剩(的),多余(的)
texture	/'tekstʃə/	n.	质感,质地
transmit	/trænz'mit/	vt.	传播,传导
vigor	/'vigə/	n.	精力,活力
visually	/'viʒuəli/	ad.	视觉上地,真实地
wavelength	/'weivleŋθ/	n.	波长
be attached to...			附属于,附着于
date back to...			追溯到……
electromagnetic spectrum			电磁波频谱
in most cases			在大多数情况下

near infrared region	近红外(线)区域
reflectance value	反射值
spectral signature	光谱特征

Vocabulary exercises

I. Match each phrase with its Chinese meaning.

1. ____ NIR   a. 电磁能
2. ____ reflectance value   b. 纳米
3. ____ spectral signature   c. 目测
4. ____ electromagnetic spectrum   d. 红外区域
5. ____ visual observation   e. 电磁光谱
6. ____ infrared region   f. 近红外区域
7. ____ electromagnetic energy   g. 反射值
8. ____ nanometer   h. 光谱特征

II. Fill in each blank with the right phrase from the following box.

readily identified	attached to	associated with	dates back to
accessible to	are unique to	centers near	is reversed
measured in	without physically touching them		

1. Leaves are _____ the stems of a plant in a different way when the plants are affected by certain diseases.
2. The green color associated with plant vigor has a wavelength that _____ 500 nm.
3. When farmers or ranchers observe their fields or pastures to assess their condition _____, it is a form of remote sensing.
4. Agricultural remote sensing is not new and can be traced back to the 1950s, but recent technological advances have made the benefits of remote sensing _____ most agricultural producers.
5. Wavelengths are _____ micrometers (μm 微米) or nanometers (nm 纳米).
6. Reflected energy bounces off leaves and is _____ by human eyes as the green color of plants.
7. Stressed sugarbeets have a higher reflectance value in the visible region of spectrum from 400—700 nm. This pattern _____ for stressed sugarbeets in the non-visible range from about 750—1200 nm.
8. The relationship between reflected, absorbed and transmitted energy is used to determine

spectral signatures of individual plants. Spectral signatures _____ plant species.

9. Low pressure areas are usually _____ unstable weather, due to a high pressure area moving in.

10. The history of people's monitoring possible disasters in agriculture and forestry _____ thousands of years ago, but only in recent decades can people obtain accurate (确切的) information.

Listening

Learn the following words and phrases and then listen to a lecture to fill in the missing information.

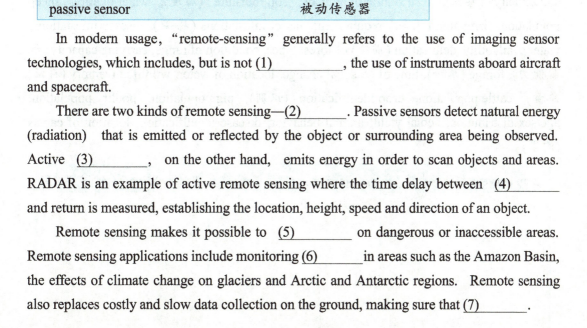

Words and phrases			
Antarctic	/æn'tɑːktik/	a.	南极的
Arctic	/'ɑːktik/	a.	北极的
glacier	/'glæsjə/	n.	冰山
imaging	/'imædʒiŋ/	n.	成像
inaccessible	/ˌinæk'sesəbəl/	a.	达不到的,不可及的
active sensor			主动传感器
Amazon Basin			亚马逊流域
passive sensor			被动传感器

In modern usage, "remote-sensing" generally refers to the use of imaging sensor technologies, which includes, but is not (1)_____, the use of instruments aboard aircraft and spacecraft.

There are two kinds of remote sensing—(2)_____. Passive sensors detect natural energy (radiation) that is emitted or reflected by the object or surrounding area being observed. Active (3)_____, on the other hand, emits energy in order to scan objects and areas. RADAR is an example of active remote sensing where the time delay between (4)_____ and return is measured, establishing the location, height, speed and direction of an object.

Remote sensing makes it possible to (5)_____ on dangerous or inaccessible areas. Remote sensing applications include monitoring (6)_____ in areas such as the Amazon Basin, the effects of climate change on glaciers and Arctic and Antarctic regions. Remote sensing also replaces costly and slow data collection on the ground, making sure that (7)_____.

Speaking

I. Read the following paragraph and have a discussion.

Agricultural resources are among the most important renewable, dynamic (动态的) natural resources. Comprehensive (全面的), reliable and timely information on agricultural resources is very necessary for a country that heavily depends on agriculture. Agriculture surveys are presently conducted in order to gather information and associated statistics on crops, rangelands (牧场), livestock (牲畜) and other related agricultural resources. These data are most important for the implementation (执行) of effective management decisions at local, district and national levels. In fact, agricultural survey is a backbone (主力, 支柱) of planning and allocation (分布, 分配) of the limited resources to different sectors (部门) of the economy.

Study the following factors concerning agricultural remote sensing and work together to group them into the suitable category. Some factors can fall into more than one category.

crop acreage (面积), types of farm buildings, crop vigor (活力), crop density (密度), crop maturity, growth rates, yield forecasting (预测), soil fertility (肥沃), effects of fertilizes, soil toxicity (毒性), distribution of animals, soil moisture (湿度), water quality, sheep population, irrigation (灌溉) requirement, insect infestations (感染), disease infestations, water availability, delineation (描绘) of forest types, condition of range, carrying capacity (承载能力), forage (草料), time of seasonal change, location of water, wildlife inventory (存活, 总量), cattle population, crop identification (识别), pig population, poultry population, age/sex distribution, actual yield, animal behavior, disease identification, location of canals (沟渠)

crop survey (作物调查)	range survey (农场调查)	livestock survey (牲畜调查)

II. Study the picture carefully. Based on what you've learned about active and passive sensors, briefly describe with a partner the working processes of an active sensor and a passive sensor respectively.

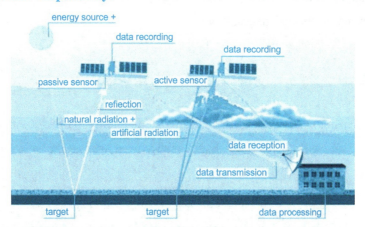

Discussion assistant

when..., after that, finally; while...; ...is reflected from...to ...

transmit; reflect; collect; receive; produce; generate

active sensor; passive sensor; energy source; data recording; target; natural radiation (自然发光); reflection (反射); artificial radiation (人工发光); data transmission; data reception (接收); data processing (处理); in the beginning; first; then; upon the data reception

III. Satellite-borne remote sensing can provide quantitative (定量的) measurements relevant to soil conditions, crop health and economic potential (潜力). There is difference in the reflectance between wet and dry soils and that of vegetation (植被). The following diagram shows such differences. Look closely and describe the differences in red light region and near infrared (近红外线的) region respectively. Then discuss with a partner the implication of such differences in interpreting remote-sensing images.

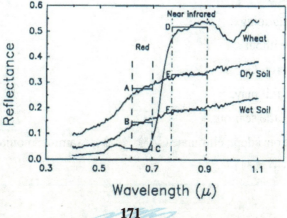

> **Discussion assistant**
>
> show; rank the top; appear; interpret; red light region; low; high; middle; pattern; image; range; remote sensor; bright; dark; the highest/lowest reflectance value; diagram; remote-sensing images; thus

Writing

Besides remote sensing, man has used electromagnetic energy in other ways. Look at the following picture and write a passage to describe how man has applied electromagnetic energy to life and work.

Application of Electromagnetic Energy

> **Writing assistant**
>
> ...can do...
>
> ...is used for.../ to do
>
> ...enable...to do
>
> ...function to do...
>
> ...is capable of.../doing...
>
> ...can hardly...without...
>
> If there had been no...
>
> ...has put...into full play.
>
> ...leaves no or little scar on...
>
> depend on; live on; adopt; eliminate (切除, 铲除); examine; monitor; transmit; entertain; facilitate (使……便利)

sunlight; electromagnetic energy; in recent decades, doctor; gamma rays; tumors (肿瘤); human bodies; X-ray; bone structure; microwave ovens; reality; "cook without fire"; longer wavelength; TV and radio signals; modern people's lives

Part II   Applications of Remote Sensing to Conservation of Forest Ecosystems

Warming up

I. Discussion

Discuss the following questions with a partner.

1. How is forest important to human beings?
2. When forest fires happen, what can we do to prevent such fires from further spreading and to put them out?

II. Listening

Learn the following words and phrases and then listen to a passage and fill in the missing information.

> **Words and phrases**
>
> ERS-SAR (Earth Resources Satellite- Safety Analysis Report) 地球资源卫星—安全分析报告
> Landsat Thematic Mapper 地球资源探测卫星专题制图仪
> NOAA-AVHRR (National Oceanic and Atmospheric Administration-Advanced Very High Resolution Radiometer) 美国海洋大气局—高级甚高分辨率辐射计
> SPOT (Satellite Positioning and Tracking) 人造卫星定位及跟踪

With the long hot days of summer, wildfires in many parts of the world happen.

The first (1)_____ against forest fires is early detection. In Northern California computerized cameras are (2)_____ traditional lookouts and fire towers. The camera has been the first alert (警报，警戒) on several fires. The forest staff can tell whether it's going to be (3)_____ right away. When the camera spots (察觉，认出) something the computer instantly maps the exact location.

Remote sensing also finds its (4)_____ in detecting forest fires. High resolution (高分辨度) satellite data such as Landsat Thematic Mapper, SPOT and ERS-SAR combined with low resolution satellite images such as NOAA-AVHRR offer new (5)_____ to monitor forest fires. They have a number of advantages: it is possible to view vast expanses (广阔的区域) of land; detection (探测) can be (6)_____ for the same area and recorded in different wavelengths, thus providing information on the state of forest resources.

Reading

Applications of Remote Sensing to Conservation of Forest Ecosystems

Question 1: Why is forest important to use? (Para. 1)

1   Forests cover about 30 percent of the land area, and contain the majority of the planet's land-based species. They also regulate the global atmospheric cycles that make biological life possible on Earth. Therefore, it is vital to forest protection.

2   Satellite-based remote sensing is probably the only way to record the change in global forest ecosystems and assess the success of conservation efforts.

Climate Change Predications

3   Remote sensing imageries show the change in global forest coverage and conditions, primarily through deforestation and biomass burning. Since deforestation and biomass burning always result from changes in climate, those imageries are also indicators of climate change.

Question 2: Why do we need higher-resolution sensors in order to precisely predict the climate change? (Para. 4)

4   However, if precise predications, such as forest age and composition, are to be obtained, we will have to await the development of global-scale sensors with higher spatial and spectral resolution. The detection of forest conditions is a complicated process. The strength of a forest area depends on the age and composition of the forest. A regenerating tropical forest typically absorbs more carbon dioxide in its growth phase than a mature forest. Furthermore, different plant species have very different carbon dioxide responses. To get more precise interpretation of remote-sensing imageries, higher-resolution sensors are expected.

Assessing the Success of Protected Areas

5   Protected areas are a key strategy used to conserve biodiversity from human activities. Remote sensing is being used to determine how successful protected areas are at reducing human impact.

Question 3: What's the purpose of citing so many numbers? (Para. 6)

6   A study both inside and outside of protected areas in the Sarapiqui region of Costa Rica showed that protected areas were dramatically controlling the rate of deforestation. The deforestation and fragmentation rates within national parks remained below 0.56% over the twenty-year study, and decreased further towards the end of the period. Deforestation rate declined from 1.7% to 1.4% over the period in private conservation land. Outside protected areas deforestation rates were between 3.6% and 3.2%.

7   We must also note that to better understand the effectiveness of protected areas and develop more feasible policies, it is essential to integrate remotely sensed information with human population, behavior, and socio-economics.

Species Conservation

8   Remote sensing is being applied to protecting species, such as the jaguar on an isolated mountain system in Northern Mexico. Jaguar sightings show significant correlation with tropical deciduous and oak forests between 400m and 900m in altitude. With the acreage of oak forests decreasing, fewer jaguars are observed. Therefore, remote-sensing imageries of oak forest cover reflect the living conditions of jaguars. That makes it possible to decide the amount of emphasis to be put on a certain conservation land, thus conserving species more effectively.

Question 4: How could we get estimates of species richness and distribution? (Para. 9)

Biodiversity Assessment

9   Remote sensing is an important technique for measuring global biodiversity in forest ecosystems. At the local scale remote sensing can provide structural information about forest stands, such as the nature of the canopy surface, the layering within the canopy and even individual tree identification. Now this information is being linked with ecological species information gathered from ground sampling. So we can get estimates of species richness and distribution over much larger scales than before.

10   With the improvements in remote sensors and their wider application, remote sensing in forestry is to be a burgeoning area of research in the near future.

Vocabulary

acreage	/ˈeikəridʒ/	n.	英亩数；面积
altitude	/ˈæltitjuːd/	n.	高度，高地，海拔
burgeon	/ˈbəːdʒən/	n.&vi.	迅速发展
canopy	/ˈkænəpi/	n.	树冠，罩棚，华盖
complicated	/ˈkɔmplikeitid/	a.	难懂的，复杂的
composition	/kɔmpəˈziʃən/	n.	构成，合成物
conservation	/ˌkɔnsəˈveiʃən/	n.	保护，保存
correlation	/ˌkɔriˈleiʃən/	n.	相互关联
coverage	/ˈkʌvəridʒ/	n.	覆盖范围，报道量
deciduous	/diˈsidʒjsuəs/	a.	每年落叶的
deforestation	/diːˌfɔriˈsteiʃən/	n.	采伐森林
distribution	/ˌdistriˈbjuːʃən/	n.	散布，分布，分发
dramatically	/drəˈmætikli/	ad.	剧烈地
feasible	/ˈfiːzibəl/	a.	可行的
fragmentation	/ˈfrægmenteiʃən/	n.	分割，破碎
frequency	/ˈfriːkwənsi/	n.	频率，频繁
imagery	/ˈimidʒəri/	n.	意象，塑像，画像
indicator	/ˈindikeitə/	n.	指示器，指示物
integrate	/ˈintigreit/	vt.&vi.	(使)成为整体，(使)融入
isolate	/ˈaisəleit/	vt.	使隔离，使孤立
jaguar	/dʒægjuə/	n.	(中南美洲的)美洲虎
Landsat	/ˈlændsæt/	n.	(美国)地球(资源探测)卫星
layer	/ˈleiə/	n.	层，层次
oak	/əuk/	n.	橡树
predication	/ˌpridiˈkeiʃən/	n.	论断，判断
regenerate	/riˈdʒenərit/	vt.	再生，新生
regulate	/ˈreɡjuleit/	vt.	控制，调节，管理
response	/risˈpɔns/	n.	回应，反应
sighting	/saitiŋ/	n.	被看见，露面
spatial	/ˈspeiʃəl/	a.	空间的，立体的
atmospheric cycle			大气循环
Costa Rica			哥斯达黎加[拉丁美洲]

derive from...	起源于……
forest stand	林分,林段
ground sampling	地面采样
land cover	土地覆盖
Sarapiqui	哥斯达黎加北部一地区
spatial resolution	空间分辨率
spectral resolution	光谱分辨率

Vocabulary exercises

I. Match each phrase with its Chinese meaning.

1. ___ biodiversity   a. 光谱分辨率
2. ___ tropical forest   b. 大气循环
3. ___ ground sampling   c. 高分辨率
4. ___ forest stand   d. 林段
5. ___ high-resolution   e. 地面采样
6. ___ forest coverage   f. 热带森林
7. ___ atmospheric cycle   g. 生物多样性
8. ___ spectral resolution   h. 森林覆盖率

II. Fill in each blank with the right word or phrase from the following box. Change the form when necessary.

| derive from | the majority of | feasible | integrate...with... |
| composition | distribution | altitude | spatial |

1. The most effective farming should be based on the analysis of the _____ of a particular piece of land.

2. Scientists have been devoting themselves to the research into a remote sensing system with higher _____ resolution in order to obtain clearer and more reliable images.

3. Every year vast areas in forests are destroyed by fires _____ hot weather or human errors.

4. In order to get accurate descriptions of a particular piece of land, scientists must _____ remote sensing imageries _____ ground sampling data.

5. To some degree the _____ of animals is a sign of the changes in natural environment, such as climate and availability of food.

6. With the _____ increasing, animal population shows closer co-relationship with the

density of forestry since life depends more on forest resources on high mountains.
7. Forests cover approximately 30 percent of the land area, and contain _____ the planet's land-based species and they regulate the global atmospheric cycles.
8. Up to now human beings have not come up with a _____ way to precisely predict the happening of an earthquake.

Listening

Listen to the following dialogue and fill in the missing information.

Interviewer: The 29th Olympic Games has just ended in Beijing. And we know that many new (1)_____ have been applied to ensure its success. Mr. Wang, could you please tell us some of the new tech?

Wang: Well, Chinese scientists have (2)_____ Olympic avenues (林荫道) landscape and surrounding environment through a remote sensing program. They compared the real-time data with the (3)_____ airborne (空中拍摄的) images in 2002 and 2003 in the Olympic central area, as well as the images from 1983 until now.

Interviewer: So those images work differently from conventional ways?

Wang: Yes. Gathering data from 1998 to 2008, the system (4)_____ stereo (立体声的) observation from space-borne, airborne and ground remote sensing methods. It comprehensively and continuously surveyed ecological environment, (5)_____, environmental pollution and traffic flows.

Interviewer: That sounds amazing.

Wang: Besides the service for the Beijing Olympics, the remote sensing also provided airborne images of Sichuan after (6)_____ on May 12, 2008. Together with other satellite images, those images were used for post-disaster damage assessment.

Speaking

I. Besides agriculture and forestry, remote sensing is also widely applied in fishery. During the past decades, with the improvement in fishermen's fishing equipment and their more knowledge of the waters, fishermen could achieve greater catch (捕获量) than before. However, problems come along due to the irrational (不合理的) fishing habits of fisher folks. More and more juvenile fish (幼鱼) is killed. The emergence of remote sensing has helped both the fishermen and the fish.

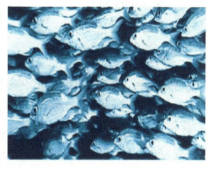

Discuss with your partner about how remote sensing has helped fishermen and fish. The following words and phrases may serve as hints.

> *Discussion assistant*
> Without touching or being close to...
> ...being combined with...
> After...
> ...can advise people on...
> ...prove to be...
>
> detect; predict; help; track (跟踪); identify; protect; grow up; water bodies; temperature of waters; weather conditions; ground sampling; the whereabouts (行踪) of fish; fish shoal (鱼群); species; types; remote-sensing imageries; a large-eyed or small-eyed net (小眼/大眼的渔网); depth of water; track the fish shoal; fish catch (捕鱼量); coastal; juvenile fish (幼鱼); more fish; win-win (双赢的)

II. Remote sensing is an interesting and exploratory (探险性的) science. It provides images of areas in a fast and cost-efficient manner. The combination of remotesensing and field surveys is an important source of information. Still, arguments arise regarding the benefits and limitations of remote sensing. Discuss with a partner the advantages and disadvantages of remote sensing.

Discussion assistant

pros and cons (赞成的观点和反对的观点)

...require us to...

to take... into consideration

For example...

acquire; compared with; obtain; interpret; look the same; lead to; against reality; confuse; measure; interfere (干扰); data; regions; samples; phenomena; imageries; land surveys; geographical area; up-to-date information; classification (分类) errors; a complicated process; geographical areas; detailed; inaccessible (不可进入的); invisible; economical; cheap; rapid; indirect; exact; distinct (清晰的); confused; artificial and natural; precise; undesirable (不受欢迎的); coarse (粗糙的); detailed (详细的); in a practical way; especially

Background Reading

What is magnetic spectrum?
What is Landsat Program?
Remote Sensing in China

Please refer to the attached disk.

Unit 10

Carbon Sequestration

碳 汇

Part I   Carbon Sequestration in Agriculture and Forestry

Warming up

I. Which four places do the above photos show? Can you connect them with carbon dioxide (CO_2)?

II. Learn the major six greenhouse gases leading to the growing global warming listed in the following chart. Which one do you think is on the top of the list contributing to the worsening climate?

Greenhouse Gases (GHGS)	Molecular Formula	Chinese
carbon dioxide	CO_2	二氧化碳
nitrous oxide	N_2O	一氧化二氮
methane	CH_4	甲烷
hydrofluorocarbon gases	HFC	水碳氟化合物气体
perfluorocarbons	PFC	全氟碳化物气体
sulphur hexafluoride	SF_6	六氟化硫

III. Brainstorm any words related to the word CO_2.

VI. Please briefly describe the chart on the right and then discuss what contributes to the increasingly serious global warming?

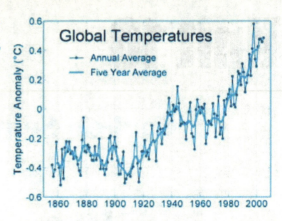

Discussion assistant

rise; increase; fall; decrease; fluctuate (波动); discharge (排放); pour into; consume (消耗); contribute to (导致); lead to; upturn the soil (翻地); fossil fuel; coal mine; oil wells; backward equipment; careless management; wars; self-ignition (自燃); forest fire; unplanned; deforestation; desertification; photosynthesis (光合作用) capability; exhaust (尾气、废气); glass walls of modern buildings

Reading

Carbon Sequestration in Agriculture and Forestry

Question 1: What's the topic sentence of paragraph 1?

1   The Earth has a natural carbon cycle. Carbon is naturally exchanged between terrestrial vegetation and the atmosphere through photosynthesis and respiration. Carbon flows from one reservoir to another over time scales ranging from days to decades to millennia. The major components or reservoirs of carbon include the terrestrial vegetation, soils and oceans, and the atmosphere. This carbon cycle helps regulate the amount of carbon dioxide (CO_2) present in our atmosphere, and is therefore a major component of the climate system.

Question 2: When are global temperatures expected to rise? (Para. 2)

2   It is crucial to maintain habitable temperatures. If there were significantly less CO_2 in the atmosphere, global temperatures would drop below levels to which ecosystems and human societies have adapted. As CO_2 levels rise, global temperatures are also expected to rise as increasing amounts of solar radiation are trapped inside the "greenhouse." The concentration of CO_2 in the atmosphere is determined by a continuous flow among the stores of carbon in the atmosphere, the ocean, the earth's biological systems, and its geological materials.

Question 3: Why has the past balanced carbon cycle been broken? (Paras. 3—4)

3   Over the millennium before the Industrial Revolution, atmospheric concentrations of CO_2 were relatively stable. This is because the two major carbon fluxes—between terrestrial vegetation and the atmosphere; and between the ocean and the atmosphere—were generally in balance.

4   The burning of fossil fuels and deforestation has introduced an additional flux into the carbon cycle. These activities combined now emit almost eight billion metric tons of carbon to the atmosphere every year, about 20% of which is the result of land-use change such as tropical deforestation. Roughly half of these human-induced carbon emissions remain in the atmosphere (for up to a century or more), while the remainder is taken up in nearly equal amount by the oceans and land vegetation.

Question 4: When can we find a carbon sink? (Para. 5)

5   Carbon sequestration, also known as terrestrial sequestration, is the process through which CO_2 from the atmosphere is absorbed by trees, plants and crops through photosynthesis, and stored as carbon in biomass (tree trunks, branches, foliage and roots) and soils. The term "sinks" is also used to refer to forests, croplands, and grazing lands, and their ability to sequester carbon. Agriculture and forestry activities can also release CO_2 to the atmosphere when agricultural tillage practices stir up soils or when biomass decays and burns. Therefore, a carbon sink occurs when carbon sequestration is greater than carbon releases over some time period.

Question 5: What's the function of carbon sequestration? (Para. 6)

6   Carbon sequestration can improve carbon storage in trees and soils, preserve existing tree and soil carbon, and reduce emissions of the greenhouse gases: CO_2—the most important global warming gas emitted by human activities, methane (CH_4), and nitrous oxide (N_2O). Therefore, it slows the rate of climate change, primarily global warming and its serious results.

Question 6: How long does it take for forest and agricultural carbon sequestration to reach saturation? (Para. 7)

7   In forests, carbon can be sequestered over decades or even centuries, until mature ecosystems reach a stage of carbon saturation; however, natural decay and disturbances such as fire or harvesting can release carbon back into the atmosphere as CO_2. Carbon from forests can also be stored in wood products like furniture and housing lumber for years to decades. Thereafter, the carbon in wood products may decay and be released as CO_2 back to

the atmosphere. In agricultural soils, carbon can be sequestered for 15 years or longer, depending not only on the type of soil but also on the type, continuity and length of management practice.

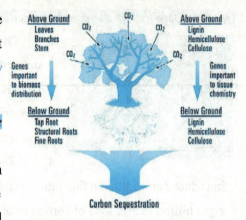

Question 7: What are the major means to increase carbon sequestration? (Para. 8)

8   Then how to enhance the carbon sequestration capability of agriculture and forestry? There are three general means by which agricultural and forestry practices can help reduce greenhouse gases, mainly CO_2:

- Avoid emissions by maintaining existing carbon storage in trees and soils.
- Increase carbon storage by, e.g., tree and grass planting, conversion from conventional to conservation tillage practices on agricultural lands, and preventing desertification.
- Substitute bio-based fuels and products for fossil fuels, such as coal and oil, and energy-intensive products that generate greater quantities of CO_2 when used.

9   At the global level, it is estimated about 100 billion metric tons of carbon over the next 50 years could be sequestered through forest preservation, tree planting and improved agricultural management. This would offset 10—20% of the world's projected fossil fuel emissions.

Question 8: What methods are generally taken to measure carbon sequestration of forest and agricultural soil and why is it harder to measure the soil carbon sequestration? (Para. 10)

10   Carbon sequestration rates vary by tree species, soil type, regional climate, topography and management practice. Several methods can be used to measure the carbon and—more importantly for the atmosphere—the changes in carbon in above-ground and below-ground biomass, soils, and wood products. Statistical sampling, computer modeling and remote sensing can be used to estimate carbon sequestration and emission sources at the global, national and local scales. Current forest carbon estimates are generally more accurate and easier to generate than soil estimates. Estimating changes in soil carbon over time is generally more challenging due to the high degree of variability of soil organic matter—even within small geographic scales like a corn field—and because changes in soil carbon may be small compared to the

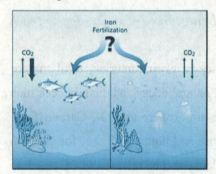

total amount of soil carbon.

11 Besides terrestrial vegetation and soil carbon sequestration, there is also a growing interest in storing carbon in underground geologic formations and possibly in the oceans. The theoretical potential for both underground and deep oceanic storage is very large. However, there are still many tough issues to be settled, including the costs, energy requirements, long-term effectiveness, and ecological consequences, especially for oceanic storage.

Vocabulary

adapt	/əˈdæpt/	vi.	(to)适应
combine	/kəmˈbain/	vt.	(使)结合/联合
component	/kəmˈpəunənt/	n.	成分,构成
conservation	/ˌkɔnsəˈveiʃən/	n.	保存,保持
continuity	/ˌkɔntiˈnjuiti/	n.	连续,继续
continuous	/kənˈtinjuəs/	a.	连续的
conventional	/kənˈvenʃənəl/	a.	常规的,传统的
conversion	/kənˈvəːʃən/	n.	变化,转化
crucial	/ˈkruːʃəl/	a.	至关重要的
decade	/ˈdekeid/	n.	十年,十
decay	/diˈkei/	n.	腐烂;衰减
desertification	/ˌdezəːtifiˈkeiʃən/	n.	沙漠化
emission	/iˈmiʃən/	n.	发射,散发
emit	/iˈmit/	vt.	发出,散发
flux	/flʌks/	n.	流量
foliage	/ˈfəuliidʒ/	n.	树叶(总称)
formation	/fɔːˈmeiʃən/	n.	构成
generate	/ˈdʒenəreit/	vt.	使产生
geographic	/ˌdʒiəˈgræfik/	a.	地理学的,地理的
geological	/dʒiˈɔlədʒikəl/	a.	地质学的,地质的
habitable	/ˈhæbitəbəl/	a.	可居住的,符合居住环境的
lumber	/ˈlʌmbə/	n.	木材
methane (CH_4)	/ˈmeθein/	n.	甲烷,沼气
millennia	/miˈleniə/	n.	一千年
modeling	/ˈmɔdliŋ/	n.	建模,造模

offset	/'ɔːfset/	vt.	抵消, 减少
photosynthesis	/ˌfəutəu'sinθəsis/	n.	光合作用
potential	/pə'tenʃəl/	n.	潜力
projected	/'prɔdʒektid/	a.	规划的, 预测的
radiation	/ˌreidi'eiʃən/	n.	辐射
remainder	/ri'meində/	n.	剩余物
reservoir	/'rezəvwaː/	n.	储存器/所; 水库
respiration	/ˌrespi'reiʃən/	n.	呼吸
sample	/'saːmpl/	vt.	取样
saturation	/ˌsætʃə'reiʃən/	n.	饱和, 饱和度
sequester	/si'kwestə/	vt.	吸收
sequestration	/si'kwestreiʃən/	n.	吸收
sink	/siŋk/	n.	水槽; 接收器
statistical	/stə'tistikəl/	a.	数据的
theoretical	/θiə'retikəl/	a.	理论的
tillage	/'tilidʒ/	n.	耕耘, 耕作
topograph	/'tɔpəgraːf;-græf/	n.	地形, 地貌; 地形学
tropical	/'trɔpikəl/	a.	热带的
variability	/ˌveəriəbiliti/	n.	可变性
human-induced			由人类导致的
nitrous oxide (N_2O)			氧化亚氮, 笑气
terrestrial vegetation			陆地植被
time scale			时间量程/范围
conservation tillage (= non-tillage)			保护性耕作法; 免耕耕作法

Vocabulary exercises

I. Match each word with its explanation.

1. ____ saturation   a. a part or an element of a system or a unit
2. ____ sequestrate   b. the condition of being full to or beyond satisfaction
3. ____ regulate   c. to adjust to a particular specification or requirement
4. ____ potential   d. to put or use (a person or thing) in place of another
5. ____ substitute   e. seize, absorb
6. ____ component   f. the inherent ability or capacity for growth, development, or coming into being.

II. Fill in each blank with the right word from the following box.

combines	greenhouse	primarily	regulate	enhance
respiration	warmer	takes up	estimate	rotational

1. When you breathe in air, it transforms (转化,转变) and when you breathe it out again it becomes Carbon Dioxide or CO_2. This process is called _____.

3. So far we've learned that carbon dioxide (CO_2) acts as the "earth's sweater." The sweater _____ help _____ our climate by trapping heat and holding it in a kind of warm air blanket that surrounds the planet.

7. Using computer climate models, scientists _____ that by the year 2100 the average global temperature will increase by 1.4 degrees to 5.8 degrees Celsius (摄氏温度).

10. In the context of climate change, mitigation (减缓) refers to a human intervention (干涉) to reduce the "sources" of greenhouse gases or _____ the "sinks" to remove carbon dioxide from the atmosphere.

Listening

Look at the following chart and then fill in the blanks with words you hear from the speaker. Meanwhile, learn where CO_2 comes from.

Out of all the CO_2 emissions in Japan, about 40 percent comes from the industrial sector such as (1) _____. _____ coming into being. _____ amount of CO_2 is (2) _____ when something is burned or machinery is operated by (3) _____ in industrial plants or factories.

The second largest emitter is the transportation sector, which (4)_____ people and goods, and accounts for about 20 percent of the CO_2 emissions. Total CO_2 emissions from cars are much larger than those from (5)_____. Although there are many trucks that carry products from factories to stores, about (6)_____ the CO_2 emissions in the transportation sector is from cars.

About 13 percent of the CO_2 emissions is from (7)_____. You also produce CO_2 from the time you get up to the time you (8)_____ (in addition to breathing). For example, you (9)_____ CO_2 by watching TV, turning on lights and air-conditioners, taking a bath, washing clothes, or cooking.

Speaking

I. Look at the following diagram (图表) and explain:

1. How does CO_2 cycle work?
2. What's carbon sequestration?

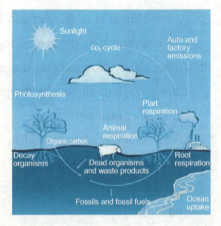

> ***Describe a process***
>
> first/firstly; secondly/then/in the next step; finally/at last
>
> after; before; when; while; as; until; at the same time; meanwhile
>
> We describe a process from the first step to the last, but we can explain a cycle from any link (环节). For this picture, we can take auto and factory emissions as a start. Eg., First, autos and factories emit CO_2 into the sky. Animals and plants also respire CO_2. Then...
>
> respire (呼吸); deposit (沉淀); circulate (循环); produce; absorb (吸收); release (释放); discharge (排放); inhale (吸入); exhale (呼出); take in; give out; soak up; take place; cycle/circulate (循环); oxygen (氧气); belowground/underground (地下的)

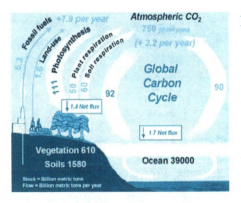

II. The following diagram shows global CO_2 flux and cycle and where the extra carbon or CO_2 comes from. The 2 broad white arrows between the ocean and the atmosphere indicate the CO_2 output and intake of the ocean, which is almost in balance. Two more billon tons of CO_2 are taken in by the ocean each year. The 3 narrow white arrows between the trees (green vegetation of the earth) and soil, and the atmosphere suggest that the vegetation and soil of the earth absorbs 111 billion tons of CO_2 and discharge 110, with 1 extra intake. The 2 red arrows on the left reveal that because of human activities such as land use and burning of fossil fuels, 7.9 extra CO_2 is emitted into the air. However, not like the ocean, the vegetation and the soil, humans can produce CO_2 but cannot sequester it. Can you so far find out anything? Please explain what and who break the balance of CO_2 fluxes in the nature.

(Note: the unit is billion tons. 1 billion tons = 1015 g. In the atmosphere, CO_2 is 99.6% of the total gases).

III. It can be seen from the following picture that productive land on the earth is used for various purposes and provide different resources for us. Please simply describe the different usages of land based on the information of the picture and the following model.

> Model
> Some lands can produce energy such as fossil fuels and they are energy lands.

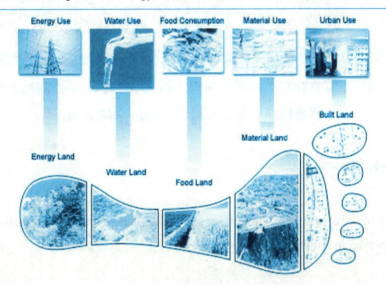

IV. The theme of 2008 World Environment Day (世界环境日, June 5th) is Kick the Habit! Towards a Low Carbon Economy! (转变传统观念，推行低碳经济！) How can we reduce CO_2 in the atmosphere?

Writing

A low carbon economy and society should be developed. Please write a passage to discuss the air-friendly measures that are taken to protect the environment in terms of cutting down CO_2 in the atmosphere.

How to Achieve a Better Environment by Cutting CO_2

Writing assistant

lead to; global warming; serious results; weather changes; natural disasters; harm; living environment; damage; human's health; as well as; urgent; governments; individuals; take measures to; reduce; CO_2 emissions; international cooperation efforts; necessary; required;

Governments: encourage; invention of more energy-efficient and energy-saving vehicles; equipments for industries; household appliances; cut down; fossil fuels; enterprises; charge high emission fees; in this case; decrease; in addition; encourage; use public transit; license plate numbers (车牌号); discourage people from; private cars; public propaganda (公众宣传); promote; people's environmental protection awareness.

Individuals: citizens; choices; clean energy; renewable energy; transboundary cooperations; necessary; share technologies, experiences, and efficient policies; lessen

Part II Farmers Cashing in on Carbon Credits Contracts with Firms Aiming to Reduce CO_2 Emissions

Warming up

I. Discussion

To reduce CO_2 in the atmosphere, more trees should be planted and no-till practices (免耕法) should be employed in crop fields.

1. If you were director of a giant oil company, would you pay for some farmers who would do the above to help reduce CO₂ produced by your company? And why?
2. Likewise, if you were a farmer, would you like being paid to plant more trees and employ no-till practices? And Why?

II. Listening

Learn the following words and phrases and then listen to a passage to answer the following questions.

Words and phrases

currently	/ˈkʌrəntli/	ad.	目前,当前
purchase	/ˈpəːtʃəs/	vt.&n.	购买
target	/ˈtɑːgit/	n.	目标
security	/siˈkjuəriti/	n.	安全
commodity	/kəˈmɔditi/	n.	商品
economic	/ˌikəˈnɔmik/	a.	经济的
set	/set/	a.	固定的,固定好的
quota	/ˈkwəutə/	n.	配额
award	/əˈwɔːd/	vt.	奖励
Carbon-Emissions Reduction(CERs)			碳减排量
Kyoto Protocol			京都议定书

Questions
1. What's the percentage does China take up in the global supply of CERs?
2. Which country is the second largest one and what's its share in the global supply of CERs?
3. When and where was the Kyoto Protocol signed?
4. If a carbon credit holder has one carbon credit, how many tons of CO₂ is he allowed to emit?
5. If a steel producer's CO₂ emission is more than its set quota, what two things can it do to meet the quota?

Reading

Farmers Cashing in on Carbon Credits—
Contracts with Firms Aiming to Reduce CO₂ Emissions

Amy Rinard

1   Increasing concern over global warming has made carbon credits, or offsets, a hot commodity.

Question 1: What are the usual measures taken to reduce CO₂ emissions? (Para. 2)

2   To lessen the warming, many countries, factories, companies, universities, individuals and even local governments begin to take actions to reduce their CO₂ emissions because they are a cause of global warming. They reduce their dependence on fossil fuels, increase the use of renewable energy, expand forests, and make lifestyle choices that help to sustain the environment. One way to reduce carbon emissions is to offset them by entering into a contract with someone who is doing something to reduce those emissions.

Question 2: How can a company earn his carbon credit? (Para. 3)

3   Essentially, if a large company wants to be a good citizen and help reduce global warming, it pledges to voluntarily reduce its CO₂ emissions by a certain amount annually. If, after doing all it can to cut emissions from its manufacturing processes and other business operations, the company still comes up short of its goal, it can pay farmers to take steps to reduce their carbon emissions—and earn credit for the reduction from what the farmer would normally have produced. It's a win-win deal.

4   In Wisconsin, USA, 400 members that have bought the contracts range from giant corporations to local governments. On the list are DuPont, Rolls-Royce, Ford Motor Co., Honeywell International Inc., Bayer Corp., Safeway Inc., IBM, Sony Electronics, Bank of America Corp., Monsanto Corp., Amtrak, Michigan State University, the states of Illinois and New Mexico and the cities of Berkeley, Calif., and Melbourne, Australia.

5   Chad Martin, a soil specialist, said the number of companies and governments buying carbon credits will only keep growing.

6 "They see the regulations coming and when they do come, they want to be able to say they're already playing an active role in reducing global warming," he said.

7 "They want to get as many feel-good points as they can."

8 The Wisconsin Farm Bureau Federation wants as many Wisconsin farmers as possible to start cashing in on the growing demand.

Question 3: What does the italic word "bureau" in line 1 mean? (Para. 9)

9 The Farm *Bureau*, the state's largest organization of farmers with more than 40,000 members, has started holding informational meetings around the state for landowners interested in selling carbon credits.

Question 4: What are the responses of companies and farmers to carbon credits, the newly emerging commodity? (Para. 10)

10 The response by farmers, so far, has been overwhelming. It's a supply and demand thing; the landowners and farmers have the supply, and the demand is coming from big corporations.

Question 5: What kind of croplands can measure up to the standards for carbon credits? (Paras. 11—14)

No-till farms qualify.

11 For cropland to qualify for carbon credits, it must be farmed with no-till or conservation tillage practices. Not tilling up the land each season means CO_2 in the soil is not released into the atmosphere.

12 A farmer has to adhere to certain specific land management practices. But many farmers in Wisconsin are already doing this and have been for some time. If farmers are already practicing no-till or conservation tillage, why not they get paid for just doing what they're already doing?

13 Rundahl, who with his two sons raises beans and corn and some cattle on their farm near La Crosse, said the family has been farming entirely with no-till and conservation tillage practices for the last 12 years and is pleased with the results. He said entering into a carbon credit contract required the family to change nothing about the way it farms. The hardest part of the process is completing the contract application, which requires verification of soil types and number of acres.

14 Credits for cropland are calculated based on soil quality and number of acres. Credits for forest land placed under contract are based on the age and species of trees. Grassland also may be placed under a carbon credit contract.

Question 6: What does the italic part in line 2 mean? (Para. 15)

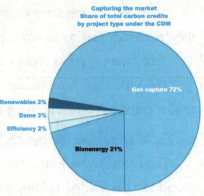

Capturing the market
Share of total carbon credits by project type under the CDM

15 Contracts run for five years, but the credit prices *are not locked in at the start*. Landowners get paid twice a year under the contract at the current price of the credits on the Climate Exchange.

16 Just like the stock market, the prices paid for carbon credits can fluctuate hourly and have ranged from 80 cents to $5 per credit since they started to be traded on the Climate Exchange in 2003. As the market grows, it would not be surprising to see a carbon credit trading for $15 by 2012.

Vocabulary

credit	/ˈkredit/	n.	信用；声望；荣誉；信任
federation	/ˌfedəˈreiʃən/	n.	联合会；联邦，联邦政府
fluctuate	/ˈflʌktʃueit/	vi.	波动，变动
Melbourne	/ˈmelbən/	n.	墨尔本(地处澳大利亚东南部)
overwhelming	/ˌəuvəˈwelmiŋ/	a.	在影响和势力上势不可挡的，不可抗拒的
pledge	/pledʒ/	vi.	(to) 保证
qualify	/ˈkwɔlifai/	vt.	使合格，使符合条件
sustain	/səˈstein/	vt.	持续；维持；支撑
verification	/ˌverifiˈkeiʃən/	n.	查证，证实
no-till		a.	免耕的
win-win		a.	双赢的
come up short of			短缺
enter into a contract			签订合同
feel-good points			感觉良好的分数
Amtrak			(美)"美铁"；美国国家铁路客运公司
Bayer Crop.			(德)拜耳公司(以药为主，多种经营)
Climate Ex Change			北美唯一一家自发组织的合法温室气体排放源和抵消源(免耕地、林木、草地等)间的贸易体系
DuPont			杜邦公司(主要经营科技产品和服务)

Ford Motor Co.	(美)福特汽车公司
Honeywell International Inc.	(加)霍韦尼尔国际公司(高新技术产品生产商)
Monsanto Corp.	(美)孟山都公司(主要经营高新农产品及技术)
Rolls-Royce	(英国)劳斯莱斯汽车公司
Safeway Inc.	(美)萨夫威连锁超市公司
Sony Electronics	(日)索尼电子公司

Vocabulary exercises

I. Finish the following exercises by the models.

1. 由人类引起的 (n. + v.ed =a.) human-induced

   以自我为中心的 _____

   以消费为导向的 _____

   与健康有关的 _____

   以经济为基础的 _____

2. biomass = biological mass

   ecosystem =

   bio-based =

   medicare =

   email =

   brunch =

   miniskirt =

3. Find words with the following prefixes as many as possible.

   bio- (biological):

   photo- (light):

   de- (reduce, degrade):

   en- (to cause to be):

   geo- (earth, geography):

   auto- (self, automatic):

II. Fill in each blank with the right word or phrase from the following box. Change the form when necessary.

be a cause of	come short of	run for	be locked in
hold information meetings	cash in on	take steps	earn credit for

1. It is a good opportunity to _____ raising pet pigs since people are nowadays crazy about special pets.

2. The contact _____ 3 years before one party finally broke it by paying a big sum of compensation (补偿, 补偿金), but without any explanation.

3. His money invested in the stock market _____ for quite a long time before the market thrived again.

4. The local environmental bureau _____ to push the enforcement of specific laws to protect the endangered wild plants and animals.

5. The Forestry Ministry _____ to declare China will make greater efforts to reduce its CO_2 emission.

6. Many agricultural projects have not be put into practice since the government _____ funds.

7. He _____ his family because of his brave performance of having saved a drowning child.

8. The driver of the car and that of the trunk both _____ the serious accident and should be criticized.

Speaking

I. Read the following introduction to carbon credit and then discuss: Has it gone public and does it have a fluctuating stock value? Please turn to the Internet and other materials for help if necessary.

A carbon credit, also known as carbon offset, is a financial instrument representing a reduction in greenhouse gas emissions. Carbon offsets are measured in metric tons of carbon dioxide-equivalent (CO_2e). One carbon offset represents the reduction of one metric ton of carbon dioxide, or its equivalent in other greenhouse

gases. Two parties are involved. Producers of carbon credits, namely, farmers, and the buyers, namely industries, governments and all entities (实体) that buy them. The more trees, grass and green crops a farmer grows and the more he uses no-till practices, the more carbon credits he earns.

II. Find out with a partner all possible means to reduce greenhouse gases and pollution, and to protect our living environment and the earth. The following pictures may be good clues.

Background Reading

What's the Kyoto Protocol?
What's carbon credit/offset?
Six Major Greenhouse Gases

Please refer to the attached disk.

Vocabulary

A

at interval 间隔 — Unit 2
a five-and-one-quarter percent chlorine solution 5.25%的氯溶液 — Unit 5
abate /əˈbeit/ vi.&vt. 使(数量，程度等)减少 — Unit 8
abbreviate /əˈbriːvieit/ vt. 缩写 — Unit 4
accelerate /əkˈseləreit/ v. 加速 — Unit 8
access /ˈækses/ n. 接近，进入；接近的机会，进入的权利；使用；通道，入口 — Unit 6
accessible /əkˈsesəbl/ a. 容易取得的，容易达到的 — Unit 9
accommodate /əˈkɔmədeit/ vt. 容纳，使适应 — Unit 2
accounting /əˈkauntiŋ/ n. 清算，核算；会计 — Unit 4
accumulate /əˈkjuːmjuleit/ vt.&vi. — Unit 1
achieve /əˈtʃiːv/ vt. 获得，达到(目标) — Unit 4
acid /ˈæsid/ n.&a. 酸；酸性的 — Unit 1
acre /ˈeikə/ n. 英亩 — Unit 7
acreage /ˈeikəridʒ/ n. 英亩数 — Unit 1
adapt /əˈdæpt/ vi. (to)适应 — Unit 10
additive /ˈæditiv/ n. — Unit 1
adequate /ˈædikwit/ a. 适当的，足够的 — Unit 2
advance /ədˈvɑːns/ vt. 提出 — Unit 4
advocate /ˈædvəkit/ vt. 提倡，鼓吹 — Unit 8
advocator /ˈædvəkeitə/ n. 拥护者，提倡者 — Unit 2
aeration /ˌeiəˈreiʃən/ n. 通风 — Unit 2
aeroponic /ˌɛərəuˈpɔnik/ a. 太空的 — Unit 2
aesthetically /iːsˈθetikəli/ ad. 审美地，美学地 — Unit 1
affordable /əˈfɔːdəbl/ a. 能担负得起的；买得起的 — Unit 5
agent /ˈeidʒənt/ n. 制剂 — Unit 3
agro-tourism /ˈægrətuəriəzəm/ n. 农业生态旅游 — Unit 6
agrobacterium tumefaciens 根癌土壤杆菌 — Unit 3
agrochemical /ˌægrəuˈkemikəl/ n. 农药 — Unit 1
alarmingly /əˈlɑːmiŋli/ ad. 令人担忧地 — Unit 8
alder /ˈɔːldə(r)/ n. 桤木 — Unit 8
allowable /əˈlauəbəl/ a. 可准许的 — Unit 5
alteration /ˌɔːltəˈreiʃən/ n. 变更，改造 — Unit 2
alternative /ɔːlˈtəːnətiv/ a.&n. 二者可选其一的(事物) — Unit 2
altitude /ˈæltitjuːd/ n. 高度，高地，海拔 — Unit 9
Amazon rainforest 亚马逊热带雨林 — Unit 8
amino /əˈmiːnəu/ a. 氨基的 — Unit 3
Amtrak (美)"美铁"；美国国家铁路客运公司 — Unit 10
anaerobic digestion 厌氧消化 — Unit 8
analytical /ˌænəˈlitikəl/ a. 分析的 — Unit 5
antibiotic /ˌæntibaiˈɔtik/ n.&a. 抗生素(的) — Unit 5
antioxidant /ˌæntiˈɔksidənt/ n. 抗氧化剂 — Unit 2
appeal /əˈpiːl/ n. 吸引力 — Unit 5
appliance /əˈplaiəns/ n. 用具，器具 — Unit 4
appropriate /əˈprəupriət/ a. 适当的 — Unit 2
approve /əˈpruːv/ vt. 赞同，核准，证实 — Unit 3
aquaculture /ˈækwəˌkʌltʃə/ n. 水产业 — Unit 3
aquatic /əˈkwætik/ a. — Unit 1
architect /ˈɑːkitekt/ n. 建筑师 — Unit 7
architecture /ˈɑːkitektʃə/ n. 建筑学 — Unit 7
artificial /ˌɑːtiˈfiʃəl/ a. 人工的 — Unit 2
assess /əˈses/ vt. 估定(数量，价值等) — Unit 4
asset /ˈæset/ n. 资源，资产 — Unit 4
assimilate /əˈsimileit/ vt. 同化；吸收 — Unit 3
asthma /ˈæsmə/ n. 哮喘 — Unit 4
atmospheric cycle 大气循环 — Unit 9
automated /ˈɔːtəmeitid/ a. 自动化的 — Unit 2
autonomous /ɔːˈtɔnəməs/ a. 自治的；自治权的；自主的 — Unit 6
availability /əˌveiləˈbiliti/ n. 可用性 — Unit 8
available /əˈveiləbl/ a. 可用的，可得到的 — Unit 1
average /ˈævəridʒ/ a. 平均的 — Unit 4
award /əˈwɔːd/ vt. 奖励 — Unit 10

B

Bacillus thuringiensis (Bt) 昆虫病原细菌苏云金杆菌 — Unit 3

Vocabulary

backup /ˈbækʌp/ n. 备用	Unit 7
bacteria /bækˈtiəriə/ n. 细菌	Unit 7
bacterium /bækˈtiəriəm/ n. 细菌(复数 bacteria)	Unit 3
balanced /ˈbælənst/ a. 平衡的	Unit 4
baled /beild/ a. 打包的	Unit 8
bark /bɑːk/ n. 树皮	Unit 2
barren /ˈbærən/ a. 贫瘠的	Unit 4
barrier /ˈbæriə/ n. 障碍物,屏障	Unit 8
Bayer Crop. (德)拜耳公司(以药为主,多种经营)	Unit 10
BBI Produce Inc. in Dover (美国)多佛 BBI 农产品生产公司,创立于 1990 年,主要生产 "Berry Boss" 牌草莓,现为佛罗里达州最大的草莓生产和供应商。	Unit 2
be attached to... 附属于,附着于	Unit 9
be disinfected with chemicals 用化学药品消毒	Unit 5
be exposed to 遭受,使曝露于……,使接触……	Unit 2
be involved in 涉及	Unit 7
be singled out 被挑选出	Unit 5
be superior to 优越于……	Unit 2
bean /biːn/ n. 豆类	Unit 1
biodegradable /ˌbaiəudiˈgreidəbəl/ a. 可生物降解的	Unit 8
biodiversity /ˌbaiəudaiˈvəːsiti/ n. 生物多样性	Unit 1
biomass /ˈbaiəumæs/ n. (单位面积或体积内)生物的数量	Unit 8
biorefinery /ˌbaiəriˈfainəri/ n. 生物炼油厂	Unit 8
biosafety /ˌbaiəuˈseifti/ n. 生物安全	Unit 3
biosphere /ˈbaiəsfiə/ n. 生物圈	Unit 4
bird flu 禽流感	Unit 5
bird-watching (在大自然中)观察研究野鸟	Unit 6
blemish /ˈblemiʃ/ n. 缺点,瑕疵	Unit 2
bole /bəul/ n. 树干,树身	Unit 8
bonus /ˈbəunəs/ n. 红利,额外收获	Unit 1
boom /buːm/ n. 繁荣	Unit 8
boon /buːn/ n. 恩惠,实惠	Unit 8
bounce /bauns/ vi.&vt. 弹回	Unit 9
Brazilian /brəˈziliən/ a.&n. 巴西的;巴西人	Unit 6
break down 分解	Unit 5
breed /briːd/ n.&vt. 物种;繁殖	Unit 3
British Petroleum 英国石油公司	Unit 8
Bt 抗虫基因	Unit 3
buckwheat /ˈbʌkwiːt/ n. 荞麦属植物	Unit 1
burgeon /ˈbəːdʒən/ n.&vi. 迅速发展	Unit 9
butanol /ˈbjutənəul/ n. 丁醇	Unit 8
byproduct /ˈbaiˌprɔdʌkt/ n. 副产品	Unit 5

C

canopy /ˈkænəpi/ n. 树冠,罩棚,华盖	Unit 9
capacity /kəˈpæsiti/ n. 生产量;容量	Unit 4
capitalize /ˈkæpitlaiz/ vt. 用大写字母写	Unit 4
capture /ˈkæptʃə/ vt. 捕获	Unit 7
Carbon-Emissions Reduction(CERs) 碳减排量	Unit 10
carbon-induced a. 由碳导致的	Unit 4
carbonhydrate /ˌkɑːbəuˈhaidreit/ n.&a. 碳水化合物(的)	Unit 8
carving /ˈkɑːviŋ/ n. 雕刻;雕刻品	Unit 6
caterpillar /ˈkætəˌpilə/ n. 毛虫	Unit 3
cellulosic /ˌseljuˈləusik/ a. 有纤维质的	Unit 8
center /ˈsentə/ vi.&vt. 居中,使……聚在一点,以……为中心	Unit 9
certifier /ˈsəːtifiə/ n. 见证者	Unit 7
chain store 连锁店	Unit 5
challenge /ˈtʃælindʒ/ n. 挑战	Unit 2
characteristic /ˌkæriktəˈristik/ n.&a. 特点,特征;特有的,典型的	Unit 1
chemical /ˈkemikəl/ n. 化学制品;化学药品	Unit 6
chlorine, iodine or bromine 氯,碘酒或溴	Unit 5
chlorophyll /ˈklɔrəfil/ n. 叶绿素	Unit 9
chromosome /ˈkrəuməsəum/ n. 染色体	Unit 3
circular /ˈsəːkjulə/ a. 圆形的	Unit 7
civil and criminal prosecution 民事和刑事诉讼	Unit 5
clear /kliə/ vi. 扫除,清除	Unit 8
Climate Ex Change 北美唯一一家自发组织的合法温室气体排放源和抵消源(免耕地、林木、草地等)间的贸易体系	Unit 10
clone /kləun/ vt. 克隆	Unit 3
code /kəud/ n. 法规	Unit 5
collaboration /kəˌlæbəˈreiʃən/ n. 合作	Unit 8
collapsing /kəˈlæpsiŋ/ a. 崩溃的,倒塌的	Unit 4
collective /kəˈlektiv/ a. 集体的	Unit 4
colonist /ˈkɔlənist/ n. 殖民主义者	Unit 1
combine /kəmˈbain/ vt. (使)结合/联合	Unit 10
combustion engine 内燃机	Unit 8
come up short of 短缺	Unit 10

commercialization /kəˌmɜːʃəlaiˈzeiʃn/ n. 商品化 Unit 3
commercially /kəˈmɜːʃəli/ ad. 商业上 Unit 2
commissioner /kəˈmiʃənə/ n. 委员, 专员 Unit 5
commitment /kəˈmitmənt/ n. 许诺, 承担义务 Unit 5
commodity /kəˈmɔditi/ n. 商品 Unit 10
community-based tourism 乡村生态旅游 Unit 6
compare /kəmˈpeə/ vt. (with / to) 比较 Unit 4
comparison /kəmˈpærisən/ n. 比较, 对照 Unit 5
compete with 和……竞争 Unit 8
complex /ˈkɔmpleks/ a. 复杂的 Unit 4
compliance /kəmˈplaiəns/ n. 依从, 顺从 Unit 5
complicated /ˈkɔmplikeitid/ a. 难懂的, 复杂的 Unit 9
component /kəmˈpəunənt/ n. 成分, 构成 Unit 10
composition /ˌkɔmpəˈziʃn/ n. 组成, 合成物, 成份 Unit 3
compost /ˈkɔmpɔst/ n. 混合肥料, 堆肥 Unit 2
compound /ˈkɔmpaund/ a. 综合的, 复杂的 Unit 4
compress /kəmˈpres/ n. 压缩 Unit 8
concept /ˈkɔnsept/ n. 观念, 概念 Unit 4
concern /kənˈsɜːn/ n.&v. 关注 Unit 5
concrete /ˈkɔnkriːt/ n. 混凝土 Unit 7
conduct /kənˈdʌkt/ vt.&vi. 进行 Unit 2
conservation /ˌkɔnsəˈveiʃn/ n. 保存, 保持 Unit 10
conservation /ˌkɔnsəˈveiʃn/ n. 保护, 保存 Unit 9
conservation tillage (= non-tillage) 保护性耕作法; 免耕耕作法 Unit 10
conservation-oriented 节约(能)型的 Unit 6
conserve /kənˈsɜːv/ vt. 保护, 保存 Unit 1
consistent /kənˈsistənt/ a. 一贯的, 一致的 Unit 3
constantly /ˈkɔnstəntli/ a. 持续地 Unit 7
consume /kənˈsjuːm/ vt. 消耗, 消费 Unit 4
consumer /kənˈsjuːmə/ n. 消费者, 用户 Unit 3
consummation /ˌkɔnsəˈmeiʃn/ n. 消费 Unit 7
consumption /kənˈsʌmpʃn/ n. 消费 Unit 4
contaminant /kənˈtæminənt/ n. 污染物 Unit 5
contaminate /kənˈtæmineit/ vt. 弄脏, 污染 Unit 3
contamination /kənˈtæmineiʃn/ n. 污染 Unit 5
continuity /ˌkɔntiˈnjuiti/ n. 连续, 继续 Unit 10
continuous /kənˈtinjuəs/ a. 连续的 Unit 10
contribute /kənˈtribjuːt/ vi. 有助于, 促成 Unit 3
conventional /kənˈvenʃənəl/ a. 常规的, 传统的 Unit 10

conventionally /kənˈvenʃənəli/ ad. 按照惯例地, 照常套地 Unit 2
conversion /kənˈvɜːʃn/ n. 变换, 转化 Unit 8
convert /kənˈvɜːt/ vt. (使)转变 Unit 8
coordinate /kəuˈɔːdinit/ vt. 使协调 Unit 1
correlation /ˌkɔriˈleiʃn/ n. 相互关联 Unit 9
corrosive /kəˈrəusiv/ a. 腐蚀的 Unit 8
Costa Rica 哥斯达黎加[拉丁美洲] Unit 9
coverage /ˈkʌvəridʒ/ n. 覆盖范围, 报道量 Unit 9
craft /krɑːft/ n. 工艺(品); 手艺 Unit 6
credit /ˈkredit/ n. 信用; 声望; 荣誉; 信任 Unit 10
crisis /ˈkraisis/ n. 危机(复数 crises) Unit 7
crooked /ˈkrukid/ a. 弯曲的 Unit 8
crop picker 作物采摘机 Unit 7
crucial /ˈkruːʃəl/ a. 至关重要的 Unit 10
cucumber /ˈkjuːkʌmbə/ n. 黄瓜 Unit 2
cull /kʌl/ n. 杂质 Unit 8
cultivate /ˈkʌltiveit/ vt. 耕种, 耕作 Unit 7
curbside /ˈkɜːbsaid/ n. 路边, 街头 Unit 4
curiosity /ˌkjuəriˈɔsiti/ n. 好奇心 Unit 4
currently /ˈkʌrəntli/ ad. 目前, 眼下 Unit 6
custom-built /ˈkʌstəmˈbilt/ a. 定制的, 定做的 Unit 3

D

date back to... 追溯到…… Unit 9
decade /ˈdekeid/ n. 十年, 十 Unit 10
decay /diˈkei/ n. 腐烂; 衰减 Unit 10
deciduous /diˈsidʒjuəs/ a. 每年落叶的 Unit 9
decompose /ˌdiːkəmˈpəuz/ vt. 变坏, 分解 Unit 1
decorative /ˈdekərətiv/ a. 装饰的 Unit 2
dedicate /ˈdedikeit/ vt. (为某一特殊用途)奉献 Unit 4
defective /diˈfektiv/ a. 有缺陷的, 有欠缺的 Unit 8
deficiency /diˈfiʃnsi/ n. 缺乏, 不足 Unit 2
deficit /ˈdefisit/ n. 赤字, 亏损 Unit 4
deforestation /diːˌfɔriˈsteiʃn/ n. 森林采伐 Unit 4
degradation /ˌdegrəˈdeiʃn/ n. 降格, 退化 Unit 5
demanding /diˈmɑːndiŋ/ a. 苛求的; 要求高的 Unit 6
demographic /ˌdeməˈgræfik/ a. 人口统计学的 Unit 5
dense /dens/ a. 密集的, 浓厚的 Unit 8
deny pests a place to live 以防有害动植物的滋生 Unit 5
Department of Pesticide Regulation (DPR) (美

Vocabulary

国)农药管理局   Unit 5
deplete /diˈpliːt/ vt. 耗尽,使衰竭   Unit 4
deregulation /ˌdiːregjuleiʃən/ n. 违反规定, 反常   Unit 8
derive /diˈraiv/ vi. (from) 得自,由……来   Unit 8
desertification /ˌdezətifiˈkeiʃən/ n. 沙漠化   Unit 10
designated /ˈdezigneitid/ a. 指定的   Unit 6
desirable /diˈzaiərəbəl/ a. 令人想要的,希望的   Unit 3
destination /ˌdestiˈneiʃən/ n. 目的地   Unit 4
detect /diˈtekt/ vt. (a. detectable)探测,查明, 发现   Unit 9
detectable /diˈtektəbl/ a. 可发觉的   Unit 5
deteriorate /diˈtiəriəreit/ v. (使)恶化   Unit 8
determinate /diˈtəːminit/ a. 确定的   Unit 2
diarrhea /ˌdaiəˈriə/ n. 痢疾,腹泻   Unit 5
diesel /ˈdiːzəl/ n. 柴油   Unit 8
differentiate /ˌdifəˈrenʃieit/ vt.&vi. 区别,区分, 鉴别   Unit 6
dignity /ˈdigniti/ n. 尊严;尊贵   Unit 6
disarm /disˈɑːm/ vt. 解除,摘除   Unit 3
discipline /ˈdisiplin/ n. 学科   Unit 7
disparity /disˈspæriti/ n. (数量、质量等)不一致, 不等   Unit 4
displacement /disˈpleismənt/ n. 转移,移植   Unit 8
disposal /disˈpəuzəl/ n. 处理,处置   Unit 8
dispute /diˈspjuːt/ n. 争论   Unit 7
distribute /disˈtribjuːt/ vt. 分配,散播   Unit 1
distribution /ˌdistriˈbjuːʃən/ n. 分配   Unit 4
distributor /disˈtribjutə/ n. 发行人,产品配送人   Unit 1
DNA (deoxyribonucleic acid) 脱氧核糖核酸   Unit 3
documented /ˈdɔkjuməntid/ a. 备有证明文件的   Unit 5
dome /dəum/ n. 圆顶   Unit 2
domestically /dəˈmestikəli/ ad. 家庭式地,国内地   Unit 5
domesticate /dəˈmestikeit/ vt. 驯养,驯化   Unit 3
dominate /ˈdɔmineit/ vt. 支配,控制   Unit 4
donation /dəuˈneiʃən/ n. 捐赠品   Unit 4
drain /drein/ vt.&vi. 排水,引流   Unit 2
dramatically /drəˈmætikli/ ad. 剧烈地   Unit 9
drastically /ˈdræstikəli/ ad. 彻底地,激烈地   Unit 4
drip emitter 滴灌发射器   Unit 2
drip irrigation 滴灌   Unit 2
drought /draut/ n. 干旱   Unit 3

dry up 干涸;用尽   Unit 6
DuPont 杜邦公司(主要经营科技产品和服务)   Unit 8
dynamic /daiˈnæmik/ a. 有活力的,动态的   Unit 1

E

earthworm /ˈəːθwəːm/ n. 蚯蚓   Unit 1
Ebb and flow 潮差无土栽培法   Unit 2
EC: Electrical Conductivity 电导率   Unit 2
ecolodge /ˌiːkəuˈlɔdʒ/ n. 生态度假村,生态旅店   Unit 6
ecological /ˌiːkəˈlɔdʒikəl/ a. 生态学的   Unit 2
ecology /iˈkɔlədʒi/ n. 生态(学)   Unit 1
economic /ˌikəˈnɔmik/ a. 经济的   Unit 10
economical /ˌiːkəˈnɔmikəl/ a. 节约的,经济的   Unit 2
economics /ˌekəˈnɔmiks/ n. 经济情况,财务情况   Unit 8
ecosystem /ˈiːkəuˌsistəm/ n. 生态系统   Unit 1
ecotourism-related ventures 生态旅游相关企业   Unit 6
effectively /iˈfektivli/ ad. 有效地   Unit 6
efficiency /iˈfiʃənsi/ n. 效率,效能   Unit 1
efficiently /iˈfiʃəntli/ ad. 有效率的,高效的   Unit 8
effluent /ˈefluənt/ n. 废物,废水   Unit 8
electromagnetic spectrum 电磁波频谱   Unit 9
elevate /ˈeliveit/ vt. 增加;举高   Unit 3
embryo /ˈembriəu/ n. 胚胎   Unit 3
emission /iˈmiʃən/ n. 排放物   Unit 4
emit /iˈmit/ vt. 发射出,排放出   Unit 4
emulate /ˈemjuleit/ vt. 与……竞争   Unit 1
encode /inˈkəud/ vt. 编码   Unit 3
endanger /inˈdeindʒə/ vt. 危及   Unit 8
endangered /inˈdeindʒəd/ a. 濒临灭绝的   Unit 6
endeavor /inˈdevə/ n. 努力,尽力   Unit 7
energy mix 能源构成   Unit 8
energy plantation 能源林   Unit 8
enforce federal rules 执行联邦政府的规则   Unit 5
enforcement /inˈfɔːsmənt/ n. 执行,强制   Unit 5
engineer /ˌendʒiˈniə/ vt.&n. 操纵,设计;工程师   Unit 3
enhance /inˈhɑːns/ vt. 提高,增强   Unit 5
ensure /inˈʃuə/ vt. 确保,担保   Unit 1
enter into a contract 签订合同   Unit 10
environmental governance 环境监管   Unit 4
environmentalist /inˌvairənˈmentəlist/ n. 环境保护者   Unit 8

enzyme /'enzaim/ n. 酶	Unit 3
equate /i'kweit/ vi. 等同	Unit 5
equitably /'ekwitəbli/ ad. 公正地	Unit 4
equity /'ekwiti/ n. 公平,公正	Unit 1
equivalent /i'kwivələnt/ a. 相等的	Unit 5
erosion /i'rəuʒən/ n. 腐蚀	Unit 1
ERS-SAR (Earth Resources Satellite- Safety Analysis Report) 地球资源卫星—安全分析报告	Unit 9
estimate /'estimeit/ vt.&n. 估计,评估	Unit 4
ethanol /'eθɔnɔ:l/ n. 乙醇,酒精	Unit 8
ethnic /'eθnik/ a.&n. 种族,少数民族,异数的	Unit 6
evaluate /i'væljueit/ vt. 评估,估价 (n. evaluation)	Unit 3
evaporate /i'væpəreit/ v. (使)蒸发,消失	Unit 8
evolution /ˌi:və'lu:ʃən/ n. 进化,发展,进展	Unit 3
exacerbate /ig'zæsəbeit/ vt. 使恶化,使加剧	Unit 4
exceed /ik'si:d/ vt. 超出,超越	Unit 4
excess /ik'ses, 'ekses/ a.&n. 过多的,额外的;过量	Unit 1
excessive /ik'sesiv/ a. 过度的,过分的	Unit 1
exhaust fan 排气风扇,抽风机	Unit 2
expedition /ˌekspi'diʃən/ n. 远征(队),探险(队),考察(队)	Unit 6
exploit /ik'sploit/ vt. 剥削,利用,开发,开采	Unit 5
exposure /ik'spəuʒə/ n. 受影响,暴露	Unit 5
extend /ik'stend/ vt.&vi. 扩充,延伸	Unit 5
external /ik'stə:nl/ a. 外部的,外观的	Unit 1

F

facility /fə'siləti/ n. 设备,设施;(供特定用途的)场所	Unit 6
fauna /'fɔ:nə/ n. 动物群	Unit 6
feasible /'fi:zibəl/ a. 可行的	Unit 9
feature /'fi:tʃə/ n. 特征,特色	Unit 6
federal /'fedərəl/ a. 联邦的,中央政府的	Unit 5
federation /ˌfedə'reiʃən/ n. 联合会;联邦,联邦政府	Unit 10
feed /fi:d/ n. 饲料	Unit 3
feedstock /'fi:dstɔk/ n. 给料(供送入机器或加工厂的原料)	Unit 8
feel-good points 感觉良好的分数	Unit 10
fermentation /ˌfə:men'teiʃən/ n. 发酵	Unit 8
fertility /fə'tiliti/ n. 肥沃,丰产	Unit 2
fertilization /ˌfə:tilai'zeiʃən/ n. 施肥,授精	Unit 2
fertilize /'fə:tilaiz/ vt. 给……施肥	Unit 1
fertilized ovum 受精卵	Unit 3
fertilizer /'fə:tiˌlaizə/ n. 肥料,化肥	Unit 1
filter /'filtə/ n.&vt. 过滤器;过滤	Unit 7
fishery /'fiʃəri/ n. 渔业,水产业	Unit 4
flora /'flɔ:rə/ n. 植物群(尤指某一地区或某一时期的植物群)	Unit 6
fluctuate /'flʌktʃueit/ vi. 波动,变动	Unit 10
flux /flʌks/ n. 流量	Unit 10
fodder /'fɔdə/ n. 饲料,草料	Unit 8
foliage /'fəuliidʒ/ n. 树叶(总称)	Unit 10
Food and Agriculture Organization of the United Nations (FAO) 联合国粮农组织	
Food and Drug Administration (FDA) 美国食品药品管理局	Unit 5
food containers 贮存食物的容器	Unit 5
foodborne disease 食源性疾病	Unit 5
for the sake of 为了……好处(利益)	Unit 4
Ford Motor Co. (美)福特汽车公司	Unit 10
forest stand 林分,林段	Unit 9
formation /fɔ:'meiʃən/ n. 构成	Unit 10
formulate /'fɔ:mjuleit/ vt. 构想,规划,阐述	Unit 1
forum /'fɔ:rəm/ n. 论坛	Unit 3
fossil /'fɔsəl/ n. 化石	Unit 8
fossil fuel 化石燃料	Unit 8
fragile /'frædʒail/ a. 易碎的,脆的;易损坏的;脆弱的	Unit 6
fragmentation /ˌfrægmenteiʃən/ n. 分割,破碎	Unit 9
frailty /'freilti/ n. 脆弱,虚弱	Unit 6
free-living organism 非寄生生物	Unit 1
frequency /'fri:kwənsi/ n. 频率,频繁	Unit 9
frequently /'fri:kwəntli/ a. 常常,频繁地	Unit 5
fund /fʌnd/ n.&vt. 资金,基金,专款提供(事业,活动等的)资金	Unit 6
furnace /'fə:nis/ n. 炉子,熔炉	Unit 8

G

gallon /'gælən/ n. 加仑	Unit 5
gasoline /'gæsəli:n/ n. 汽油	Unit 8
gauge /geidʒ/ n.&vt. 尺度,标准;测量	Unit 4
generate /'dʒenəreit/ vt. 使产生	Unit 4

Vocabulary

genetic modification 转基因   Unit 5
genetically modified (GM) 转基因的   Unit 3
genetics /dʒi'netiks/ n. 遗传学   Unit 7
geographic /ˌdʒiə'græfik/ a. 地理学的, 地理的   Unit 10
geographically /ˌdʒi:ə'græfikəli/ ad. 地理学地, 地理地   Unit 4
geological /dʒi'ɔlədʒikəl/ a. 地质学的, 地质的   Unit 10
germ cells 生殖细胞   Unit 3
global /'gləubəl/ a. 全球的   Unit 5
global hectare (gha) 全球公顷 (1gha=2.47 acres< 英亩 >)   Unit 4
gravel /'grævəl/ a. 碎石的, 沙砾的   Unit 4
gravel substrate 沙砾培养基   Unit 2
grease /gri:s/ n. 油脂   Unit 8
greenhouse /'gri:nhaus/ n. 温室   Unit 3
ground sampling 地面采样   Unit 9
gumweed /'gʌmwud/ n. 胶草   Unit 8

H

habitable /'hæbitəbəl/ a. 可居住的, 符合居住环境的   Unit 10
habitat /'hæbitæt/ n. 栖息地, 住处   Unit 1
HACCP (Hazard Analysis Critical Control Point) 危害分析关键控制点   Unit 5
hail /heil/ n. 雹子   Unit 9
hands-on 亲自动手的, 躬亲的   Unit 6
harmony /'hɑ:məni/ n. 协调, 和谐   Unit 4
hazard /'hæzəd/ n. 危险   Unit 5
herbicide /'hə:bisaid/ n. 除草剂   Unit 3
herbicide /'hə:bisaid/ n. 除草剂   Unit 9
heritage /'heritidʒ/ n. 遗产, 继承物, 传统   Unit 6
high-level 高阶层的   Unit 5
High-level International Food Safety Forum 国际食品安全高层论坛   Unit 5
high-yielding a. 高产的   Unit 8
hiking /'haikiŋ/ n. 徒步旅行   Unit 6
Honeywell International Inc. (加)霍韦尼尔国际公司(高新技术产品生产商)   Unit 10
hormone /'hɔ:məun/ n. 荷尔蒙, 激素   Unit 5
hormone /'hɔ:məun/ n. 激素   Unit 3
horticulturalist /'hɔ:tikʌltʃərəlist/ n. 园艺家   Unit 2
household /'haushəuld/ n. 一家人; 家庭, 户   Unit 6

human-induced 由人类导致的   Unit 10
humanity /hju:'mæniti/ n. 人类   Unit 4
hybrid /'haibrid/ n. 杂种, 混合物   Unit 8
hydrogen /'haidrədʒən/ n. 氢气   Unit 7
hydroponics /'haidrəu'pɔniks/ n. 水耕法, 水栽培   Unit 2

I

identify /ai'dentifai/ vt. 认出, 识别   Unit 9
illegal /i'li:gəl/ a. 违法的, 不合规定的   Unit 5
imagery /'imidʒəri/ n. 意象, 塑像, 画像   Unit 9
impact /'impækt/ n. 影响, 作用, 冲击   Unit 1
implementation /ˌimplimen'teiʃən/ n. 实施, 执行   Unit 7
implication /ˌimpli'keiʃən/ n. 含意, 暗示   Unit 5
imported /'impɔ:tid/ a. 进口的   Unit 5
improperly /im'prɔpəli/ ad. 不适当地   Unit 5
in accordance with 依照   Unit 7
in direct proportion to 与……成正比   Unit 4
in harmony with... 与……和谐共处   Unit 6
in most cases 在大多数情况下   Unit 9
in terms of 在……的方面   Unit 7
incorporate /in'kɔ:pəreit/ vt. 包含, 合并   Unit 1
incorporate /in'kɔ:pəreit/ vi.&a. 合并; 合并的   Unit 3
indeterminate /ˌindi'tə:minit/ a. 不确定的   Unit 2
indicator /'indikeitə/ n. 指示器, 指示物   Unit 9
indigenous /in'didʒənəs/ a. 本土的, 固有的   Unit 1
indivisible /ˌindi'vizəbəl/ a. 不可分的   Unit 1
indulge /in'dʌldʒ/ vt.&vi. 沉迷于; 放纵   Unit 6
inert media /i'nə:t 'mi:diə/ n. 惰性的媒介   Unit 2
infancy /'infənsi/ n. 幼年   Unit 2
infant /'infənt/ n. 婴儿, 幼儿   Unit 5
infection /in'fekʃən/ n. 传染, 影响, 传染病   Unit 3
infestation /in'festeiʃən/ n. (v. infest)(害虫/盗贼等)群袭出没   Unit 9
infiltration /ˌinfil'treiʃən/ n. 渗透   Unit 1
influx /'inflʌks/ n. 涌进, 流入, 注入   Unit 6
infrared /ˌinfrə'red/ a. 红外(线)的   Unit 9
initial capital 创办资本, 启动资金   Unit 2
initiate /i'niʃieit/ vt. 开始, 创始, 开始实施   Unit 6
innovative /'inəu,veitiv/ a. 创新的   Unit 1
insecticide /in'sektisaid/ n. 杀虫剂   Unit 2
insertion /in'sə:ʃən/ n. (基因)嵌入   Unit 3

insoluble /in'sɔljubəl/ a. 不溶解的 Unit 1
install /in'stɔːl/ vt. 安装 Unit 4
intact /in'tækt/ a. 完整无缺的,未受损伤的 Unit 6
integrate /'intigreit/ vt.&vi. (使)成为整体,
　(使)融入 Unit 9
integrated /'intigreitid/ a. 综合的 Unit 2
intensity /in'tensiti/ n. 强烈,强度 Unit 8
intentional /in'tenʃənəl/ a. 有意识的 Unit 4
interaction /ˌintər'ækʃən/ n. (v. interact) 相互
　作用,合作 Unit 4
interfere /ˌintə'fiə/ vi. 妨碍,冲突 Unit 3
internal /in'təːnl/ a. 内部的,内政的,体内的 Unit 1
International Energy Agency Bioenergy
　Agreement 国际能源机构《生物能源协定》 Unit 8
invade /in'veid/ vt. 侵略 Unit 7
inventory /'invəntəri/ n. 存货,存量 Unit 8
investment /in'vestmənt/ n. 投资 Unit 7
irrigation /ˌiri'geiʃən/ n. 灌溉 Unit 2
isolate /'aisəleit/ vt. 使隔离,使孤立 Unit 9
isolated /'aisəleitid/ a. 孤立的,(被)隔离的 Unit 6
isolation /ˌaisə'leiʃən/ n. 分离,隔离 Unit 3
jaguar /'dʒægjuə/ n. (中南美洲的)美洲虎 Unit 9
jurisdiction /ˌdʒuəris'dikʃən/ n. 权限 Unit 5
justice /'dʒʌstis/ n. 公平,公道 Unit 4

K

Kyoto Protocol 京都议定书 Unit 10

L

label /'leibəl/ n.&vt. 标签,签条;贴标签于,
　分类 Unit 3
land cover 土地覆盖 Unit 9
Landsat /'lændsæt/ n. (美国)地球(资源探测)
　卫星 Unit 9
Landsat Thematic Mapper 地球资源探测卫星
　专题制图仪 Unit 9
landscape /'lændskeip/ n. 风景,景观,地形 Unit 1
larch /lɑːtʃ/ n. 落叶松属植物 Unit 8
Latin America 拉丁美洲 Unit 6
layer /'leiə/ n. 层,层次 Unit 9
leach /liːtʃ/ vt. 沥滤 Unit 1
legislative /'ledʒislətiv/ n.&a. 立法(的),立
　法机关(的) Unit 5

legume /'legjuːm/ n. 豆类,豆荚 Unit 1
lettuce /'letis/ n. 莴苣,生菜 Unit 2
liberate /'libəreit/ vt. 解放,释放 Unit 1
license /'laisəns/ n.&vt. 许可(证),(发)执照 Unit 5
liquidate /'likwideit/ vt. 清理,清算 Unit 4
livelihood /'laivlihud/ n. 维持生命所需的东西 Unit 4
livestock /'laivstɔk/ n. 家畜,牲畜 Unit 3
logging /'lɔgiŋ/ n. 伐木,采伐 Unit 8
lubricity /ljuː'brisiti/ n. 光滑,润滑 Unit 8
lumber /'lʌmbə/ n. 木材 Unit 8
lupine /'ljuːpin/ n. 羽扇豆 Unit 1
luxury /'lʌkʃəri/ n. 奢侈品 Unit 4

M

mad cow disease (BSE) 疯牛病 Unit 5
maintenance /'meintənəns/ n. 维修,维护 Unit 1
maize /meiz/ n. 玉米 Unit 3
majority /mə'dʒɔriti/ n. 多数,大多数 Unit 6
make a list of pest control measures 列出有害
　动植物防治措施 Unit 5
make a loss 亏损 Unit 6
make way for 为……让路 Unit 8
malfunction /mæl'fʌŋkʃən/ vi. 运转不正常 Unit 2
malnutrition /ˌmælnjuː'triʃən/ n. 营养不良 Unit 3
manipulation /məˌnipju'leit/ n. 控制 Unit 3
manufacture /ˌmænju'fæktʃə/ vt. 制造,加工 Unit 8
manufacturer /ˌmænju'fæktʃərə/ n. 生产商 Unit 5
manure /mə'njuə/ n. 肥料 Unit 8
maple /'meipəl/ n. 枫,枫树 Unit 8
margin of safety 超过实际要求的安全系数 Unit 5
marginal /'mɑːdʒinəl/ a. 边缘的 Unit 8
marine /mə'riːn/ a. 海的,海运的,海事的 Unit 1
mass /mæs/ n.&a. 大量;大规模的 Unit 5
mass tourism 大批游客旅游(游客同时涌
　入同一个旅游点) Unit 6
maximize /'mæksimaiz/ vt. 最佳化,最大化 Unit 2
maximum /'mæksiməm/ n. 最大量,最大限度 Unit 2
means /miːnz/ n. 资源物力;财力;方法 Unit 4
meaty /'miːti/ a. 肉的 Unit 2
medicinal /me'disənəl/ a. 医学的 Unit 3
Melbourne /'melbən/ n. 墨尔本(地处澳大利
　亚东南部) Unit 10
methane (CH4) /'meθein/ n. 甲烷,沼气 Unit 8

microbe /ˈmaikrəub/ n. 微生物, 细菌		Unit 5
microbiology /ˌmaikrəubaiˈɔlədʒi/ n. 微生物学		Unit 7
microinject /ˌmaikrəuinˈdʒekt/ vt. 显微注射		Unit 3
micrometer /maiˈkrɔmitə/ n. 微米, 测微计		Unit 9
migration /maiˈgreiʃən/ n. 移民, 迁移		Unit 5
milkweed /ˈmilkwiːd/ n. 乳草属植物		Unit 8
mill /mil/ n. (木材) 碾磨加工		Unit 8
millennia /miˈleniə/ n. 一千年		Unit 10
mine /main/ n.&vt. 矿, 矿井; 开矿		Unit 6
mineral /ˈminərəl/ n. 矿物, 矿石		Unit 4
miniature /ˈminətʃə/ a. 缩小的, 微型的		Unit 2
minimal /ˈminiməl/ a. 最小的, 最小限度的		Unit 4
minimize /ˈminimaiz/ vt. 最小化		Unit 5
minor /ˈmainə/ a. 次要的, 较小的		Unit 3
minority /maiˈnɔriti/ n. 少数; 少数派; 少数民族		Unit 6
mission /ˈmiʃən/ n. 使命, 任务		Unit 4
mode /məud/ n. 方式, 模式		Unit 6
modeling /ˈmɔdliŋ/ n. 建模, 造模		Unit 10
modify /ˈmɔdifai/ vt. 修改, 更改		Unit 1
moisture /ˈmɔistʃə/ n. 水分, 湿气		Unit 1
molecular /məuˈlekjulə/ a. 分子的		Unit 3
molecule /ˈmɔlikjuːl/ n. 分子		Unit 8
monitor /ˈmɔnitə/ vt. 监控		Unit 4
Monsanto Corp. (美) 孟山都公司 (主要经营高新农产品及技术)		Unit 10
multiple /ˈmʌltipl/ a. 多个的		Unit 7
mutate /mjuːˈteit/ vt. (使) 变异, (使) 突变		Unit 3
mycorrhizal fungi 菌根真菌		Unit 1

N

nanometer /ˈnænəˌmiːtə/ n. 纳米, 1/1,000,000,000 米		Unit 9
national seed boards 国家种子委员会		Unit 3
near infrared region 近红外(线)区域		Unit 9
Nepal /niˈpɔːl/ n. 尼泊尔 (南亚国家)		Unit 6
nitrate /ˈnaitreit/ n. 硝酸盐		Unit 1
nitrogen /ˈnaitrədʒən/ n. 氮		Unit 1
nitrous oxide (N_2O) 氧化亚氮, 笑气		Unit 10
no-till a. 免耕的		Unit 10
NOAA-AVHRR (National Oceanic and Atmospheric Administration-Advanced Very High Resolution Radiometer) 美国国家海洋大气局——高级甚高分辨率辐射计		Unit 9

notable /ˈnəutəbəl/ a. 显著的		Unit 1
NTF 养分膜技术		Unit 2
nursery tray 苗圃浅盘		Unit 2
nutrient /ˈnjuːtriənt/ a. 有营养的		Unit 7
nutrient-infused solution 注入了营养液的溶液		Unit 2
nutritious /njuːˈtriʃəs/ a. (有)营养的		Unit 1
nutritious /njuːˈtriʃəs/ a. 有营养成份的, 营养的		Unit 3

O

oak /əuk/ n. 橡树		Unit 9
oat /əut/ n. 燕麦		Unit 1
obligation /ˌɔbliˈgeiʃən/ n. 义务, 责任		Unit 4
obscure /əbˈskjuə/ vt. 使不明显		Unit 4
odorless /ˈəudəlis/ a. 无嗅的		Unit 8
offset /ˈɔːfset/ vt. 抵消, 减少		Unit 10
offspring /ˈɔfspriŋ/ n. 后代 (复数不变)		Unit 3
on-site 现场的		Unit 8
opponent /əˈpəunənt/ n. 反对者		Unit 7
optimum /ˈɔptiməm/ a. 最适宜的		Unit 2
orchid /ˈɔːkid/ n. 兰花		Unit 2
orderliness /ˈɔːdəlinis/ n. 整洁; 整齐, 有条理		Unit 6
ore /ɔː/ n. 矿石		Unit 4
organic /ɔːˈgænik/ a. 有机的		Unit 1
organism /ˈɔːgənizəm/ n. 有机体, 生物(体)		Unit 1
otherwise /ˈʌðəwaiz/ ad. 否则		Unit 5
outbid /autˈbid/ vt. 出高于……的价钱		Unit 7
outfit /ˈautfit/ n. 全套装备, 全套用品		Unit 6
outskirt /ˈautskəːt/ n. 市郊, 郊区		Unit 6
outweigh /autˈwei/ vt. 在……上超过		Unit 7
ova /ˈəuvə/ n. 卵子 (ovum 的复数)		Unit 3
overall /ˈəuvərɔːl/ a. 总体的		Unit 9
overshoot /ˌəuvəˈʃuːt/ n. 超出, 超出量		Unit 4
overwhelming /ˌəuvəˈwelmiŋ/ a. 在影响和势力上势不可挡的, 不可抗拒的		Unit 10

P

packing shed 包装棚		Unit 5
panel /ˈpænl/ n. 嵌板, 镶板; 壁板; 镜板		Unit 7
parasite /ˈpærəsait/ n. 寄生虫		Unit 3
particle bombardment 基因枪法; 粒子轰击法		Unit 3
particle gun bombardment 基因枪轰击技术		Unit 3
pasture /ˈpɑːstʃə/ n. 牧场, 牧草		Unit 9
pathogenic /ˌpæθəˈdʒenik/ a. 致病的, 病原的		Unit 5
patronize /ˈpeitrənaiz/ vt. 光顾, 惠顾		Unit 6

peak /pi:k/ vi. 达到高峰	Unit 1	prevailing /pri'veiliŋ/ a. 流行的，占优势的	Unit 4
pebble /'pebəl/ n. 小圆石，小鹅卵石	Unit 2	preventative /pri'ventətiv/ a. 预防性的	Unit 5
penalty /'penlti/ n. 处罚，罚款	Unit 5	preventive /pri'ventiv/ a.& n. 预防的；预防措施	Unit 1
per capita 每人，人均	Unit 4	price /prais/ vt. 给……定价；给……标价	Unit 6
percolation /ˌpə:kəleiən/ n. 过滤，渗透	Unit 1	principal /'prinsəpəl/ a. 主要的，首要的	Unit 2
pest /pest/ n. 有害物	Unit 7	privacy /'praivəsi/ n. 隐私	Unit 6
pesticide /'pestisaid/ n. 杀虫剂	Unit 1	privilege /'privilidʒ/ n. 特权	Unit 6
petroleum /pi'trəuliəm/ n. 石油	Unit 4	pro-poor /'prəu-puə/ n. 扶贫	Unit 6
pH 酸碱度	Unit 2	processed clay 加工过的黏土	Unit 2
pharmaceutical /ˌfɑ:mə'sju:tikəl/ a. 药用的	Unit 3	processor /'prəusesə/ n. 食品加工人，办理事务的人，处理器	Unit 1
photoperiod /ˌfəutəu'piəriəd/ n. 光周期（有机物每天暴露于阳光的时间）	Unit 2	productivity /ˌprɔdʌk'tiviti/ n. 生产率，生产力	Unit 1
photosynthesis /ˌfəutəu'sinθəsis/ n. 光合作用	Unit 8	project /'prɔdʒekt/ n. 项目，计划	Unit 3
photosynthetic /ˌfəutəusin'θetik/ a. 光合作用的	Unit 8	projected /'prɔdʒektid/ a. 规划的，预测的	Unit 10
picture /'piktʃə/ vt. 描绘	Unit 7	property /'prɔpəti/ n. 财产	Unit 4
places where food is handled or stored 操作和贮存食品的空间	Unit 5	proportion /prə'pɔ:ʃən/ n. 比例，均衡	Unit 8
		propose /prə'pəuz/ vt. 提议	Unit 7
plantation /plæn'teiʃən/ n. 种植园，大农场	Unit 8	protein /'prəuti:n/ n. 蛋白	Unit 3
pledge /pledʒ/ vi. (to) 保证	Unit 10	prototype /'prəutətaip/ n. 原型	Unit 7
plough /plau/ vt. 耕，犁	Unit 1	provincial /prə'vinʃəl/ a. 省的；外省的	Unit 6
poach /pəutʃ/ vt.&vi. 偷猎	Unit 6	pulpwood /pʌlpwud/ n. 纸浆用木材	Unit 8
poll /pəul/ n. 民意测验	Unit 4	pump /pʌmp/ n.&v. 泵；（用泵）抽	Unit 2
pollen /'pɔlin/ n. 花粉	Unit 2	purchase /'pə:tʃəs/ vt.&n. 购买	Unit 10
poplar /'pɔplə/ n. 白杨	Unit 8	put stress on 施加压力	Unit 8
ports of entry 进口港，入境港	Unit 5	**Q**	
pose a risk 造成危险	Unit 5	qualify /'kwɔlifai/ vt. 使合格，使符合条件	Unit 10
positive /'pɔzətiv/ a. 正面的，积极的，肯定的	Unit 1	quota /'kwəutə/ n. 配额	Unit 10
potent /'pəutənt/ a. 有力的，有效的	Unit 8	**R**	
potential /pə'tenʃəl/ n.& a. 潜力，潜能；可能的，潜在的	Unit 3	radiation /ˌreidi'eiʃən/ n. 辐射	Unit 10
potentially /pə'tenʃəli/ ad. 潜在地	Unit 9	rancher /'rɔ:ntʃə/ n. 大农场主	Unit 9
pour into 川流不息地涌入	Unit 8	range /reindʒ/ n.&vt. 范围，行列；排列，归类于	Unit 3
power grid 电网	Unit 8	rat and mouse 田鼠和家鼠	Unit 5
practical /'præktikəl/ a. 实用的，实践的	Unit 1	raw materials 原材料	Unit 6
practice /'præktis/ n. 习惯做法	Unit 2	real estate 房地产	Unit 7
practitioner /præk'tiʃənə/ n. 从业者，实习者	Unit 1	recombinant /ri'kɔmbinənt/ n. 重组体	Unit 3
pragmatist /'prægmətist/ n. 实用主义者	Unit 7	reflectance value 反射值	Unit 9
precautionary /pri'kɔ:ʃənəri/ a. 预防的	Unit 1	regenerate /ri'dʒenəreit/ vt. 再生，更新	Unit 3
predication /ˌpridi'keiʃən/ n. 论断，判断	Unit 9	regeneration /ri,dʒenəreit/ n. 再生，重建	Unit 1
predict /pri'dikt/ vt. 预知，预言	Unit 2	regulate /'regjuleit/ vt. 控制，调节，管理	Unit 9
premature /ˌpremə'tjuə/ a. 早熟的，过早的	Unit 4	regulated /'regjuleitid/ a. 管制的	Unit 5
premature death 早夭	Unit 5	release /ri'li:s/ vt. 释放，发行	Unit 1
preserve /pri'zə:v/ vt. 保护，保持	Unit 4	reliance /ri'laiəns/ n. 依靠	Unit 5

Vocabulary

remainder /ri'meində/ n. 剩余物 — Unit 10	野生动物园 — Unit 6
remarkable /ri'mɑːkəbəl/ a. 杰出的,非凡的 — Unit 2	Safeway Inc. (美)萨夫威连锁超市公司 — Unit 10
renewable /ri'njuːəbl/ a. 可更新的,可再生的 — Unit 4	sample /'sɑmpəl/ n. 样本 — Unit 2
renewal /ri'njuːəl/ n. 更新,恢复 — Unit 7	sanitation /ˌsæni'teiʃən/ n. 卫生,卫生设施 — Unit 5
replace /ri'pleis/ vt. 取代 — Unit 1	Sarapiqui 哥斯达黎加北部一地区 — Unit 9
reproductive /ˌriːprə'dʌktiv/ a. 生殖的 — Unit 3	saturation /ˌsætʃə'reiʃən/ n. 饱和,饱和度 — Unit 10
reservoir /'rezəvwɑː/ n. 小池,水库;贮液器 — Unit 2	sawtimber /'sɔːˌtimbə(r)/ n. 锯材,锯材原木 — Unit 8
reside /ri'zaid/ vi. 居住 — Unit 7	scrub /skrʌb/ n. 洗擦,擦净,净化 — Unit 8
resident /'rezidənt/ n. 居民 — Unit 4	sector /'sektə/ n. 部分,部门 — Unit 6
residential lot 居住地 — Unit 4	security /si'kjuəriti/ n. 安全 — Unit 7
residual /ri'zidjuəl/ n. 剩余部分 — Unit 8	seedling /'siːdliŋ/ n. 秧苗,树苗 — Unit 2
residue /'rezidjuː/ n. 剩余,余渣 — Unit 1	sensitive /'sensitiv/ a. 易受影响的 — Unit 5
resilience /ri'ziliəns/ n. 恢复力,弹力 — Unit 1	sequester /si'kwestə/ vt. 吸收 — Unit 10
resistance /ri'zistəns/ n. 抵抗力,反抗 — Unit 3	sequestration /si'kwestreiʃən/ n. 吸收 — Unit 10
respiration /ˌrespi'reiʃən/ n. 呼吸 — Unit 10	set /set/ a. 固定的,固定好的 — Unit 10
respiration /ˌrespi'reiʃən/ n. 呼吸,呼吸作用 — Unit 2	shavings /'ʃeiviŋz/ n. 刨花 — Unit 2
respiratory /ri'spirətəri/ a. 呼吸的 — Unit 4	shelf life 保存限期 — Unit 5
respite /'respit/ n. 休憩场所 — Unit 7	sighting /'saitiŋ/ n. 被看见,露面 — Unit 9
response /ri'spɔns/ n. 回应,反应 — Unit 9	sightseeing /'saitˌsiːiŋ/ n. 观光,游览 — Unit 6
restore /ri'stɔː/ vt. 修复,重建 — Unit 1	significantly /sig'nifikəntli/ ad. 显著地 — Unit 2
restrict /ri'strikt/ vt. 限制 — Unit 2	sink /siŋk/ n. 水槽;接收器 — Unit 10
restriction /ri'strikʃən/ n. 限制,约束 — Unit 5	skyline /'skailain/ n. 地平线 — Unit 7
retail market 零售市场 — Unit 5	skyscraper /'skaiˌskreipə/ n. 摩天大厦 — Unit 7
retrofit /'retrəufit/ n. 改造,改装 — Unit 8	small-scale 小规模的 — Unit 6
revenue /'revənjuː/ n. 收入,收益 — Unit 6	soak /səuk/ vt. 浸透 — Unit 2
reverse /ri'vəːs/ vt. 颠倒,逆转 — Unit 9	soaring /'sɔːriŋ/ a. 剧增的 — Unit 7
rewarding /ri'wɔːdiŋ/ a. 有利的,回报率高的 — Unit 4	socio-economic 社会经济的 — Unit 6
ripe /raip/ a. 成熟的 — Unit 2	soft maple 软枫 — Unit 8
ripen /'raipən/ vi. 成熟 — Unit 3	soil conditioner 土壤改良剂 — Unit 8
ripeness /'raipnis/ n. 成熟 — Unit 7	solar generator 太阳能发电机 — Unit 4
rocket /'rɔkit/ vi. 迅速上升;猛涨 — Unit 6	solar panel 太阳能电池板 — Unit 4
rockwool /'rɔkwəːl/ n. 岩石棉;石棉 — Unit 2	Sony Electronics (日)索尼电子公司 — Unit 10
Rolls-Royce (英国)劳斯莱斯汽车公司 — Unit 10	Southeast Asia 东南亚 — Unit 6
rot /rɔt/ vi.&n. 腐烂 — Unit 3	soybean /'sɔibiːn/ n. 大豆,黄豆 — Unit 3
rotation /rəu'teiʃən/ n. 旋转,轮换 — Unit 1	spare no efforts 不遗余力 — Unit 5
runoff /'rʌnɔf/ n. 流走之物 — Unit 1	spark ignited 火花点火 — Unit 8
rural /'ruərəl/ a. 农村的;田园的;有乡村风味的 — Unit 6	spatial /'speiʃəl/ a. 空间的,立体的 — Unit 9
rye /rai/ n. 黑麦 — Unit 1	spatial resolution 空间分辨率 — Unit 9
	species /'spiːʃiz/ n. 物种,种类(复数不变) — Unit 3
S	species extinction 物种灭绝 — Unit 4
sacrifice /'sækrifais/ vt. 牺牲 — Unit 2	spectral resolution 光谱分辨率 — Unit 9
safari /sə'fɑːri/ n. 狩猎旅行,狩猎的旅行队	spectral signature 光谱特征 — Unit 9
	sperm /spəːm/ n. 精子 — Unit 3

spire /spaiə/ n. 螺旋	Unit 7
SPOT (Satellite Positioning and Tracking) 人造卫星定位及跟踪	Unit 9
sprawl /sprɔːl/ vi. 蔓生,蔓延	Unit 2
spray /sprei/ n.&vt. 喷雾器;喷雾	Unit 3
sprout /spraut/ vi. 萌芽	Unit 2
stabilize /'steibilaiz/ vt.&vi. (使)稳定,(使)稳固	Unit 1
stake /steik/ n.&v. 木桩;用木桩系住	Unit 2
stand /stænd/ n. 林分,(一块地上的)林木	Unit 8
staple /'steipəl/ n.&a. 主要产物,副食;主要的	Unit 3
starter /'stɑːtə/ n. 起动器	Unit 2
starvation /stɑːˈveiʃən/ n. 饥饿	Unit 7
statistical /stəˈtistikəl/ a. 数据的	Unit 10
stem borer /stemˈbɔːrə/ n. 螟虫	Unit 3
stock /stɔk/ n. 储存,储存量	Unit 4
storage areas 贮藏货物的地方	Unit 5
straightforward /streitˈfɔːwəd/ a. 直接的,率直的	Unit 3
strain /strein/ n. (动植物的)系,品系,类型	Unit 3
strawberry /'strɔːbəri/ n. 草莓	Unit 2
strengthen /'streŋθən/ vt. 加强,巩固	Unit 5
stress /stres/ v.&n. 强调,压力,施压力于……	Unit 9
stump /stʌmp/ n. 树桩	Unit 8
Sub-Sahara 撒哈拉以南	Unit 7
sub-zero 低于零度	Unit 3
submit /səbˈmit/ vt. 提交,递交	Unit 5
subscribe /səbˈskraib/ vi. 赞成,赞许;订购(书籍等)	Unit 6
subsistence /səbˈsistəns/ n. 生存,存活	Unit 4
substitute /'sʌbstitjuːt/ vt.&n. 替代,替代物	Unit 8
sugarbeet /'ʃugəbiːt/ n. 甜菜	Unit 9
superior /sjuːˈpiəriə/ a. 质量或品种较高级的	Unit 2
supervisor 监督人	Unit 5
supplement /'sʌplimənt/ vt. 增补,补充	Unit 1
supplemental /ˌsʌpliˈmentl/ a. 补足的,补充的	Unit 2
surpass /səˈpɑːs/ vt. 超越,胜过	Unit 4
surplus /'səːpləs/ n.&a. 过剩(的),多余(的)	Unit 9
survive /səˈvaiv/ vi. 生存,生还	Unit 3
suspend /səsˈpend/ vt. 吊,悬挂	Unit 2
sustain /səˈstein/ vt. 支撑,使继续	Unit 1
sustainability /səˈsteinəbiliti/ n. 可持续性	Unit 4
sustainable /səˈsteinəbəl/ a. 可持续的	Unit 3
switch /switʃ/ v. 转换,转变	Unit 2
switchgrass /'switʃgrɑːs; -græs/ n. 柳枝稷	Unit 8
synthetic /sinˈθetik/ a. 合成的,人造的	Unit 1

T

target /'tɑːgit/ vt. 把……作为目标(或对象)	Unit 6
target /'tɑːgit/ n. 目标	Unit 10
temperate /'tempərit/ a. 温带的	Unit 3
tend /tend/ vt.&vi. 照顾;倾向,易于(to)	Unit 1
tendency /'tendənsi/ n. 趋向,倾向	Unit 2
terrestrial vegetation 陆地植被	Unit 10
territory /'teritəri/ n. 领土,地域	Unit 2
test data 测试数据	Unit 5
texture /'tekstʃə/ n. 质地	Unit 5
The American Society of Travel Agents (ASTA) 美国旅行社协会	Unit 6
the Buddha 佛祖;佛像	Unit 6
the first line of defense against pests 预防有害动植物的第一道防线	Unit 5
the host country 主办国,东道国	Unit 6
The International Eco-tourism Society (TIES) 国际生态旅游学会	Unit 6
The National Institute of Health (美国)国家卫生研究院	Unit 5
theoretical /θiəˈretikəl/ a. 理论的	Unit 10
theoretically /θiəˈretikli/ ad. 理论上,理论地	Unit 8
thermostat /'θəːməstæt/ n. 自动调温器	Unit 2
threaten /'θretn/ vt. 威胁	Unit 3
thrift stores 廉价旧货店	Unit 4
thrive /θraiv/ vt. 兴盛,兴隆	Unit 1
tillage /'tilidʒ/ n. 耕耘,耕作	Unit 10
time scale 时间量程/范围	Unit 10
tissue /'tiʃuː/ n. 组织,薄纸	Unit 1
tobacco /təˈbækəu/ n. 烟草	Unit 3
tolerance /'tɔlərəns/ n. 耐受性	Unit 5
topograph /'tɔpəgrɑːf; -græf/ n. 地形,地貌;地形学	Unit 10
tough /tʌf/ a. 强硬的	Unit 5
township /'taunʃip/ n. 小镇;镇区	Unit 6
toxic /'tɔksik/ a. 有毒的,中毒的	Unit 5
toxicity /'tɔksisəti/ n. 毒性	Unit 2
toxin /'tɔksin/ n. 毒素	Unit 3
trace /treis/ n. 痕迹,微量	Unit 5

Vocabulary

trace element 微量元素	Unit 1
traceable /'treisəbl/ a. 可追踪的,起源于	Unit 5
trail /treil/ n. 路线,小路	Unit 6
trait /treit/ n. 特征,特点,特性	Unit 3
transboundary /ˌtræns'baundəri/ a. 超越国界	Unit 4
transgenic /trænz'dʒenik/ a. 转基因的	Unit 3
transit /'trænsit/ n. 运输(尤指公交系统)	Unit 4
transmit /trænz'mit/ vt. 传播,传导	Unit 9
transnationally /trænz'næʃənəli/ ad. 跨国地	Unit 5
transplantation /ˌtrænsplɑːn'teiʃn/ n. 移植	Unit 3
transportation /ˌtrænspɔː'teiʃn/ n. 运输	Unit 7
tray /trei/ n. 浅盘	Unit 2
trend /trend/ n. 趋势,倾向	Unit 1
trial /'traiəl/ n. 试验	Unit 8
tropical /'trɔpikəl/ a. 热带的	Unit 3
tulip /'tjuːlip/ n. 郁金香	Unit 2
tumor /'tjuːmə/ n. 肿瘤	Unit 3
turnaround /'təːnəraund/ n. 周转时间	Unit 5

U

undermine /ˌʌndə'main/ vt. (暗中慢慢)破坏	Unit 4
unique /juː'niːk/ a. 唯一的,独一无二的;独特的	Unit 6
unmodified /ʌn'mɔdifaid/ a. 未更改的	Unit 8
unsurpassed /ˌʌnsə'pɑːst/ a. 非常卓越的	Unit 2
untamed /ʌn'teimd/ a. 未驯服的;未被抑制的;未开发的	Unit 6
update /ʌp'deit/ vt. 更新;使……跟上时代	Unit 5
urban /'əːbən/ a. 城市的	Unit 7
urbanization /ˌəːbənai'zeiʃn/ n. 都市化	Unit 5
US Environmental Protection Agency (EPA) 美国环境保护局	Unit 5
utilize /'juːtilaiz/ vt. 利用	Unit 6

V

vacant /'veikənt/ a. 空白的	Unit 7
valid /'vælid/ a. 有效的,有根据的	Unit 1
variability /ˌveəriəbi liti/ n. 可变性	Unit 10
variety /və'raiəti/ n. 品种,种类,变种	Unit 2
vary /'veəri/ vt. 改变	Unit 2
verification /ˌverifi'keiʃn/ n. 查证,证实	Unit 10
verify /'verifai/ vt. 查证,核实	Unit 3
vertical /'vəːtikəl/ a. 垂直的	Unit 7
verticality /ˌvəːti'kæləti/ n. 垂直,垂直状态	Unit 7
victorious /vik'tɔːriəs/ a. 获胜的	Unit 7
Vietnam 越南	Unit 5
vigor /'vigə/ n. 精力,活力	Unit 9
vine /vain/ n. 藤,蔓	Unit 3
violate /'vaiəleit/ vt. 违反或藐视	Unit 5
vision /'viʒn/ n. 先见之明,幻想	Unit 8
visual /'viʒuəl/ a. 视觉的,形象的	Unit 5
visually /'viʒuəli/ ad. 视觉上地,真实地	Unit 9
voluntary /'vɔləntəri/ a. 自愿的,主动的	Unit 5

W

water holding capacity 水容量	Unit 1
wavelength /'weivleŋθ/ n. 波长	Unit 9
weather-related 与天气相关的	Unit 7
website 网页	Unit 5
well-being /ˌwel'biːŋ/ n. 健康,幸福	Unit 1
wholesale market 批发市场	Unit 5
wich system 毛细传送系统	Unit 2
willow /'wiləu/ n. 柳树	Unit 8
win-win a. 双赢的	Unit 10
windmill /'windˌmil/ n. 风车	Unit 4
with a view to 着眼于,考虑到	Unit 2
with regard to 关于	Unit 1
woodlot /'wudlɔt/ n. 植林地	Unit 8
yield /jiːld/ n. 产量	Unit 1

Y

Yushi 玉狮(云南省兰坪县普米族居住区)	Unit 6

北京市高等教育精品教材立项项目

农林英语

尊敬的老师:

您好!

为了方便您更好地使用本教材,获得最佳教学效果,我们特向使用该书作为教材的教师赠送本教材配套参考资料。如有需要,请完整填写"教师联系表"并加盖所在单位系(院)公章,免费向出版社索取。

北京大学出版社

教 师 联 系 表

教材名称		农林英语	
姓名:	性别:	职务:	职称:
E-mail:	联系电话:	邮政编码:	
供职学校:	所在院系:		(章)
学校地址:			
教学科目与年级:	班级人数:		
通信地址:			

填写完毕后,请将此表邮寄给我们,我们将为您免费寄送本教材配套资料,谢谢!

北京市海淀区成府路 205 号
北京大学出版社外语编辑部　李　颖
邮政编码:100871
电子邮箱:evalee1770@sina.con

邮 购 部 电 话:010-62752015
市场营销部电话:010-62750672
外语编辑部电话:010-62767315